1913

America
Between Two Worlds

THE MACMILLAN COMPANY
NEW YORK • CHICAGO
DALLAS • ATLANTA • SAN FRANCISCO
LONDON • MANILA

IN CANADA
BRETT-MACMILLAN LTD.
GALT, ONTARIO

1913

America

Between Two Worlds

ALAN Chester VALENTINE

New York

The Macmillan Company

1962

First Printing

The Macmillan Company, New York
Brett-Macmillan Ltd., Galt, Ontario

Printed in the United States of America

Library of Congress catalog card number: 61–12703

Foreword

The differences in values and habits of thought between our sons and our fathers are greater than those between any other three generations, as men so variant in experience as Henry Adams and Robert Oppenheimer have pointed out. When and why did those changes come about? Does any single year epitomize the turning point?

It is a cliché that World War I destroyed the Old World and ushered in the New. In that case, 1913 represented the final year of the older culture. Americans of 1913, products of the nineteenth century, were faced with the new problems of the twentieth. How easily did they meet the challenge of change? As I surveyed that year, I felt forced to revise my concept of it, for I found in it the embryo of nearly every development that symbolizes modernity in the Nuclear Age. It was as much a preface to the Age of Anxiety as a postlude to the Age of Complacency. Like every other year, it was a year of transition.

Yet 1913 still seemed as good a point as any other from which to look backward and forward. But there was no resting there, for its character was not static but kinetic, a series of action pictures rather than a still life one could study at leisure. To keep up with its movement one had to pursue it ardently in all directions. Instead of looking at a pathologist's specimen under a microscope, I found myself trying to observe and understand the physiology of living change.

The chronicle of that year is too complex to yield clear answers to my questions. Men moved across its span indifferent to their collective significance, and events did not fall accommodatingly into consistent patterns. Facts in their diversity laughed at my search for unity. Plunging for principles beneath the crosscurrents of its surface, I may have brought up only what my own limited perspective reveals to me. Like the patient on the analyst's couch, the chronicler can only talk himself into understanding a little better why he is here.

That would be true of any year, but in 1913 the sudden acceleration of change made its patterns especially confusing. It is difficult enough to perceive their pattern, but even more difficult to judge whether the general direction of their movement was upward. What seemed at the time a gain may now appear a loss, for the correction of one fault may have bred another no less grievous. Conversely, an evil of yesterday may have caused, by the reaction of later years, a virtue of today.

De Tocqueville wrote that some men assisted democracy by their talents, and others by their vices. Half a century does not give hindsight enough to assess with confidence the vices and virtues of the forces of 1913, or to conclude with finality whether its corporations or its labor leaders, its muckrakers or its bosses, its affirmers or its dissenters, were the heroes or the villains. In the words of Yeats: "A man walked, as it were, casting a shadow, and yet no one could say which was man and which was shadow, or how many the shadows that he cast."

Only a few things seem clear. Our own confused values and our own anxious minds—indeed our own atomic world—were determined largely by the way the men and women of 1913 thought, felt, and acted under the pressures of change. Adjustment to events involves not only the mind but also the emotions, and they do not adjust with equal speed and thoroughness. Americans of 1913 were notable victims of the conflict between the legendary America of their emotional traditions and the real America of their reason and practice. Americans of 1960 wallow in the same conflict with no greater success.

Any reader can criticize my choice of what to include and not to include in this picture of the year. I have left out much that is important and kept in some events outwardly less significant. I can defend my choices only by saying that I have been partly guided by the emphasis of the time as reflected in the periodicals and headlines and partly by an attempt to interpret the forces of change. This is not a history of America just before the first great war, as we see it in the perspective of 1962, but an estimate of how Americans looked to themselves in 1913.

It is impossible to acknowledge properly all the sources from which I have had help, not only because they are so numerous but also because many of them are so intangible, and after much reading I cannot always trace the origin of an idea. I can only record my gratitude to all my sources and plead, both as to the facts and the fancies in this undertaking, an incorrigible interest in the ironies of human endeavor.

Contents

Nostalgia

The squeak of sleigh runners and the crunch of winter-sharp horse-shoes on the packed snow.

Fringed hammocks across corners of clematis-curtained front stoops.

The smell of saddle soap and old leather in the livery stable next to the Farmers' Grange.

The dead air in the front parlor when it was opened for Sunday-afternoon callers.

The bandstand, the horse trough, Sousa's marches, and the smell of citronella.

The player piano, and the Edison Gramophone with cylindrical records and a big horn.

Trimming the wick on the kerosene lamp, and putting a new Wels-bach gas mantle into the glass globe over the living-room table.

"Pony Boy," "Alexander's Ragtime Band," "A Perfect Day."

The horsecars on lower Broadway, the wedgelike wonder of the Flatiron Building.

Girls' bathing suits, with black bloomers bulging below black skirts and over the knees of black cotton stockings.

Homemade dandelion wine, root beer, raspberry shrub, and cherry bounce.

White duck pants, long recitations, and saw-toothed Eton collars at high-school commencements.

Mackinaw coats and corduroy knickerbockers fastened at the knees, that whispered loudly as you walked to the dictionary in study hall.

Gray-blue agateware pans on pantry shelves, with a quarter-inch of yellow Jersey cream rising to the top.

Gas flares, white cotton dresses, June bugs, and William Jennings Bryan outside the Chautauqua tent.

Carrying endless pails of water to the elephant on circus-day morning, for a free ticket to the afternoon show.

Coaling up the furnace at bedtime, and shaking her down in the morning.

Christy Mathewson, Three-Fingered Mordecai Brown, and Home-Run Baker.

St. Nicholas *magazine, the* Youth's Companion, *and the* Outlook *at home; the* Police Gazette *at the barbershop.*

The Wright Brothers, Barney Oldfield, Admiral Peary.

Maude Adams as Peter Pan, and William Gillette as Sherlock Holmes.

Lou Tellegen, Francis X. Bushman, and Pearl White in The Perils of Pauline.

"Speak softly and carry a big stick."

"They gotta quit kickin' my dawg aroun'."

"We stand at Armageddon, and we battle for the Lord."

"Twenty-three, skiddoo."

"Watchful waiting."

Reality

Germany increased its standing army to some 850,000 and other European nations took balancing steps. The United States Army had some 35,000 men ready for active duty within the national boundaries, and army appropriations had been reduced regularly since 1910.

In the Balkans wars 35,000 Bulgarians fell in ten days, and Sir Edward Grey told the House of Commons it was impossible to exaggerate the horrors and atrocities of the fighting.

Secretary of State Bryan said that "conditions promising world peace were never more favorable than now," and Andrew Carnegie said war with Germany had never "even been imagined."

In number of airplanes of all sorts, the United States was tenth, and the amount spent on aeronautical development was less than one-fortieth of what was spent by Germany or France.

On a net income of $4,001 the new income tax would be one cent; on a net income of $100,000 the tax would be $2,260. The New York Times editorially questioned both the equity and efficiency of an income tax.

The new Underwood tariff set the lowest import duties since the Civil War, and Charles M. Schwab of the Bethlehem Steel Corporation said it would lead the nation into its most serious depression in history. The former chairman of the House Banking and Currency Committee said the new Federal Reserve System was certain to bring overwhelming calamity to the country.

Men's suits cost from $10 up, but a clerk's wages were $15 a week, the average family income was under $1,000 a year, and thousands of girls were working a 50-hour week for less than $4.

There were forty-five officially recognized lynchings during the year, and in various strike riots several men and women were killed by gunfire.

Andrew D. White stated that city government in the United States was the worst in the world—the most expensive, the most inefficient, and the most corrupt.

Governor William Sulzer of New York was impeached for perjury and attempting to suppress evidence by threats to witness, but less than a month later was elected to the State Assembly with twice the number of votes secured by the Democratic and Republican opponents together.

Women were arrested for wearing slit skirts; Mrs. Emmeline Pankhurst was refused entry on grounds of moral turpitude, and Annapolis midshipmen were ordered not to dance the Turkey Trot or hold a girl's hand on the dance floor.

Preparation

A thirty-one-year-old Harvard graduate resigned from the New York State Senate to become Assistant Secretary of the Navy, and his cousin Theodore sent young Franklin a correct but not very warm note of congratulations.

Cadet Eisenhower was learning football, and other things less brilliantly, with two more years to go at West Point; and after two years in a Kansas City bank Harry Truman was putting in his seventh year on the family farm near Independence. Francis and Hannah Nixon of Yorba Linda, California, became, on January 3rd, the proud parents of a son, Richard.

William Averell Harriman graduated from Yale with an inheritance of some $69,000,000 and arrived in Omaha in his private car to begin work in the locomotive shops of the railroad he controlled. While there he would live in the house of the Union Pacific president and two years later would be vice president of the railroad at the age of twenty-four.

A nine-year-old Jewish boy was already far ahead of his class at school, and would graduate from Harvard in the same class with young Neil McElroy from Berea, Ohio, who had no idea then what part he or Robert Oppenheimer would play in nuclear developments.

After nine years of hardscrabble farming and one of teaching in New Hampshire, Robert Frost, already thirty-nine, had scraped together funds to spend an economical year in England, hoping to publish a book of verse. He did not know another aspiring poet named T. S. Eliot, who was putting in his third year of graduate study at Harvard and who would follow him to England.

Neither seemed very likely to meet there another literary aspirant who had fought in the Boer War, served as Undersecretary of State for the Colonies and then as Home Secretary, and in 1913 was completing his second year as First Lord of the Admiralty. People would later confuse him with an American author named Winston Churchill.

Setting out on Good Friday from his home in the village of Günsback in the Münster Valley after long study and preparation, a tall young Alsatian doctor named Albert Schweitzer hoped that a European war would not upset his plan for a life of missionary service in Central Africa.

A twenty-one-year-old journeyman locksmith—the seventh son of a Croatian farmer named Broz—was just completing his two-year term of compulsory service in the army of the Austro-Hungarian Empire. He had never heard of an assistant to the mayor of Cologne named Konrad Adenauer, sixteen years older than Tito, who was urging the establishment of a university at Cologne.

Neither had heard of an eighteen-year-old factory clerk named Bulganin in a city then called Nizhni Novgorod, or of Joseph Vissarionovich Dzhugashvili, at thirty-four a hunted man. Joseph had recently escaped from Siberia, and in January made his way to Cracow to talk subversion with a man then known as Ulyanov and later as Lenin. Then Joseph went on to Vienna to talk with another fellow conspirator he never really liked, called Trotsky. From there Joseph went to Moscow, where the Czar's police would pick him up and send him back to Siberia for another four years. Americans would later know this revolutionary as Stalin.

I

The New Dawn

March 4, 1913, drew the largest inaugural crowd in history. The morning was dark with rainclouds, but just before the ceremonies began the sun broke through, and this was pronounced a happy augury for four years of peace and progress.

It was a great day for the Democrats, who had not had the power and patronage of the White House since Grover Cleveland. They came to Washington in thousands, and their jubilation was unrestrained. It was a great day, too, for Princeton men, many of whom paraded in a Democratic procession for the first and last time. Most of the intellectuals of the country were happy too, though they were less prominent in the festivities. Woodrow Wilson was a man of their kind; and at Princeton and Trenton he had challenged entrenched economic and political power.

There were other favorable omens. The President-elect had been the first to be driven to his inauguration in an automobile, and this typified American progress and his determination to keep up with it. His personal insistence that there should be no inaugural ball appealed to the austere and frugal citizens, even if it disappointed congressmen's wives and political socialites. The fact that Chief Justice Edward Douglass White, who administered the oath of office, was a Roman Catholic and former Confederate soldier seemed to assure an end to the old divisions and prejudices. Domestic sentiment approved the fact that the Bible the Chief Justice used for the swearing was Mrs. Wilson's. When he opened it at random, Mr. Wilson's lips touched the 119th Psalm, which included these prophetic words:

"With my lips have I declared all the judgments of thy mouth.

. . . I have sworn, and I will perform it, that I will keep thy righteous judgments."

There was promise, too, of a new spirit of national unity and good feeling after a campaign that had not been without rancor. When Mr. Taft and Mr. Wilson, squeezed somewhat tightly together in the back of an open barouche, drove down Pennsylvania Avenue, the retiring President seemed at his most genial, and appeared to enjoy the cheering, even though most of it was for his successor. Mr. Wilson reciprocated cordiality as much as his more self-conscious dignity would permit, and, turning to Mr. Taft, said spontaneously, "You're a darned good sport!" Mr. Taft beamed still more, and seemed to observers more relaxed than Mr. Wilson— perhaps with reason.

Optimism was in evidence almost everywhere in America that March morning. The New York *World* began the day by pronouncing that "Woodrow Wilson's inauguration marks the beginning of a new political epoch. The United States has entered on a new phase of popular government." The *Century Magazine* had already pointed out another reason for expecting good government: "No president has ever entered office so free from obligations as he will be," and this pleased even the myriad seekers for federal office and federal favors, for the fewer the previous commitments, the more room for them and their friends.

Mr. Wilson appealed especially to the idealism of youth. Ardent and inexperienced young liberals expected miracles of reform and progress from this academic Galahad "who scorned alike the support of the bosses and the support of Plutocracy." He seemed to personify all the qualifications and virtues extolled in high-school textbooks on government. Even the leaders of organized labor forgot for a day to be cynical, and newspaper men were talking and writing quite sincerely about "the new dawn of freedom."

To those carried away by the spirit of the occasion, the road to a more equitable and elevated democracy seemed clear. Americans had but to follow and support this man of demonstrated character and political idealism as he pushed aside the powers of reaction on the way to the promised land of democratic equality. Government would be "restored to the people"; bosses would be overthrown; Wall Street would be put in its place, and the wealth released by the new income tax would be spent for the benefit of all. The weak would be protected from the strong, the wage earner from the capitalist, and the farmer from the railroads. Almost no prediction of a coming Utopia seemed too farfetched to be heard on that afternoon in the lobby of the New Willard Hotel, the less-upholstered lounges of faculty clubs, and the columns of the liberal journals. Those who had their doubts were temporarily drowned in the wave of enthusiasm.

Cooler heads, of course, stuck to more modest but sanguine expectations. In spite of Mexican revolutions and European war scares, there was little fear of American entanglement. Even if Europe went to war, America would keep out of it under a President less buoyantly aggressive than Theodore Roosevelt and not so susceptible to dollar diplomacy as Mr. Taft. Mr. Wilson's program was concentrated on domestic reforms; in foreign affairs he would mind his own business. He had the support of a majority in House and Senate, and the mandate of the electorate. Though corporations, bankers and businessmen were not happy about his regulatory intentions, they were somewhat reassured by the more pacific tone of his inaugural address, and the stock market was steady in early March.

There was certainly little or nothing in the President's inaugural address to shake the general optimism. He did not strike very hard at big business, and what he said was surprisingly characteristic of all acceptance speeches. He was dignified, idealistic, diffuse. He referred, of course, to the need for lower tariffs, currency control, and trust regulation, but the effects of these had already been discounted in business and on the exchanges. It was only Mr. Wilson's more thoughtful friends and idealistic supporters who were a little disappointed; they privately thought his address a little uninspired and uninspiring, a little lacking in force—too vague, too academic. . . .

There were, of course, some clouds on the horizon that the inaugural celebrants ignored, and there were some private prophecies less flattering to the new President. Henry Adams, from his watchtower opposite the White House, measuring the new political deal against the perspective of history and the precedents of Europe, and filtering the prospects through the fine mesh of his disillusioned mind, reached conclusions at variance with the popular ones on Pennsylvania Avenue. In late January he had written to his niece, Mabel La Farge: "I expect trouble, and already see a big scare around me. Mr. Woodrow Wilson does not inspire confidence." He had also written to his English friend Sir Ronald Lindsay: "I know less of the President-elect Wilson, but I apprehend he will quarrel with everybody at once, and especially with his friends if he has any. Not one of his old group is now with him." And six weeks after the inaugural, Adams wrote to another confidante, the wife of Senator Ralph Cameron: "The confusion and consternation here are startling. If it were a question only of a Democratic administration, they are resigned to that, but no one knows whether the people want representative government at all. They seem to want an Athenian democracy without representation."

That last was more of an alarm about the American people than about the new President, and Adams's concern about coming mobocracy was not shared by the majority, who would have laughed off his alarms as the unimportant irritabilities of an elderly and disappointed conservative watching his friends go out of power and a new crowd come in. He was expressing merely the point of view of a vanishing élite who never again would, or should, control American politics or culture.

For even more obvious reasons, Theodore Roosevelt's estimate of the new President should be heavily discounted, though its restraints (which would change before the year was out) made it more significant. On January 28th T. R. wrote to Governor Hiram Johnson of California, his running mate on the Progressive ticket:

Wilson was from their [the Democrats'] standpoint the best man they could have nominated. I do not regard him as a man of great intensity of principle or conviction, or of much reality of sympathy with our [reform] cause. He is an adroit man, a good speaker and writer, with a certain amount of ability of just the kind requisite to his party under present conditions. He showed his adroitness during the campaign . . . talked ardent but diffuse progressiveness.

The most illuminating comment on Mr. Wilson's qualities of leadership came from his stanchest friend and supporter. Colonel Edward M. House declined the President's offer of his choice of several Cabinet posts, feeling that he could serve more effectively as an independent friend and adviser. Commenting on his decision, Colonel House wrote privately to a friend, "Had I gone into the Cabinet I could not have lasted eight months."

Businessmen respected Mr. Wilson's integrity, and preferred him to a demagogue like William Jennings Bryan, but the new President's greater ability made his opposition to big business more alarming. Their fears of what he might do to banks and corporations had risen and fallen each week as the President-elect had spoken more or less belligerently about businessmen. His proposed tariff revisions were unpalatable to most of them, but they hoped to whittle down the decreases he intended. His currency reforms probably could not be defeated, but they might be steered; in any case they would not be fatal to profits, and some bankers even favored them. But how much further would Mr. Wilson go in four years or perhaps eight? Did he intend only remedial measures or would he move to punitive ones?

The conciliatory inaugural address was only mildly reassuring in view of some of Mr. Wilson's earlier threats. At the annual dinner of the Southern Society in New York on December 17th he had said he would choose his chief advisers from the leftward wing of the party, for that, he said, was the obligation imposed on him by the vote—though it was difficult to understand how he interpreted the returns as so clear a leftward mandate. He had added that he would "build a gibbet as high as Haman's" for anyone who attempted to discredit his administration by starting an "unnatural" panic. Since a panic was the last thing Wall Street and businessmen wanted, it was a little alarming that Mr. Wilson suggested they might deliberately create one simply to discredit him. But suppose a slump in business did occur? Who, businessmen wanted to know, would decide who was to blame for it? Would the new President act personally as both judge and hangman?

In the *World's Work Magazine* of January the President-elect had declared the country to be in the grip of a heartless economic system that had destroyed the freedom of American industry and enterprise, in which a few men controlled the fate of all the rest. Many small businessmen agreed with him, but how far down the line was Mr. Wilson thinking when he spoke of "a few"? And in a speech at Staunton, Virginia, he had asserted, after referring to business: "The presidency is an office in which a man must put on his war paint." Such remarks from a campaigning candidate need not be taken seriously, but from a President-elect they were disturbing.

The President-elect had certainly taken a more critical position toward business than Professor Woodrow Wilson had taken only a few years earlier. In a speech in 1907 he had ascribed the panic of that year to "the aggressive attitude of legislation toward the railroads," and had declared that government regulation of railways would "merely mean taking the power away from the people and putting it in the hands of political discontent." Later that year he had attacked federal regulation of corporations as based on a theory "compounded of confused thinking and impossible principles of law." And in an open letter in 1909 Professor Wilson had written, "I am a fierce partisan of the Open Shop and of everything that makes for individual liberty."

The President had his own worries on inaugural day. In spite of the ovation, he was already encountering obstacles and disillusionment. Important men in his own party, whose support he could not afford to lose, had begun to make embarrassing demands. They expected him, by extensive use of the spoils system, to fatten a Democratic organization lean after years of federal famine. Then there were the endless requests, some more like demands, to appoint a deserving party worker or a personal friend to some important or lucrative post, with little or no regard to the man's qualifications. To ensure necessary political support he had already been led to regrettable expediencies, such as the appointment of Mr. Bryan to the highest post in the Cabinet—though only Mr. Bryan could think himself really qualified to be Secretary of State.

There were other appointment troubles. The new President inherited some 1,500 nominations to the federal services, and several hundred promotions in the army and navy, put forward by Mr. Taft but still unconfirmed on March 4th by progressive Republicans and recalcitrant Democrats. Whatever action Mr. Wilson took on Mr. Taft's nominations would be criticized as either partisan or weak, yet the posts had to be filled without delay. Even in the selection of his Cabinet he had been compelled to pass over some of his first choices in the interests of geography and party solidarity. The result was a Cabinet on the whole undistinguished, but what Mr. Wilson disliked most about it was that its composition made it patent to the public that he had compromised with expediency.

New York State was the best represented in numbers, with William G. McAdoo as Secretary of the Treasury and William C. Redfield as Secretary of Commerce. Both were able men, but neither had been considered outstanding ones. The same could perhaps be said for the Far West's only representative, Franklin K. Lane, of California, as Secretary of the Interior. The all-important South had contributed three men: Josephus Daniels, of North Carolina, as a distinctly dry and landbound Secretary of the Navy; Albert Burleson, of Texas, to the ubiquitously political post of Postmaster General; and, as Attorney General, James C. McReynolds, of Tennessee—who on later appointment to the Supreme Court proved to be no John Marshall. The only other man from the east was Lindley M. Garrison, of New Jersey, as Secretary of War. Apart from Mr. Bryan, of Nebraska, the Middle West had to be content with David F. Houston, of Missouri, as Secretary of Agriculture. Mr. Wilson had wanted the best; now he could only hope for the best!

Some of Mr. Wilson's other disappointments were more personal, and that made them hurt all the more. He had expected that he could draft almost any friend or former colleague to serve in his great crusade. If men of high caliber, who knew him and appreciated his aims, did not feel it a duty and pleasure to serve when called upon, how could government be properly manned and democracy ably served? Yet he had received some refusals where he least expected them, and was having to climb down the ladder of his preferences to get men to fill top diplomatic posts.

Early in the year he had offered the post of Ambassador to Japan to Charles W. Eliot, president emeritus of Harvard University, and hence an old colleague of the former president of Princeton. Mr. Eliot had declined. On March 19th Mr. Wilson asked Mr. Eliot to accept the most distinguished of all diplomatic appointments—Ambassador to the Court of St. James'. Dr. Eliot again declined, and more than hinted at his reason in terms not overdiplomatic: "I had already seen in the newspapers that Mr. Bryan was to be Secretary of State, and the function of Ambassador to the Court of St. James, or any other court, had no attraction for me." It was a personal criticism as well as a personal rebuff, and Princeton has never taken kindly to rebuffs from her big sister at Cambridge.

As if that were not discouraging enough, Richard Olney, Secretary of State in Grover Cleveland's Cabinet, also declined the London post because of "obstacles of a personal and family nature." Must Woodrow Wilson scour the country to find a Democrat of ability and character who would accept his top diplomatic position? The ultimate appointment of Walter Hines Page proved a very satisfactory one, especially to the British government, but even Page was not happy with his diplomatic chief. In a private letter to Colonel House on December 12, 1914, he let the colonel understand that he regarded the conduct of the State Department under Mr. Bryan as worse than unfortunate.

As Ambassador to Germany, certainly in 1913 a post of crucial importance, Mr. Wilson first invited his former dean at Princeton, Henry B. Fine. Since Dean Fine would be unable to finance from his own pocket the heavy costs of diplomatic life Unter den Linden, Mr. Wilson appealed personally to another old friend and Princeton trustee. Cleveland H. Dodge agreed to supplement by a personal gift, "up to fifteen or twenty thousand a year," the ambassadorial salary of

Dean Fine, but in spite of this the dean declined. James W. Gerard was appointed to Berlin, and devoted much of his time, just a year before the war broke out, to finding suitably imposing quarters for his embassy. The President offered the ambassadorship to the new Chinese Republic to Dr. John R. Mott, "a robust Christian," a missionary leader, a man known and admired in China, but he too declined. It was difficult not to feel a little disillusion, perhaps even a little irritation.

Such personal disappointments were of course minor compared with the national problems the President encountered the day after his inauguration. Though the nation had, on the whole, nearly as much confidence in its new leader as he had confidence in himself, there was one domestic issue that neither he nor the public showed any inclination to face squarely. That was the relationship between capital and labor, which was rapidly deteriorating. Since the beginning of the year there had been several big strikes and many smaller ones: a railroad stoppage threatened, and the rising cost of living would bring further demands for higher wages.

This was not a new problem, but no one had found a basic solution for industrial strife. Each labor dispute had been dealt with as a separate and isolated issue. When a strike ended, the government and the public sighed with relief and hoped another would not soon begin, but they gained little from each experience that helped to deal with the next. There was no canon of industrial law, no accepted standard by which to measure industrial justice or guide procedure. The right of employees to bargain collectively was not universally accepted; the right to establish a closed shop or maintain an open shop was still undetermined by any series of consistent court decisions; the right of factory owners to use force to defend their property against strikers was not clear. There was no consistency in the actions of local governments toward strikers or toward asking for state troops to keep order, or in the action of state troopers when put in charge. The responsibilities and powers of the federal government in connection with industrial strife were unsettled in public opinion.

Perhaps the only way to reach the right answers was to let them evolve from painful experience and the ultimate building up of a corpus of consistent legal rulings and a body of public opinion. But that was an expensive way, and industrial strife might get much worse before it began to get better. Could not something be done from the White House that would at least clarify the rights and define the proper procedures of the participants? If Mr. Wilson thought so he did not say so. If he had any plan for fundamental approach to industrial problems he had not revealed it at the time he took office. His only concrete proposals were in connection with a federal board for arbitration: that would be helpful, but it did not cope with the underlying causes of the issue.

Events would allow the new administration little time to think about such matters, for there were pressing external problems to be faced in the cold light of the morning after the inauguration. On the western horizon lay clouds between California and Japan, and trouble with the Great Powers over the terms of a loan to the new Chinese Republic. To the south were the more immediate dangers of Mexican political banditry, and on the east loomed the chaotic Balkan situation. In the dispute over the Panama Canal tolls, Britain was distinctly annoyed and Congress likely to be very stubborn.

Americans applauded every move toward world peace, so long as the United States did not get involved in any international commitments or responsibilities—a condition that made effective leadership toward world peace impossible. Beyond that general and unrealistic policy, the attitude of most Americans toward other nations was nebulous. They were impatient with European rivalries, confident of America's moral superiority, and critical of the manners and methods of professional diplomats. Public opinion believed Europe's rivalries might be settled if only the disputing parties would tackle them the American way, by straight talk, common sense, give-and-take, and the Ten Commandments—with all the cards, of course, face up on the table. Elihu Root, drawing on his experience as a former Secretary of State, described the current American attitude in a few words: "In this country international law was regarded as a rather antiquated branch of useless learning, diplomacy as a foolish mystery and the foreign service as a superfluous expense."

Americans were in emphatic disagreement regarding American policy toward its own defense. Mr. Bryan was enthusiastically applauded and roundly condemned when, on the eve of the inauguration, he declared it to be the "imperative duty of the United States . . . to set a shining example of disarmament." The American army was a mere fraction of that of Germany or France or Russia, and the United States Navy had two oceans to patrol and a Monroe Doctrine to defend. Although few men took the international opinions of private citizen Bryan very seriously, one could not ignore the opinions of the new Secretary of State, and he was beginning his Cabinet career somewhat incautiously.

The New Freedom had been born on a sunny day and had been given a magnificent welcome. March 5th was another day, when the promising infant of the rosy dawn began to be looked over more critically, even by indulgent aunts and rich uncles. And the bills for the birthday party would soon begin to come in.

II

Reformers

The American affirmation of unity in freedom was never unanimous, for one of its tenets was independent judgment, and that meant minority dissent. There was always more of the spirit of protest in American society than its politics and surface complacencies revealed. Some of it found release in literary expression, some in moving westward away from whatever was unsatisfactory at home. Some, with that curious distortion of liberalism that was the Puritan spirit, found its outlet in efforts to make other men better by legal compulsions, from blue laws to Prohibition. Only part of minority dissent expressed itself in reform, and then often in support of some panacea, like abolitionism, the single tax, or free silver.

The more balanced political dissent came from those who professed a more consistent liberalism. It was they who urged state and local legislation against economic injustice, and prepared the way for the social security of recent decades. Usually they were politically ineffective in comparison to their talents, for the liberal of the old school was too much of an individualist to cooperate fully or to compromise happily. He was not an organization man in a society where, increasingly, only organization was influential. American liberal movements in the nineteenth century were temporary alliances between forces in disagreement upon almost everything except a single mutual dislike, and were usually only sporadic, with a tendency toward centrifugal movement, constantly throwing off individuals from the nucleus. Since liberals were never more than a minority, it was only when some external force pushed other voters into their camp that they strongly influenced national politics.

That was what began to develop at the opening of the new century, when the natural liberals gained temporary support from others discontented or in search of change. Many Americans who usually kept clear of reform movements had been stirred by painfully visible social and economic infelicities. The instinct for protest that had lain fallow since the Civil War reasserted itself in solid Midwest farmers, small eastern businessmen, and skilled factory workers. Prosperous and hence convinced supporters of private enterprise, they were nevertheless disturbed by some of its excesses that seemed to stem from economic oligarchy. Many a citizen of 1912 was thinking as Edward Bellamy had thought twenty-five years earlier: "How shall an equal opportunity for the pursuit of happiness be guaranteed to all save by a guarantee of economic equality?" Senator Albert Beveridge had written in 1906 of men like these: "I have been carefully studying the present unrest . . . it is not a passing whim, but a great and natural movement such as occurs in this country . . . once about every forty years."

The dissenters and worriers, mentally conditioned by the thought patterns of mechanical progress, turned instinctively to mechanical remedies for human ills, and set out to improve society by improving its organization and machinery. Randolph Bourne described that instinct, but though he placed it in the future it was potent as he wrote in 1913:

> The religion that will mean anything to the rising generation will be based on social ideas and a growing belief in political machinery. Since there seems little hope of making men more moral, perhaps better machinery will make it more difficult for them to be immoral.

Most reformers of the time believed the flaws in economic and social life could be corrected by government action. First they attempted reforms through local politics, but soon became convinced that local ills were derived from wider causes, and turned to state and national politics. Since few Americans want to step out of the two-party system or change their allegiances within it, these disturbed citizens tried to liberalize their own parties. The natural liberals and the newly vocal workingman turned chiefly to the Democratic party, which professed great social concern partly because it had been so long out of power. There was some irony in this, for that party contained as many would-be Mark Hannas as the Republican organization did: southern senators, labor leaders, urban professional men, machine bosses, intellectual liberals, and economic underdogs made as strange bedfellows in the Democratic party in 1912 as in 1948. The intellectual liberals supported Woodrow Wilson against the Democratic old guard, but it was agrarian resentment against the urban elements of the Democratic party in 1912 that was most vocal at the 1912 convention. The chants of Champ Clark's Midwestern supporters had deep significance:

> Every time I come to town
> The fellers keep kickin' my dawg aroun',
> I don't care if he is a houn';
> They gotta quit kickin' my dawg aroun'.

That protest, more than anything else, made the Democratic party the party of the people and hence of change, but it did not attract into its ranks many who were temporarily aroused from their natural conservatism. Had these men—Republican by instinct or tradition—had no option to voting for Mr. Taft or Mr. Wilson in 1912, they would have voted for Mr. Taft, but Theodore Roosevelt provided them with an alternative. This shift of disturbed conservatives from Mr. Taft to Mr. Roosevelt elected a liberal Democrat they did not want.

The Progressive party of Theodore Roosevelt was not really a political party. It was a combination of an admiration society and a protest vote, short-lived because it had only one leader and because many of its members never voted comfortably except under the Republican eagle. Half the Progressives were less devoted to measures than to a man, and the rest were voting in protest against the domination of their own party by reactionaries. Roosevelt, in his new incarnation of virtuous rebel, led many of his supporters further leftward than they would otherwise have gone. Their 1912 revolt was rightly named the Progressive and not the Liberal party.

The sudden ebullient surge to T. R.'s Bull Moose banner was not an isolated phenomenon in American political history. Political crusades centered upon a single leader had happened before and would happen again. Such a movement was due in 1912, for in cyclical intervals, as Senator Beveridge had pointed out, a segment of the American public takes off on what its members believe to be a noble crusade and its opponents call merely an emotional jag. The Bryan fervors and the Willkie fervor of 1940 were other examples, but created no moments with quite the significance of those when, at the opening of the Bull Moose convention, Oscar Straus, Jewish philanthropist, led the entering New York delegation down the aisle singing "Onward Christian Soldiers."

The appeal of any political crusade is primarily to the young in years or spirit, and youthful ardor was especially characteristic of the 1912 Progressives. The average age of the leading Progressives in California was thirty-eight, and the reform leaders in all three parties were generally younger than the men they opposed. William Jennings Bryan, after his long career of oratory and defeat, was only fifty-three in 1913; Robert La Follette, for over a decade the warhorse of the corn-belt Progressives, was fifty-eight. Woodrow Wilson was but fifty-seven, and Roosevelt had been the youngest President to enter the White House, and after two terms and then three years of travel and exuberant fulmination was still younger than many Presidents before and since.

Even the elderly Progressives had never fully recovered from the enthusiasms of their youth, when they had listened to the protesters and the hopefuls of the eighties and nineties and then to the muckrakers and municipal reformers of the new decade. William Allen White was one of them, and he found the Bull Moose delegates in startling contrast to the supporters of earlier third parties. The Greenbacks and the Populists had drawn much of their strength from itinerant workmen, misfits and long-haired reformers; farmers with big mortgages, teachers who could not make the grade, less successful lawyers, and ministers whose intentions were better than their political judgments, hopefuls with more enthusiasm than understanding, and neurotics full of hates. Men of that sort had frightened away from earlier liberal movements the prosperous and practical men who could bring social standing and financial support to liberalism. The Progressive movement of 1912 had a wider appeal. White wrote, years later:

> When the Progressive convention assembled in Chicago, I looked down upon it [from the reporter's stand], and saw that here was another crowd. . . . Here were the successful middle-class country-town citizens, the farmer whose barn was painted, the well-paid railroad engineer, and the country editor. It was a well-dressed crowd. We were, of course, for woman suffrage, and we invited women delegates and had plenty of them. They were our own kind too—women doctors, women lawyers, women teachers, college professors, middle-aged leaders of civic movements, or rich young girls who had gone in for settlement work. I figured there was not a man or woman in the crowd who was making less than two thousand a year, and not one, on the other hand, who was topping ten thousand. Except for George Perkins [a Morgan Partner] from Wall Street . . . who had known Roosevelt in Harvard, loved him and misunderstood him.
>
> The Progressive party . . . was a party of middle-class protest . . . ripening into middle-class rebellion at the slow-moving economic progress being made by our government . . . in the main and in its heart *petit bourgeois* . . . a movement of little businessmen, professional men, well-to-do farmers, skilled artisans from the upper brackets of organized labor . . . the successful middle-class citizens. They were not lineal descendants of the Greenback, the Populist and the early agrarian movements.

To Amos Pinchot, who was also present, the Progressive convention was not quite so wholeheartedly admirable. He saw among its members: "socialists in a hurry and impatient of the tactics of their party; sentimentalists more moved by their emotions than by any processes of their minds . . . cynical, hard-faced professional politicians with no ideals and no purpose beyond the possible collection of the loaves and fishes that Roosevelt's popularity might put within their reach"—in short, the camp followers that are the liability of every crusade.

Theodore Roosevelt was a liberal more by circumstance than by nature, and that made his Progressive party more palatable to men to whom even the mildest radicalism was distasteful. He gave reform the reassuring flavor of safe Americanism, and his platform, concerned largely with the welfare of the small salaried men, the farmer, the skilled workman, and the middle-class consumer, made his brand of liberalism seem less *outré* to solid citizens. Though he borrowed liberal doctrines from reformers and even from the Democratic platform, he was as firm as any Old Guard Republican in his opposition to the "lunatic fringe"—by which he meant those whose ideas did not have the sanction of a conventional American approach. With no sense of inconsistency he could justify some purely political expediency by a biblical allusion, such as, "We stand at Armageddon and we battle for the Lord"—though he would have been angry if someone had pointed out that in bringing the Bible to the ballot box he was imitating William Jennings Bryan, who had opposed letting the Republicans "crucify mankind upon a cross of gold."

A platform as well as a political opportunity was waiting almost ready-made for T. R. when Old Guard domination of the Republican party induced him to form his own. In 1911 the insurgent Progressive Republicans led by Senator La Follette had organized the national Progressive Republican League and had called for a complete revision of domestic policy. They had attacked the corporations, the bankers, and the private interests that were exploiting the nation's natural resources, and demanded that "government be returned to the people" (a phrase more original then than now) through such devices as the direct election of senators, the initiative, referendum and recall, and national presidential primaries instead of boss-dominated nominating conventions. This was a program hand-tailored to attract the leadership of T. R., and on his return from Africa and Europe he had joined the league, which later provided the nucleus of an organization and platform for his own Progressive party.

Liberalism has different meanings to different generations, and tends to become whatever men who claim to be liberals say it is. Neither the liberalism of the Roosevelt Progressives nor that of the

Wilson Democrats was the liberalism of the nineteenth century, and that change is highly significant in political history. The only common ground in the liberalism of Gladstone or Cleveland and that of Wilson or T. R. lay in their mutual desire to improve human welfare and oppose conservatism. In their concepts of what conservatism is, or how to achieve human welfare, or the function of the state, they were poles apart.

Nineteenth century liberals sought progress through the individual; liberals of the twentieth century seek it through the group. The Victorian liberal believed government should regulate individuals only to the minimum essential to the common good. He did not defend rampant laissez faire, but he did believe the state should not assume direct responsibility for the private welfare of the individual. His political philosophy was influenced and nourished by the traditions of religious nonconformity. It was, for example, moral pressure from religious nonconformists that led Gladstone to repudiate Parnell because he was a convicted adulterer. And when the Methodist preacher Hugh Price thundered from his pulpit, "What is morally wrong can never be politically right," liberals of Victorian times were sincere in their agreement—at least in principle.

But by 1912 liberalism was no longer fortified by religious convictions and moral imperatives, and though it worked for human improvement it had somewhat less "respect for the dignity and worth of the individual," as John Morley had put it. The liberals of the new century sought political reforms, not as expressions of the will of God, but as steps toward the Good Society. They believed that the increasing complications of modern civilization rendered the individual incapable of solving his own economic and social problems, and though they praised the common man at least as fulsomely as earlier liberals had done, they had less faith in his unaided capacities. Society must care for those unwilling, as well as those unable, to care for themselves. Central government must be not only a good Samaritan but also a good nurse and headmaster. Instinctively they turned to federal legislation and supervision to remedy economic flaws and human frailties, and if a man was faced with a situation too big for him, they thought, There ought to be a law—or at least a new federal agency. They overlooked the remark of De Tocqueville: "Men do not change their characters by uniting with one another."

This new point of view had been developing for over a generation. Edward Bellamy's *Looking Backward* pictured in 1887 a Utopian American of the year 2000—a slightly saccharine blend of Plato, Karl Marx, St. Paul, and Aldous Huxley's *Brave New World*. The book went through several editions, and influenced many intellectuals who never really read it. Its happy citizens bought all their food and clothing from government stores, and paid, not with money, for there was none, but from credit cards issued by the state—for man could work for no one else. The honor of serving the state was man's strongest incentive and highest achievement.

Lester Frank Ward had published in 1883 his *Dynamic Sociology* to stimulate liberal thinking in the direction of state paternalism. In 1906 Ward went further, and presented the first clear-cut American version of the welfare state, in which "scientific sociologists" would solve all "questions of social improvement, the amelioration of the condition of all people, the removal of whatever privations still remain, and the adoption of means to the positive increase of the social welfare, in short the organization of human happiness." The idea naturally appealed more to those ready to be "scientific sociologists" than to the millions who would become their full-time patients. Those who thought themselves wiser than other men were in favor of an all-powerful benevolent state in which their own wisdom would rule.

Henry George influenced liberal thought even more widely with his version of the ever-popular idea of spreading the wealth. He argued that since land was a natural resource it should be the property of society as a whole, and its use the single source of taxation, with unearned increases in its value appropriated by the state for the benefit of all. By 1905 more than two million copies of his *Progress and Poverty* had been sold, and many men who did not accept all of George's ideas were impressed by his emphasis on the common right to a nation's natural resources. Thorstein Veblen was already talking of an engineer-managed economic system—a preview of the technocracy of the 1930's, and Brooks Adams, though more individualistic than the new liberals, expressed their thinking in the *Atlantic Monthly* for April, 1913:

> The social progress of the immediate future resolves itself into the maintenance of order, and order is only another form of words for expressing the notion of competent sovereignty . . . under modern conditions no sovereignty can be competent which is not so powerful that all private interests, great and small, shall be equal before it.

Thus the older liberal emphasis on the individual as the source of social advance became twisted into emphasis on society as the improver of the individual. The old liberal fear of big government was replaced by a new liberal demand for big government. The new liberals would advocate and achieve many needed reforms, but not without intellectual arrogance. They knew what was the best for their neighbors, and felt they had a mandate to organize and regiment society accordingly. Liberalism, without changing its name, had reversed its operating philosophy, and in doing so had diminished the personal status of the individual.

Curiously enough, Theodore Roosevelt's Republican-derived progressivism went further along the road to the welfare state than Woodrow Wilson's Democratic liberalism. The Wilson program advocated reform through the states; he and his fellow Democrats said little or nothing before the election about adding to the powers of the federal government. Roosevelt was at once more radical and more realistic, for he saw that the reforms his platform called for could be achieved only by a greatly widened and strengthened federal government. In terms of modern liberal philosophy, T. R. was therefore more liberal than Mr. Wilson; to the Victorian liberals he would have seemed less so.

It was ironic that the most rugged individualist in America, by leading the Progressive parade to "common principles of right and fair dealing," arrived at a position to the left of his Democratic opponent. T. R. did his best to defend himself against the charge of advocating state paternalism, and in doing so he phrased better than

Mr. Wilson what more and more Americans were conceiving as the proper function of democratic government:

> I do not ask for over-centralization, but I do ask that we work in a spirit of broad and far-reaching nationalism . . . for what concerns our people as a whole. . . . The new nationalism puts the national creed before sectional or personal advantage. . . . The new nationalism regards the executive power as the steward of human welfare.

But he did not convince the New York *Times,* among others, that his program would not lead to state socialism. In its year-end review its editors commented:

> The most disturbing agitation of the year was doubtless that in which Mr. Roosevelt was the prime mover, for his Progressive party formulated a program of action that aimed at grave changes in the structure of our government. It would have changed not alone the government, but the habits of the people.

President Nicholas Murray Butler of Columbia University wrote with disapproval of "the new American revolution" in which the people were yielding their power and might later yield their freedoms to the federal government for the sake of economic security. Frederick Jackson Turner, the historian of the frontier, and psychologist William McDougall would soon voice similar concerns. But, in spite of such warnings, Americans were getting ready to create a new bureaucratic federal army that their ancestors might have resisted as vehemently as they resisted the quartering of the king's troops in their homes. They would accept the new invasion of government because each separate end seemed at the time sufficiently desirable to make its means tolerable. They did not visualize in advance the cumulative effect of their concessions.

Abstract considerations like these did not trouble most voters in 1912. It did not matter very much, in long-term realities, which of the candidates they elected in 1912, for forces greater than Presidents and political parties were pushing the nation toward standardization and statism. Industrialized economy and popular sovereignty were in the saddle, and they would inevitably change the United States from a federated republic of limited powers to a total democracy with almost limitless powers. They would turn Americans from the pursuit of personal freedom to personal security, from pride in an independent personality to pride in the conformity of "togetherness." The Progressives and liberals of 1912 were not to be blamed for that, if blame is appropriate. They did not see where the pursuit of the new liberalism would lead them. If they had seen, many would not have liked it, but they could not have prevented it.

III
Congress

The new year of 1913 dawned, according to the New York *Times*, "burdened with good promise." Before the year was out many a congressman would feel the burden of that promise, as well as of campaign promises of his own. A French aristocrat, asked what he did during the Revolution, replied with some feeling, "I survived!" By the end of 1913 the politicians of Washington might feel like congratulating themselves on having survived tariff revisions, banking legislation, war scares, the high cost of living, reforms, the pressures of patronage, the suffragettes, slit skirts, and William Jennings Bryan.

These trials lay still ahead when the Sixty-third Congress convened, in an atmosphere of "cautious confidence," to hear the President read his message in person. No President had done so since Thomas Jefferson, and this reassertion of democratic directness seemed another good augury.

Congress expected its chief work to be in economic legislation, which would not only curb the malefactors of great wealth but also enhance prosperity. Even the bankers, though they groaned over coming currency and tariff laws, expected a prosperous year. James Forgan, president of the First National Bank of Chicago, stated in a New Year release: "For the coming year I see no reason to anticipate anything but good business and continued prosperity. The change of administration should not cause real apprehension. The tariff will, of course, be revised, which will cause hesitation in some lines of business, but the President-elect has promised that business interests have nothing to fear from the administration."

Some of Mr. Forgan's fellow bankers did not share his confidence in the cordiality of the new administration, but the old year had ended cheerfully on the New York Stock Exchange, the money market was quiet, and commodities like wheat and cotton were encouragingly steady. Year-end reviews said the prospect of Balkan peace was more hopeful; there was a cheerful feeling on the London exchange, and the financial situation in Berlin was easier than had been feared.

The *Times* was almost jaunty in its new-year prophecies: "We are still messing up the corporations a good deal, but public opinion is coming to accept them as being for the general good. . . . The reformers are in full cry after the money trust and the Stock-Exchange," but the bark of the reformers was usually worse than their bite. Though labor unions were threatening serious strikes and many businessmen were preparing to fight the unionization of their plants, collective bargaining was recognized in fact if not always in principle, and the nation had displayed a consoling ability to survive strikes and reformers. It was only the Industrial Workers of the World that really disturbed the *Times:* "The prevailing opinion in American communities is that this organization is a power for evil."

There was widespread agreement that the economic system needed some regulation and that the federal government must make both management and labor more considerate of the public welfare. Theodore Roosevelt had made a beginning toward curbing economic irresponsibility, but his trust busting had been far from complete, and Mr. Taft, though moved to some measures by the pressures of a Democratic majority in the House, had left much to be done. The Wilson administration had promised a thorough inquisition of the suspected offenders, and the public settled back to enjoy the coming show.

Henry Adams also anticipated fireworks, though with less pleasure. In late September, 1912, he had written to John Franklin Jameson: "By the time I get back I expect to see you all settled down to Mr. Wilson's regime, and as that amounts to the death and burial of my friends, I hope to pack up and git, the Lord knows where, till the revolution is over. The new world will not concern me."

Adams did not object to reasonable regulation of the railroads,

banks, and corporations, for every Adams had opposed, at least in
theory, the plutocratic powers. What Adams foresaw and disliked
was a far more fundamental change, a shift downward in the control
of national power. He wrote to his English friend Milnes Gaskell, the
day after Mr. Wilson's inauguration:

. . . after all, these governments merely reflect the majority of society, and
we know pretty well what intellectual stage that is. We started to straddle
an upper-middle class. Matt Arnold and others told us what that was. It
very rapidly broke down, and dropped us in the dust. The lower-middle
class then took its place, and naturally left us on our backs. I take it that
you in England are now beyond any middle class, and are being run by the
laboring class, or something near it.

Adams's long-term worries were not troubling Congress or the
people, who were interested in more immediate and concrete events.
During the first two years of Mr. Taft's Presidency, Congress had been
Republican-controlled, but in the elections of 1910 the Democrats
had secured a majority in the Senate. Though the *Times,* reviewing
the Sixty-second Congress, had called it "a fussy, excited, confused
body which undertook much and brought about little," it had set in
motion forces that determined the pattern of action of the next
Congress.

That "fussy, excited, confused body" had voted the first federal
income tax, and the Sixteenth Amendment permitting the tax received its necessary state ratifications in the last weeks of the Taft
administration. That Congress which "brought about little" had legislated the direct election of senators, and the Seventeenth Amendment
authorizing the change received its thirty-sixth state ratification and
became law on May 9th. The same split-party Congress had established the parcel-post system, which added greatly to public convenience and retail trade, and was welcomed as one of the most useful
steps taken by recent administrations. When it went into effect on
the stroke of midnight of January 1, 1913, the first package delivered
in Philadelphia was for President Taft: fifty-eight silver spoons from
former Postmaster General John Wanamaker. The first package de-

livered in Princeton reached the President-elect seven minutes after
the new year had begun. It was a gift of two dozen apples (doubtless
well polished) from the Woodrow Wilson Club of Princeton, and
few noted the pleasing paradox that it was the Republican President
who accepted free silver. The new system was so popular that on
August 15th the allowable weight per package was raised from eleven
to twenty pounds, and five months later to fifty pounds.

The same Sixty-second Congress had enacted an important amendment to the pure-food law; it had broken the ice toward a general
eight-hour workday when it voted an eight-hour law for all work
under government contract; it had passed a "dollar-a-day" pension
act; it had admitted Arizona and New Mexico as states, and it had
ratified several treaties with Britain and France. Perhaps equally important in the long run were the investigations initiated by this "confused body" leading toward legislation on working conditions and
financial controls. These investigations and the popular opinions they
helped form made it easier for the Wilson administration to legislate
its economic program.

Of course, the "lame duck" session from November to March postponed some legislation so that the new administration could act on it,
but the record of the Sixty-second Congress in that final session is not
without achievement. It amended the Interstate Commerce Act "providing for a valuation of several classes of property of carriers subject
thereto, and securing information concerning their stock, bond and
other securities." It established a Department of Labor in the Cabinet,
a bill reluctantly signed by Mr. Taft in deference to the expressed
wish of the President-elect. It revised the laws on immigration, ex-
cluding all aliens over sixteen who could not read English or some
other language, excepting parents and grandparents of existing citizens. The President vetoed that bill, and the Senate passed it over his
head, but the House failed to do so and the bill did not become law.

The "lame duck" session also adopted the Webb-Kenyon bill to
assist the states in the enforcement of state prohibition laws, though
Mr. Taft had opposed it as "a violation of the Interstate Commerce
clause of the Constitution, in that it is in effect a delegation by Con-

gress to the state of the power of regulating interstate commerce in liquors, which is vested solely in the Congress." The House passed a bill dealing with working conditions for seamen, but Mr. Taft pocket-vetoed it on the grounds that it conflicted with treaty obligations. The Senate voted a resolution to amend the federal Constitution and limit the term of the President and Vice President to a single term of six years. In the House, the Judiciary Committee had reported favorably on a similar bill in 1902, but no final action was taken.

Anxious to begin his ambitious program of legislation, President Wilson summoned the new Congress for an extra session beginning on April 7th. He had good prospect of legislative support. Democrats controlled the Senate by a majority of six or seven, and in the House there were 291 Democrats, 127 Republicans, 7 Progressive Republicans, 9 Progressives, and one Independent. It was significant, though not necessarily encouraging, that 56 of the Senators and 248 of the Representatives held law degrees.

Even before Congress met, the Democratic leaders had agreed on the main outlines of the new tariff bill—an issue sure to rouse strong opposition. The administration was committed to large reductions in import duties, and these were certain to be opposed by powerful interests in business and agriculture. The Underwood Tariff bill, promptly laid before the House and Senate, proposed reductions of from 42 per cent to 26 per cent and the free list was increased by some hundred items, while seventy others previously free were to become dutiable. Like any tariff bill, the Underwood bill represented infinite compromises between special interests, but not compromises enough to suit several large industries with powerful lobbies in Washington. In its final form the bill was of course less drastic in its reductions than had been initially hoped and feared.

As a historian President Wilson was presumably prepared for the activities of lobbyists and the pressures of special interests, but apparently their number, power, and methods surprised as well as angered him. How much of this wrath was calculated it is difficult to know, but his outbursts were well timed to bring added support to the Underwood bill. Early in May he was quoted in the press across the nation as having remarked that there were so many tariff lobbyists in Washington that he "couldn't throw a brick without hitting one . . . . There is every evidence that money without limit is being spent to sustain this lobby. . . . The Government ought to be relieved of this intolerable burden."

The average American did not like lobbyists, except of course those lobbying for his own special interests, and the President received strong public support for his proposed investigation of lobbies by a joint House-Senate committee. Those investigations, though they failed to produce the startling scandals that some had hoped for, did tend further to discredit the opposition to the Underwood bill. The testimony of every senator was taken by the committee, and some senators named persons who had used, or tried to use, improper methods to influence legislation, especially in the case of the sugar and wool tariffs. The American public was apparently more shocked by lobbies in 1913 than it was by the activities of the Five Percenters thirty years later.

The most sensational testimony was that of one Martin M. Mulhall, who said under oath that agents of the National Association of Manufacturers and other interested groups had attempted to bribe certain members of Congress. Mulhall's charges were found to be without foundation except in the case of Representative James T. McDermott, of Illinois, whom the committee found guilty of "grave acts of impropriety." The investigation, like Mr. Wilson's remarks, was well timed to aid the passage of the tariff bill.

The House, voting on party lines, passed the Underwood bill on May 8th by 281 to 139, but the fight had only begun, for in the Senate the Democratic majority was less dependable. Nearly every item marked for reduction was strenuously argued through the summer, with those who opposed the free entrance of sugar the most vehement of all. Even the automobile manufacturers, whose sales were mounting every year, insisted that the new tariff of only 45 per cent on imported motorcars would flood America with cars made in Europe, and stifle the new industry. Charles M. Schwab, president of the Bethlehem Steel Corporation, said that the proposed reductions

would bring the country the most serious depression it had ever
known. In the *Century Magazine* Theodore Roosevelt, without taking a position on individual tariffs, called the tariff bill "a red herring
. . . to divert people from the real issues." Finally, on September 9th,
the Senate approved the bill by 49 to 37, and the President signed it
on October 3rd. Its rates were the lowest since the Civil War.

Bankers and businessmen disagreed among themselves about
some features of the proposed economic controls, and the stock-
market fluctuations probably reflected these differences more sensi-
tively than they reflected the danger of war in Europe. Every leader
in industry and finance must have wondered when his turn would
come to appear before the Pujo Committee or the Senate Committee
on Interstate Commerce, or the currency committee headed by
Senator Carter Glass, or one of the other congressional committees
or Department bureaus investigating the ocean-shipping "trust," railroad wrecks, factory working conditions, canning-factory hours and
wages, the cost of living, or oyster-bed pollution. Even before the new
administration had set up various new committees of inquiry, the
Times had said, on January 19th: "Never in the history of the United
States have so many investigations been underway as at present . . .
trying to unearth graft or wrong-doing. The Federal Government is
setting the pace."

Heads of business and finance sometimes fought back in their
testimony before Congress, in newspapers and magazines, and
through their political influence at home and in Washington. Since
they were the largest contributors to the treasuries of both parties,
their political influence was considerable. Business men had a good
over-all case for the merits of their system as a whole, and many of the
attacks on them were untrue or unjustified. Most of the economic experts supported the financial system, though some of them did so less
downrightly than Sir George Paish, editor of the London *Statist,* a
financial authority respected on both sides of the Atlantic. He wrote
in January that the alleged United States "money trust" had made for
progress in America and that the influence of the large banking houses
had been wholly beneficial.

When Mr. Wilson embarked upon his promised antitrust program, the public was with him, provided, of course, that he did not go "too far." Legislative activity began almost immediately on a broad front. A Senate committee urged immediate enactment of amendments that would strengthen the antitrust laws, and recommended the creation of a federal commission with jurisdiction over all corporations, partnerships, and individuals engaged in interstate commerce—an arrangement similar to the Interstate Commerce Commission's control over the common carriers. Senator La Follette and others introduced bills to regulate business, and in early March the Federal Commission on Corporations announced that the International Harvester Company held an illegal monopoly. Its president, Cyrus McCormick, promptly protested the statement and the government's method of attack through press release before a hearing, but the public assumed the federal authorities would eventually win its case.

"The Boot and Shoe Trust," as it was promptly christened by journalists, was accused of fixing the prices of nearly 80 per cent of the boot and shoe lasts in the United States, and just before Mr. Wilson took office Judge Arthur Tuttle of the United States District Court in Detroit issued a decree dissolving the trust. Presumably there would be an appeal, but the climate of opinion under the new administration was likely to result in a legal decision supporting the judge.

The Taft administration deserves credit for the amendment to the Interstate Commerce Act voted in early 1913. That amendment was more significant than at first appeared, for it authorized the Commission to make a fiscal valuation of railroad properties as the first step toward arriving at a just basis for determining fair rates. The idea that the federal government should regulate the railroads in the interests of the public had been voiced by a few citizens when the Union Pacific Railroad was completed across the continent at the close of the Civil War, and very mild legislation to that end had been introduced into Congress in 1874 and 1878. In 1885 a Senate Committee had declared:

"It is the deliberate judgment of the Committee that upon no public question are the people so nearly unanimous as upon the proposition that Congress should undertake in some way the regulation of interstate commerce."

An Interstate Commerce Act was passed two years later, but by 1890 certain court decisions had made it almost impotent. Between 1887 and 1905 the railroads took sixteen decisions of the Commission to the Supreme Court, and that Court had found in favor of the railroads in fifteen of them. Similar actions by the courts had weakened the operations of the Sherman Antitrust Act, which became law in 1890. As a result there was much bitter criticism of the courts by liberals, farmers, small producers, and organized labor. In 1906 the Hepburn Act finally gave the Interstate Commerce Commission some real control over unreasonable or discriminatory railroad rates, but not control over the means of finding the facts to determine what was a fair rate.

By the middle of 1913 it was generally believed that the President was considering the advisability of government ownership of the nation's telegraph and telephone system. Theodore N. Vail, president of the American Telegraph and Telephone Company, commented somewhat cryptically: "We should not be averse to any government action which would result in reducing the expense of operating our long distance service." The *Times* came stalwartly to the defense of private enterprise: "There is nothing new about the government telegraph idea, and there is nothing good about it." The company had been under investigation by the Department of Justice for some time, and before 1913 ended it agreed to divest itself of all its holdings in the Western Union Telegraph company, and reorganize "in full conformity with the terms of the Sherman Act." By December a number of other large companies, including the New Haven Railroad and the American Sugar Refining Company, were said to be arranging with the Department of Justice to settle their cases by consent decrees or out of court.

During the Taft administration there had been much talk of currency reform and the creation of a Federal Reserve Bank and Board. Opinion in conservative financial circles supported this plan, and the *Wall Street Journal,* a decade earlier in 1903, had described the banking world as "not merely a normal growth, but concentration that comes from combination, consolidation, and other methods employed to secure monopolistic power. Not only this, but this combination has not been along the lines of commercial banking. The great banks of concentration are in close alliance with financial interests ultimately connected with promotion of immense enterprises, many of them being largely speculative."

Some bankers doubted, however, the ability of Congress to formulate without their aid a wise and workable currency system and Reserve Board. Even the draft of a bill prepared by a Senate committee under the able leadership of Carter Glass of Virginia did not please them. In his June message Mr. Wilson urged Congress to give "the business men of this country a banking and currency system by means of which they can make free use of freedom of enterprise and of individual freedom"; but that appeal did not win the support of Charles N. Fowler, former chairman of the House Banking and Currency Committee, who said the new bill "exhibits more ignorance of banking economics and involves more danger to business and government than any other serious proposal in fifty years," and that the measure was "certain to bring overwhelming calamity to this country." Mr. Fowler could not have been more wrong, and he certainly did not express the opinion of many bankers and financial experts.

After much debate the House passed the Glass committee's bill on September 18th by the overwhelming vote of 286 to 84, but there was still strong opposition in the Senate, including Democratic Senators James A. Reed and James A. O'Gorman. But the November election returns with their added Democratic gains were generally interpreted as popular support of the President's program, and the two senators agreed to support the bill. Even then Mr. Wilson had to adopt extraordinary measures to secure its passage. He insisted that Congress continue in session until the currency bill had been dealt with. Since Christmas was imminent and there were political fences to be mended at home, the Senate finally passed the bill in mid-December, and Mr. Wilson signed it two days before Christmas. In spite of earlier reservations, the banks of the nation promptly took up membership in the Federal Reserve System. It was a hard-won but notable victory for Mr. Wilson and the legislation proved to be highly successful. The historian Samuel Eliot Morison has since called the Federal Reserve Act "the most important piece of financial legislation since Hamilton."

The new income tax was still more significant and, alas, at least equally enduring. The idea of an income tax was not a new one, and the credit or blame for its creation cannot go to Mr. Wilson. In his annual message to Congress on December 3, 1906, Theodore Roosevelt had written: "There is every reason why, when next our system of taxation is revised, the National Government should impose a graduated inheritance tax, and, if possible, a graduated income tax." But T. R. did not press for income-tax legislation, and it is doubtful that it would have been voted in the Taft administration if the Democrats had not been so strong in the House.

Many citizens, and particularly those with large incomes, believed a tax on personal income to be wrong in principle and dangerous in practice. They claimed that it invaded the right of the individual to his earnings and to privacy regarding them; that it was equivalent to government confiscation, and that although the tax might be small in the beginning it would increase until it amounted to socialistic redistribution of private property. The *Times* doubted both the equity and the efficiency of an income tax, and said it was popular because it taxed only the richest 10 per cent of the population, but it would become less popular later as the rates were raised or the exemptions lowered. But the bill was passed, and the necessary constitutional amendment ratified by the thirtieth state on February 13, 1913, and Secretary Knox proclaimed it law only a week before Mr. Wilson took office. As compared with present income-tax rates and coverage, the tax was far from painful. The basic tax was 1 per cent of income, and the first $4,000 of income was exempt from any tax. Incomes that after deductions were in excess of $20,000, and less than $50,000, were taxed 2 per cent; those between $50,000 and $75,000 were taxed 3 per cent, and even in the highest brackets of income the percentage increases were not steeply graduated.

So the year's legislation grated on, enlivened by investigations and delayed by debates over Mexico, industrial strife, and military budgets. The President did not relax his determination to press forward with further progressive legislation as rapidly as Congress and the distractions of a misbehaving world would permit. But antitrust legislation soon lost its initial appeal as a crusade against evildoers, for the inquisitions revealed fewer great iniquities and sins than had been predicted by the liberals, and the public was reaching the conclusion that there had been more political smoke than economic fire. Despite the rising cost of living and the disquiet of farmers and organized labor, the nation was prosperous, and prosperity put a damper on drastic change. What was more, public attention was increasingly directed toward Mexico, Europe, and the question of American military preparedness.

Even the most ignorant or indifferent citizen could not be sure that Europe might not erupt into war and that the effects on America might not be incalculable. It now seems strange that during 1913 there was not more firm leadership from the President to prepare the nation's defenses, intellectual as well as military, against that possibility. The United States Army and Navy were inadequately financed, and the Regular Army was almost infinitesimal. Yet there was no clear proposal directly from the White House to strengthen them. If the people of America judged the seriousness of the situation by the words and actions of the President, they had no reason to think themselves unprepared. The situation in Mexico seemed to bulk larger in the administration's concern than worry over the threat of Europe's armament race. Were American diplomats in Europe failing to apprise Mr. Wilson of the real danger, or was Mr. Bryan soft-pedaling their reports, or was Mr. Wilson refusing to read the handwriting on the wall?

As the year progressed there was increasing public concern about rising costs of living, but it brought little or no effective action from Washington. The President appointed a commission to study what could be done, but in his public utterances he did not stress the problem as one of great concern to the White House. He made no concrete proposals regarding it, even in his December message to Congress. Rural credits were under discussion, but legislators and the White House gave the matter only lip service.

On December 2nd, in his first annual message to Congress, the President urged further federal regulation of trusts and monopolies and, somewhat less forcefully, a system of rural credits, but most of his other specific recommendations were on peripheral issues. He recommended a national primary for the nomination of presidential candidates, the extension of citizenship to Puerto Ricans, more self-government for Hawaii, ultimate independence for the Philippines, development of the resources of Alaska and, later, a "free territorial government" there. For a President opposed to "manifest destiny" and concerned with domestic affairs, the message seemed remarkably centered on the outposts of the empire. So far as industrial legislation was concerned, the President's proposals ignored the heart of the matter. He advocated an employers' liability act for railways, alleviation of working conditions for sailors, and steps to increase safety and economy in mining. A man from Mars, reading that message, might assume that America was faced with no economic or military threats that could not be coped with by a little more tinkering with the machinery of government.

A man who demands a great vision and strong actions of others when the power is in their hands sometimes falls silent when power is in his own. Viewed with the hindsight of 1960, President Wilson's year-end plans of 1913, at the height of his national influence, seem strangely lacking in realism and in fundamental attacks on the chief problems of the nation. By taking no clean-cut position on military preparedness, he seemed to deny its importance, yet the press and public opinion did not seem strongly critical of this omission. During 1913 men and women were killed in strike riots, federal and state troops were called out in half a dozen states, and the right of labor, employers, and the public in industrial disputes were far from clear. Though wage increases over the previous decade had not equaled cost increases, working hours often exceeded fifty per week, and women and children were working in textile plants and canning factories at incredibly low wages, the President did little to alter these conditions. It was true that he had pressed Congress into creating a federal mediation board just in time to avert a railway strike, but mediation boards are more palliative than remedial, and none of the proposed industrial legislation struck at the heart of economic problems.

Mr. Wilson had, in fact, demonstrated that even he could sometimes compromise principle to expediency. When the Appropriations bill came to him from Congress for his signature, it contained a rider exempting labor organizations and farm organizations from prosecution under the Sherman Act. Mr. Taft called this rider "class legislation of the most vicious sort," as indeed it was, but Mr. Wilson needed the money, and the Democratic party would need the farm and labor votes. He signed the bill.

In spite of these retrospective criticisms, the legislative record of 1913 was good, and the public so regarded it. The President deserves the credit for that record. Though the income tax was not a measure of Mr. Wilson's, he had driven through the Federal Reserve bill and the Underwood Tariff bill with adroit and courageous leadership. At the end of the year the *American Yearbook* said: "American history has been made in 1913 more rapidly than in any other year since the beginning of the century. . . . After sixteen years of Republican rule a Democratic administration has come into power infused with new ideas and dominated by the earnest and powerful personality of President Wilson."

There was much truth in the statement, and if 1913 had been a normal year, with only normal issues and dangers facing the nation, Mr. Wilson's first year might have seemed the beginning of a truly great Presidency. What he had seen and achieved in that first year was on the whole good; it was what he failed to see, or ignored, that troubles the historian. Though he ended the year with the praises and confidence of the American people, it was also true that some of his own supporters were privately a little disappointed. The only major legislation for which he could take great credit was in tariffs and the currency. And there were other men, of both parties, who saw more clearly than he did the danger to America inherent in the European crisis, but whose warnings did not rouse the White House to more than the traditional approach to international peace.

The reaction of one contemporary figure is interesting and, in spite of its emotional bias, significant. Theodore Roosevelt had never liked Mr. Wilson personally, though in 1912 the two men had been advocating similar progressive policies. In spite of the animosities engendered by the campaign, T. R. had emerged from it with respect for Mr. Wilson's astuteness and ability. But as the year wore on, his opinion altered. On September 9th T. R. wrote privately to his friend Senator Henry Cabot Lodge: "I regard Wilson with contemptuous dislike. . . . He is a ridiculous creature in international matters . . . a narrow and bitter partisan, and he is intellectually thoroughly dishonest."

Those were strong words and unjustified opinions, but they indicated how the wind, but for the crosscurrents created by the war, might have begun to blow. What Mr. Wilson's record as a President would have been had not the European war deflected the administration's normal course, it would be futile to try to guess. This much is clear, however: his first year in office proved the only one in which he could move forward relatively undisturbed with his program for domestic affairs. After August, 1914, all internal politics and legislation were colored by international considerations. The President became in effect a war President, and the people of the United States developed, in spite of themselves, a war psychology. The legislative year had begun with optimism tempered by social unrest. It ended with its thinking muddied and distorted by the complications of change and the perturbations of imminent war.

IV
Diplomatic Distractions

On one matter Americans of 1913 were unanimous. They wanted peace. They wanted to be left alone to concentrate on the internal problems brought about by change. Most of them believed the United States need never fight another major war. The majority were by no means pacifists, and were prepared to fight if the nation was attacked, but they did not believe any nation would dare attack them.

What most of them did not see clearly was that in the modern world America might be attacked in ways other than by an army of invasion. There were, of course, some Americans whose professions or businesses led them to think in international terms, who were conscious of how narrow the Atlantic had become, and who saw that America might need to defend itself by fighting outside its own Hemisphere. But there were far more, especially in America's heartland, to whom the affairs and animosities of Europe and Asia seemed safely remote. They had not adjusted themselves to the implications of their nation's new status as a world Power. They did not admit that reality partly from lack of perspective, but partly, too, because it raised issues they did not want to face. America's ability to avoid foreign entanglements was already a myth, but its people could not bring themselves to discard it.

No one had denied the danger of a major war in Europe, but wishful thinkers encouraged their fellow Americans to minimize the danger. They pointed out that a few men had been alarmist about a European war for over a decade but that no major war had taken place. They said the danger of war had been greater than now when the Kaiser had sent his warships to Agadir, but conflict had been avoided then, and future crisis would also be solved at the eleventh hour. Nations like Britain, France and Germany were too civilized, or at least too sensible of their own interests, to attack one another, and too powerful to be attacked. The Great Powers were working together to prevent wars in the Balkans from spreading, and this was proof in spite of saber waving they did not want war. The war talk was inspired by a few jingoists and unscrupulous adventurers with axes to grind, or by military specialists who could not see that modern nations would not make wars without the consent of their people, now too civilized to want to destroy one another. The armaments race was incendiary and should be stopped, but even if it led to war in Europe that war could not last very long, and America need not, and would not, be drawn in. In 1913, a year before Germany invaded Belgium, not one American in ten thought that within five years his country would be sending a million men to fight overseas.

America might bicker with Britain over minor differences, such as the Panama Canal tolls, but it was inconceivable that the two nations would ever fight each other again. A Franco-American war was equally out of the question. As for Germany, Americans had developed a friendly admiration for its culture and efficiency, and for over a decade professors and scientists had been telling their fellow Americans that Germany was the most civilized country in the world. Its schools and universities had become a Mecca for American scholars and scientists, who were even modeling American graduate schools and research on the German system. Its municipalities were models for America to imitate, and American experts like Frederic C. Howe, in the *Outlook* magazine for February 25th, were saying that German cities "have developed the most democratic administration in the world." The efficiency of German industry and labor made even American industrialists envious; the rapid growth of its industry and trade; the tens of thousands of German immigrants who had become good American citizens; the *Gemütlichkeit* of its dominant and well-educated middle class; the sentimental charms of *Stille Nacht* and German family life; the increasing appreciation in America of Goethe,

Heine, and Wagner—all these portrayed a nation too civilized to attack America or begin a war in Europe.

Like the people, the new President wanted to be left alone to devote himself to internal improvements. That was where most of his interest and all his experience lay. As a professor of politics Mr. Wilson had concentrated on American history and governments; as a college president he had devoted himself to educating Princetonians "in the nation's service," and as governor of New Jersey he had not been called on to consider foreign affairs. As a presidential candidate he had limited his references to foreign affairs to the usual platitudes about peace, good will, international justice and moral leadership. Like most other Americans, he regarded professional diplomacy with mild distaste and suspicion, and a few days before his inauguration he had remarked, "It would be the irony of fate if my administration had to deal chiefly with foreign affairs." But no sooner had he taken office than his domestic program began to be interrupted by the irrational or wicked people in other parts of the world who kept doing things he could neither ignore nor control. Like naughty Princeton sophomores they took his time and distracted his attention from the preparation of his next lecture.

Fate added further irony in the fact that political necessity—that indispensable charwoman of democratic government—had compelled the new President to appoint as his Secretary of State a man whose international experience was no greater than his own, and in whose judgment he lacked confidence. William Jennings Bryan had his virtues, but a knowledgeable and orderly approach to international affairs, and a discreet reticence before complicated world issues, were not among them. What was more, the Secretary did not wholly trust the professionals in his own Department and the Foreign Service, and they did not trust him.

Presidents and Secretaries of State inexperienced in foreign affairs were not unprecedented in Washington, but most of them had been allowed time to orient themselves before being called on to make important world decisions. Mr. Wilson and Mr. Bryan were not so lucky. Immediately on taking office they encountered grave foreign issues not of their own making. One of these involved a delicate constitutional problem as well as an international one. California dropped a neatly packaged headache on the door of the White House before its new tenant had even unpacked his belongings.

Mr. Wilson was in some ways more fortunate in that situation than a later President forced to join in the constitutional battle of Little Rock. It was not the Negroes whom Californians were determined to make victims of their discrimination but, as a congressman in Alabama put it, "only the Japs." Fortunately for the unity of his Democratic party, Mr. Wilson was therefore not faced with a solid bloc of resistance from the southern states. He was also lucky that the controversy arose at a time when his honeymoon with the electorate had not ended. But he was unlucky that the foreign country involved was the most sensitive of all the Great Powers and that California was a crucial state in national elections.

After its rapid and conclusive defeat of Russia in 1907, Japan had become the risen sun of the Pacific—a Power to be reckoned with. The Japanese were a proud nation, and especially resentful of any suggestion of inferiority to the American people they emulated and admired—and who professed democratic equality. With a population and birth rate far exceeding the economic capacities of their islands, Japanese were compelled to seek settlement in new lands. The great Western Powers, professedly so friendly, had closed door after door to Japanese in the Pacific area, and were beginning to exclude them from immigration into their own homelands. Americans as a whole had no great fear of Japan's economic aggressiveness or dislike of Japanese immigrants, but the men on the West Coast felt differently. When Japanese began to settle in relatively small though increasing numbers on the Pacific Coast, Californians conjured up an economic threat and social menace from an inferior race. There had been no flaming crosses or lynchings on Californian hillsides, but the spirit of the Ku Klux Klan was in evidence.

In spite of these discouragements, most of the Japanese who had settled in California were flourishing modestly, chiefly in agricultural pursuits. As they saved money they bought small holdings of fruit and vegetable land. The 1910 census reported 1,816 Japanese farmers in California, of whom one-third owned land. In numbers they could hardly be called a major threat to California industry or society, but their number was increasing, and California had already put special limitations on American citizenship.

Early in April, 1913, the California legislature seemed determined to pass a bill prohibiting the further owning of land by aliens not eligible for citizenship. This was a measure openly aimed at the Japanese, discriminatory in intent as well as in effect, and highly offensive to its government and people. The Japanese ambassador politely but urgently called the attention of the federal government to this impending legislation, which, he claimed with good reason, was directly in violation of the existing Japanese-American Treaty of 1911.

While Washington mulled uncomfortably over the matter, the California legislature was more brisk. On April 15th its lower House passed the bill. On April 22nd Mr. Wilson telegraphed to Governor Hiram Johnson requesting him "to act . . . in a manner that cannot from any point of view be fairly challenged or called into question." The President then sent the Secretary of State to Sacramento to present the point of view of the federal government to the governor and legislators of California, while Japan waited with a polite restraint that did not attempt to conceal strong feelings.

According to the press, Mr. Bryan had three "secret" conferences with Governor Johnson and the legislature, and urged them to postpone all land-tenure legislation. He was reported to have hinted that a new treaty with Japan was in the making, though both Japanese and Californians must have recognized that no treaty that would satisfy the Japanese would be acceptable to the Californians. Secretary Bryan's personality may not have made him the most winning of federal spokesmen on that occasion, and Governor Johnson, who had been the Vice-Presidential candidate on the Progressive ticket in the previous year, and who had some of the splenetic directness of the late Mr. Ickes, may not have found the Secretary personally congenial.

At any rate the official reactions of California to Mr. Bryan's proposals were prompt and negative. Governor Johnson, who seldom took kindly to avuncular advice, issued a statement upholding the right of a state to legislate its own internal affairs, and criticizing the federal government for its interference. Although a new bill was drafted by the attorney general of California, it was in essence like its predecessor, and President Wilson sent word to Governor Johnson that it too raised questions of "delicate legislation." But both California Houses passed the bill, and the governor signed it on May 19th.

This put the federal government in a very difficult position and created a major international issue. The Japanese ambassador delivered an official note calling the California law "obnoxious, discriminatory, unfriendly and in violation of the treaty between the two countries," and President Wilson wrote on May 16th that "the Japanese Ambassador was very nervous and gave evidence that his country looked for war."

The issue was half settled by evasion, to the satisfaction of no one except perhaps the Californians, who had their way. The legal authorities of the State Department, necessarily expert at interpreting treaties in ways to relieve national embarrassment, held that the Webb bill was not in direct violation of the existing treaty with Japan, though to any less expert legal mind this seemed a strange interpretation. Americans as a whole were probably not in sympathy with the Webb bill or with the federal government's weasel words. On April 30th ex-President Eliot of Harvard published a long letter protesting the legislation, and the *Times* was by no means the only newspaper to express general agreement with him. Educated opinion throughout the country was reflected in an editorial statement in the *Independent* magazine of May 21st:

> California, through her legislature and her Governor, utterly refuses to yield to the expressed wish of the President of the United States. . . . This is a condition that could not occur in any other respectable nation. There will be no war . . . what may happen, however, is a loss to us of the friendship of Japan.

War was avoided, but the Webb Act continued to be a major exacerbation to Japanese pride and a reason for Japanese doubt of American good will and American honesty. Japanese friendship was lost, and the Webb Act pushed the two nations closer to Pearl Harbor.

Mr. Wilson had not dealt very convincingly with his first great constitutional issue and his first great diplomatic test. Nor had he demonstrated his reputed insistence on ethical standards in international relations. Short of some federal action that might have induced Californians to talk wildly of secession, there was one step that the President might have taken. With all the prestige of his reputation for idealism and of his first weeks in office, he might have put the issue clearly before the American people and appealed to their sense of fair play and good faith. Such an appeal might have created a national sentiment so strong that California might have felt compelled to defer to it. It seems curious that a President so eager to stamp his new administration with an ethical imprint failed to make that attempt.

He was immediately offered a second opportunity to do so, and that time he rose, though somewhat slowly, to the occasion. This was easier, however, for it involved no constitutional issue and no opposing internal sentiment to make him cautious, though it did have complex European aspects. A revolution in China resulted in the establishment of a Chinese Republic that looked sincerely democratic. Most Americans assumed that Mr. Wilson would give it official recognition as soon as he took office, and were surprised when he took no such action during March and April.

The president was quite ready to recognize the Chinese Republic, but wanted to do so in a way that would not offend interested European Powers, and yet would avoid condoning or sharing in the future economic exploitation of China by the same Powers. In the nineteenth century the leading nations of Europe had forced open the doors of China and gained, sometimes under the threat of guns of their battleships, territorial rights and privileges. The results had been foreign exploitation of China and the Chinese. Although the record of the United States in China was far less sullied by military blackmail than that of some other Powers, it was by no means free of charges of dollar diplomacy.

The new Chinese Republic, in dire need of large foreign loans, was not in a position to bargain effectively over their terms. The European Powers, which with America had constituted the Six-Power Pact, were ready to give financial assistance, but on terms that seemed to Mr. Wilson to threaten the continuation of western exploitation of China. Mr. Taft's Secretary of State had given the impression that the United States would join in the Six-Power loan, and make Chinese acceptance of its terms a condition of recognition.

On March 19th Mr. Wilson announced that the United States would no longer be a party to the Six-Power loan, since it was to be secured and administered under terms and conditions "imposed" on China and hence "obnoxious to the principles on which this government rests." He thus repudiated dollar diplomacy and exploitation. His decision was bitterly criticized by some politicians and businessmen, and Huntington Wilson, first Assistant Secretary of State, resigned immediately after the President's announcement. American popular opinion on the whole seemed to approve the President's stand, and a little later the United States recognized the Chinese Republic and found its own way to give it financial support.

International morality proved in this case to be politically sound and diplomatically wise. Whatever moral prestige Mr. Wilson lost in the California-Japan impasse was ameliorated by this stroke in the Chinese affair. But the Chinese problem was easy compared to the issues raised by California, and by others the President would soon have to face. If in these first episodes he had not revealed himself a weak President in international affairs, he had not yet convinced his people and the world that he was a strong one.

V

Watchful Waiting

The California incident was painful and the Chinese problem difficult, but they were soon ended and forgotten, except by the Japanese. The Mexican mess seemed almost insoluble and endless. It too was not of Woodrow Wilson's making; the Mexicans were perennially creating their own troubles. But Mr. Wilson was to learn from Victoriano Huerta things that might help him to deal with kings and kaisers in another year.

Porfirio Díaz, virtual dictator of Mexico for thirty years, had given his countrymen something of order and the semblance of justice at considerable cost in their securities and freedoms. Order was a rare virtue in Central America, appreciated by men with business interests there, and although Americans could not approve dictatorship they had accepted and condoned Díaz. But by 1911 his hand had slipped from the controls and, unable to suppress a revolution, he had resigned. The government formed by the leader of a middle-class revolt was promptly recognized by the United States and European nations. But it soon developed that, after the manner of revolutions, the real power had fallen into the hands of the ignorant, the fanatic, and the self-seeking, whom President Francisco Madero could not control.

According to a congressional committee, there were some 75,000 American citizens resident in Mexico, and American investments there came to at least $1,500,000,000. Americans owned some 78 per cent of Mexican mines, 72 per cent of its smelters, 58 per cent of its oil, 68 per cent of its rubber, and some 66 per cent of its railways. American lives as well as property were endangered in the disorder, and Ambassador Henry Lane Wilson was reporting to Washington that everything under Madero was as bad as it could possibly be.

The peons had supported Madero in the hope of recovering the land Díaz and the upper-class semifeudal proprietors had taken from them. Madero failed to redeem his promise to the landless, and thereby lost their support. But he showed enough sympathy with the peons to alienate the large landholders and some foreign investors. Behind the usual façade of men fighting in the name of freedom, the propertied interests sponsored a movement against Madero, and in February, 1912, Pascual Orozco defeated Madero's troops. President Taft sent 100,000 regulars and reserves to the Mexican border, and many United States citizens, though by no means all of them, left Mexico in alarm.

Then a hard-fighting former general of Díaz named Huerta, nominally a supporter of Madero, crushed the revolt with volcanic efficiency and came to Mexico City to receive the popular ovation that often precedes a move toward military dictatorship. Another rebellion, this one led by Bernardo Reyes and Félix Díaz, then broke out, and President Madero had no alternative to calling on General Huerta to command the federal troops against it. After several bloody battles Huerta put down the new revolution, and reportedly shot not only any civilians who got in his way but also whole companies of his own federal troops whom he thought might be loyal to anyone other than himself.

Again the victorious hero, Huerta bargained with Reyes and Díaz, who, though reluctant, were finally persuaded by Ambassador Wilson to support Huerta's claim for "temporary dictatorship." Huerta arrested Madero and kept him confined to the National Palace, while Ambassador Wilson assembled the diplomatic representatives of the Powers, urged them to accept the Huerta regime, and led the applause to the "savior of Mexico" when Huerta entered the room.

On February 22, 1913, Madero was being escorted from the palace to the jail by Huerta's troops, but on the way he was taken out of the carriage, and shot. Huerta announced that an armed force of Madero's supporters had attacked the federal troops and that Madero had been accidentally shot in the confusion, but readers familiar with the methods of Hitler and Stalin will draw their own conclusions, and most Americans of 1913 reached similar ones. In spite of Ambassador Wilson, the American government and people had little faith in Huerta's honesty and intentions. He was apparently a villain on the Elizabethan model, cruel, able, unscrupulous, and courageous. He was also a heavy drinker and a regular taker of drugs. According to Professor H. B. Parkes, Huerta at the height of his power "lived in perpetual intoxication, and his ministers found him almost impossible to find. Processions of cars filled with high officials were frequently to be seen driving about the city in search of whatever saloon Huerta was believed to be frequenting." One is tempted to discount this picture on the theory that no constant drunkard could have dealt so skillfully with the American government or stayed so long in power.

Most Americans opposed recognizing a government that had gained office by naked force and assassination, led by a drunken dictator, and were shocked when Britain promptly did so. The State Department was equally taken by surprise, since it had received assurances from the British Foreign Office that Britain would not be in haste to recognize Huerta. When officially queried, the Foreign Office explained somewhat lamely that it had changed its mind, and many Americans suspected that British oil interests had called the turn. President Taft, in spite of the initial urging of Ambassador Wilson, refused to recognize Huerta, and was supported by American public opinion, which is never more righteous than in its judgments of the sins of others.

The British recognition of the Huerta regime increased the resentment that two other issues had created between Washington and Whitehall. During the final year of the Taft administration, Congress had legislated exempting ships under the United States flag from the payment of tolls for passing through the Panama Canal, soon to be opened to traffic, but charging tolls to ships under other flags, including the Union Jack. The British government protested that this was a direct violation of the Hay-Pauncefort Treaty ratified by both countries in the administration of Theodore Roosevelt. Mr. Wilson seemed ready to admit this British claim, but Congress was more than reluctant to retreat from legislation it had so recently enacted. National pride, face saving, and the political popularity of twisting the tail of the British lion were all involved in the congressional reaction.

Ill feeling was also augmented by commercial competition in Mexico. British private capital had investments there, and each nation suspected the other of using diplomacy to advance the interests of its own nationals at the expense of their rivals. There were heavy pressures upon both the White House and Downing Street, and Americans were further irritated by the behavior of one Lionel Carden.

Mr. Carden had served as British Minister to Cuba, where his anti-American attitude had been so objectionable that Secretary of State Philander Knox had instructed Ambassador Whitelaw Reid in London to bring Carden's conduct to the attention of the British Foreign Office. The British government not only refused to withdraw or chasten Carden but promptly knighted him. A little later the American government officially asked that Carden be withdrawn, and was refused. Now, when affairs in Mexico seemed to be at their crisis, Britain appointed Sir Lionel to be its Envoy Extraordinary and Minister Plenipotentiary in Mexico City. As if this were not bad enough, Sir Lionel was also believed to be working closely with Lord Cowdray, the head of the British oil interests in Mexico. A few days after the new knight passed through New York city en route to his Mexican post, the New York *World* published an interview with him in which he was reported to have declared that President Wilson knew nothing of the Mexican situation and that Huerta was the best man to lead Mexico through its crisis. American reactions can be imagined.

When it came to ambassadors to Mexico, the United States had little to boast about. Henry Lane Wilson, an appointee of President Taft, had been closely associated with the Guggenheim mining interests, and his repeated and emphatic advices to Washington, as well as his actions in Mexico, were certainly ill judged if not fantastic. Though President Wilson did not immediately replace him, he showed no great confidence in his ambassador and fortunately did not follow his advice.

Woodrow Wilson was inaugurated just ten days after the assassination of Madero, and he promptly made clear his policy toward Mexico. He wished friendship, but friendship would be possible "only when supported at every turn by the orderly processes of just government, based upon law and not upon arbitrary or irregular force." He proclaimed that the United States desired nothing in Central or South America except the lasting interests of the people of the two continents, the security of governments intended for the people and not some special group or interests, and the development of personal and trade relationships "which shall redound to the profit and advantage of both, and interfere with the rights and duties of neither." Since the Huerta government did not qualify under that definition, no one was surprised when on March 11th the President announced: "We have no sympathy with those who seek to seize the power of government to advance their own personal interests or ambitions."

Soon after that curtain lecture from Washington, Huerta announced that since the United States did not recognize his government he obviously could not recognize an American ambassador. Few Americans appreciated the irony of Huerta declining to recognize the man who had helped him to power and had sent repeated messages to Washington urging he be recognized, or that Huerta was doing the President a favor in providing him with an excuse to recall Henry Lane Wilson. When the President learned that his ambassador had, among other diplomatic ventures, invited Huerta to dine at the American Embassy, he sent a note to Secretary Bryan: "I think Wilson should be recalled." The ambassador was asked to resign, and since the United States could not consistently send an ambassador to a government it refused to recognize, the President appointed Mr. Bryan's friend, ex-Governor John Lind of Minnesota, as "my personal representative, to act as advisor to the American Embassy in the City of Mexico," with letters giving him broad powers of negotiation.

Mr. Lind was instructed to propose two steps to Huerta as essential to recognition by the United States. The first was that Huerta immediately end the fighting against the remains of the Madero supporters and against the Constitutionalists headed by Carranza with occasional aid from the independents, General Pancho Villa and Emiliano Zapata. The second was that Huerta arrange for an early and genuinely free election throughout Mexico, in which he would not be a candidate for the presidency or serve if elected. Huerta very naturally accused the United States of trying to dictate to Mexico in its internal affairs—as indeed it was. He rejected the proposals, though later in the summer he did announce a national election in October, and at one time stated that he would not be a candidate. But large-scale guerrilla warfare continued.

Various American interests urged the President to recognize Huerta; others urged that he intervene, with American troops if necessary, and depose him. On July 21st, for example, Senator Albert Fall of New Mexico (who ten years later would be involved in the Teapot Dome oil scandals) and Senator William J. Stone of Missouri proposed that United States troops enter Mexico to protect American citizens there. At the end of July the President made it clear that he was equally opposed to recognition and military intervention, but the public grew more and more impatient for some move from the White House that would settle the confusion and restore American prestige. Senator Beveridge wrote to Senator Moses Clapp on August 24th: "We ourselves must go there and administer her officers for the next two or three generations." Some, though by no means all, Americans would have agreed with what William Allen White later wrote in his autobiography: "Wilson was being noble and huffing and puffing at the job, treating the Mexican government as though they were little brown brothers, and Huerta was getting madder and madder."

In August, Huerta took the diplomatic offensive by giving the United States until midnight of August 19th to recognize the government. Otherwise, he said, all communications between the two governments would cease. Though the United States did not recognize his government, all communication did not cease. Mr. Lind, who had begun his mission very hopefully, found Huerta infinitely resourceful in making half-promises followed by full evasions, and got nowhere.

In late August the President told Congress that the Lind mission had failed and that the situation in Mexico had grown worse. It was reported that American consuls in certain Mexican cities were, on instructions from Washington, urging all Americans to depart, and this caused national excitement. Was the President going to war after all? Whether there had been a misunderstanding or a quick reversal of policy is not clear, but only a few days later some American consuls in Mexico were reported to be encouraging Americans to remain.

By October events seemed to be moving rapidly to the final showdown. On the 11th Huerta issued a decree dissolving the Mexican Congress, and followed it up by sending armed troops to arrest 110 deputies who objected to his personal dictatorship. Ex-Governor Lind, still hopefully in Mexico City, telegraphed to Secretary Bryan: "The United States will probably be compelled to land troops in Mexico before long." On October 15th Secretary Bryan officially informed Huerta that in view of his assumption of dictatorial powers the United States would not recognize as legal or constitutional the results of the Mexican elections of a new president and Congress set for October 26th. Huerta was also warned that the United States regarded his action of dissolving the Mexican Congress as an act of bad faith and that recognition of his government was now wholly out of the question. In a diplomatic precedent, those could readily be regarded as fighting words.

Sir Lionel Carden's activities continued to aggravate Americans and to increase resentment against Britain. His public statements seemed intended to undermine American policy in Mexico, and he appeared to be negotiating with Huerta for exclusive privileges for British oil interests. By late autumn the President and Mr. Bryan were almost convinced that the Cowdray-Carden cabal was chiefly responsible for American inability to work out a joint Mexican policy with Britain. On October 22nd Sir Lionel was reported as having said he saw no reason why the United States should intervene, diplomatically or militarily, in the Mexican situation, or why Huerta should be displaced, Americans were almost unanimously angry, and liberals in England demanded Sir Lionel's recall.

The Mexican elections took place as scheduled, with Huerta denying he had ever said he would not be a candidate for the presidency. Though too few votes were cast to make the election legal, Huerta received more votes than anyone else, and announced that he would continue to head the "provisional government." Three days later General Díaz, a leader of the opposition, tried to land in Vera Cruz but was ordered out of Mexico by Huerta's officials there. He was taken aboard the United States gunboat *Wheeling*, and later transferred to the battleship *Louisiana*, which was standing off in the bay.

Matters looked worse than ever, but undercover diplomacy went to work and brought about important results. The fact had its irony, since it was engineered by a President who would later denounce secret diplomacy and urge "open covenants openly arrived at." No one familiar with the period needs to be reminded of the part played by Colonel Edward M. House as personal adviser and alter ego of the President, but few Americans knew of his role of negotiator in the Mexican crisis. It is difficult to define the precise boundaries between a diplomatic coup and an international deal, if there is a difference, but whatever Colonel House's achievement is called, it was maneuvered with skill and success.

The British government was eager to get the canal-toll controversy settled quickly and favorably but without loss of face by either party. Ambassador Page wrote to Colonel House from London on August 20th: "If the United States will . . . repeal the Canal Toll discrimination, we can command the British fleet, British manufactures—anything we please." There was no doubt where Page stood personally in the matter; he wrote directly to the President on November 2nd: "The Panama Tolls . . . we are dead wrong on that, as we are dead right in the Mexican matter."

Since Europe regarded Colonel House as the power behind the White House throne, his standing as unofficial negotiator exceeded that of any American ambassador. On July 3rd he began private conversations with Sir Edward Grey, the British Foreign Secretary, and with Sir William Tyrrell, the permanent Undersecretary. The talks were studiedly casual, and Colonel House recorded in his diary after the first of them: ". . . we then drifted to the Panama Canal tolls question." Sir William Tyrrell later wrote to the colonel: "If some of the veteran diplomats could have heard us, they would have fallen in a faint." Each party soon caught the other's drift, and after several more unrecorded talks Sir William came to Washington and held further conversation with Colonel House, Secretary Bryan, and the President.

They were fruitful. Colonel House wrote to Ambassador Page on November 14th that after President Wilson and Sir William had discussed Mexico, "then the President elaborated upon the toll question much to the satisfaction of Sir William." One exchange, as reported by Sir William, throws light on Mr. Wilson's character. At one point, the Undersecretary said to the President:

"When I go back to England I shall be asked to explain your Mexican policy. Can you tell me what it is?"

Mr. Wilson, he said, replied, "I am going to teach the South American republics to elect good men."

Even while the talks were in progress, Britain's attitude toward Huerta became more firm, and on November 10th Prime Minister Herbert Asquith stated: "There is not a vestige of foundation for the rumours that . . . we would take a line calculated deliberately to thwart the United States," and that Britain would not consider intervening between Huerta and President Wilson. France and Germany picked up the cue and indicated that they would not fix their own Mexican policies until the United States had defined its attitude. Then, on November 15th, with what inner discomfiture one can but guess, Sir Lionel Carden led a procession of European diplomats to Huerta and formally advised him to yield to the American demand that he withdraw from the presidency of Mexico. Britain also appeared receptive to Mr. Wilson's strategy of placing an embargo on goods entering Mexico, and thus starving Huerta out.

On the military front things were also happening with the suddenness characteristic of Mexican politics. On November 5th Huerta's army moved to recapture Juárez from the Constitutionalists under General Villa, who with Carranza and Zapata had overrun much of nothern Mexico. Villa routed the Huerta troops and started south. Early in November President Wilson called on Huerta to resign immediately and not to name a personal supporter as his successor; it may not have been a coincidence that on the same day the United States Army reported that it could rapidly mobilize 500,000 men wherever needed. Two days later American opposition to Huerta became even more strong at the report that General Díaz had been shot at, point-blank, and stabbed five times, in Havana. Díaz survived, but most Americans assumed the attack had been instigated by Huerta. Mr. Lind left Mexico, openly recommending that the United States sever all diplomatic relations with the Huerta government.

An Anglo-American bargain had been struck, and it was a good one for both nations. To what extent members of Congress realized that repeal of the Canal-toll legislation had been made a bargain for Britain's backing in Mexico, it is hard to say. Professor Charles Seymour, the editor of the House letters, stated categorically that "President Wilson promised to push the repeal of the clause exempting American coast-wise shipping from the Canal tolls, providing the British would not hurry him." On December 13, 1913, Colonel House wrote to Ambassador Page: "Sir Cecil Spring-Rice [the British ambassador] will leave the Panama tolls question entirely in our hands." It was not until the following March that Mr. Wilson formally asked Congress to repeal the clause in question, and not until June that Congress acted, but the President made good on his promise—in his own good time. Colonel House had done his work well.

The military actions that followed were confused and confusing. On November 25th Tampico was attacked by anti-Huerta forces; on November 29th Mazatlán was reported to have fallen to the rebels; two days later Villa announced that he would soon march on Mexico City. The next day the Huerta forces evacuated Chihuahua City, and President Wilson announced that "Huerta's power and prestige are crumbling and collapse is not far away" and that American policy was one of "watchful waiting." Several of Huerta's generals deserted him, for to back a fallen dictator in Mexico was an unpopular form of suicide. A commission sent by Huerta or his supporters went to Juárez to feel out peace terms with the rebels.

Events in December seemed to assure the prompt fall of Huerta. Opposition forces closed in on Tampico; Huerta's family left for San Francisco; the rebels menaced Mexico City. Meanwhile Republicans like Elihu Root and Mr. Taft spoke in nonpartisan support of the President's Mexican policy. The White House seemed to have earned a merry Christmas.

Mr. Wilson's diplomacy, which had for months seemed pompous and futile to many Americans, appeared at last to be justified. Though Huerta held on until the summer of 1914, and though the Mexican troubles did not end with his fall, the President's policy at least achieved a satisfactory end of the first chapter of the Mexican drama without military action or the loss of American lives.

No man ever brought to the Presidency a greater predilection than Woodrow Wilson for urging other nations to conform to his own high ideals. But he revealed in his first year of diplomacy the defects of his own conscious virtue: he trusted few men and did not delegate power easily. Too often he saw himself as a lone crusader against human ignorance and sin, and, like many other professors and intellectuals, he lectured too much. His preaching irritated other men and nations, while his persistence in playing a lone hand annoyed Congress and tested the devotion of his own staff. He would never wholly escape from those self-created limitations, as he would never wholly escape from the problems created at home and abroad by less orderly minds and less ethical men. He had not yet finished with ruffians or ruffians with him.

VI

Balkan Dynamite

Mexico was next door, but the Balkans were far away, and there were not so many Americans or dollars in Romania, Turkey, Serbia, Montenegro, and Greece as in Mexico. Peace and stability in the distant Balkans concerned Americans less than they did in a neighboring country that lay within the province of the Monroe Doctrine. Most Americans did not think that affairs in the Balkans were so likely as the Mexican mess to draw them into war.

A few experts in world affairs realized the Balkan danger, but to the average American what happened at Adrianople was regrettable evidence of Old World instability, but nothing that could affect him personally. The Balkan battles and sudden shifts of fortune made interesting headlines in American newspapers, but some local scandal or sporting event often pushed Balkan news off the front pages. The average man in Paducah or Mankato or Punxsutawney or even in New York knew little or nothing of the history and enmities of eastern Europe. What he did read about, when he had time, was too confusing to understand, and he would have had to turn to an atlas to identify the boundaries and capital cities of the nations at war. No one knew, and only a few feared, that what was happening north of Salonika would prove a preface to world-wide Armageddon.

The United States government did very little to enlighten its citizens about the real menace of the Balkan situation, and if the President or the State Department entered in any significant way into the negotiations to end the Balkan fighting, it is not recorded in the newspapers and magazines of 1913. There must have been watchful waiting in Washington, but those who watched and waited seemed remarkably silent and undisturbed. Mr. Wilson and Mr. Bryan urged world peace and talked disarmament, but they did nothing specific to help put out the Balkan fires.

Yet because those fires alarmed the chancelleries of Europe and ultimately involved America, no survey of the year can ignore them. It is difficult to reduce their confusions and constant realignments to clarity in a few paragraphs, and to do so one must fall back on unsatisfactory generalizations. The only unity among the Balkan allies was in hatred of the Turks, and whenever the Turks were defeated the various allies turned on one another. Any conquest of new territory resulted in new wars to determine who should possess it; any political change in the Balkan nations threatened to upset the balance of power throughout Europe, for each Great Power had its commitments in the Balkans.

In fact, nearly every nation in Europe had its manipulating fingers in that hotbed of political and military rivalries. The great nations had their semisatellites and secret subsidies, and played one Balkan state off against another as pawns in the major chess game of European power politics. International schemers, soldiers of fortune, would-be dictators, groups infected with belligerent patriotic fervors, and the double-dealing agents of economic interests also were stirring the Balkan stew. The Great Powers threw their weight toward peace, for not one of them was ready for war, but even the Great Powers could not control all the discordant elements, and no one could be sure which way the Balkan cats would jump.

In 1912 the allied Balkan States had given Turkey a bad beating and had conquered most of Turkey-in-Europe. Through mediation of the Great Powers, a conference of the belligerents was held in London, and on January 1, 1913, Turkey agreed to cede to the Balkan victors nearly all of her area in Europe except Adrianople, and Greece insisted on taking over the islands held by Turkey in the Aegean. Just when it looked as though Turkey would concede Adrianople, the political party called the Young Turks suddenly overthrew their government and, determined to redeem Turkish pride and Turkish territory, refused peace on such ignoble terms. "We are going to save our national honor or perish in the attempt," they announced, and their fervor put new life into the exhausted and defeated Turks. The peace conference was broken off, and the wars began again.

Thus at the beginning of 1913 Europe abounded with nervous speculation. Lucien Wolf expressed the general alarm in the *London Graphic* when he wrote of "renewed rivalry between Austria and Russia," and added: "It is a delusion to imagine that the Eastern question is now finally at an end. . . . The balance of power in Europe is not quite the security it was taken for." The New York *Times* was more optimistic. Its editorial of February 17th stated: "A year ago it was generally believed in all the capitals of Europe that the first serious conflict in the Balkans would be the signal for a general war, and that, on the other hand, soon or later, a struggle between Great Britain and Germany was inevitable, and more probably soon than late. The interval has seen a very serious conflict in the Balkans, and has also seen Germany and Great Britain working patiently, firmly and in good faith, to preserve general European peace." The *Times* seemed to think that, as far as danger of a European war was concerned, the worst was over.

But the fighting went on, and though under the leadership of the Young Turks the Turkish Army fought like demons, Turkey was unable to hold its own against the combined forces of Bulgaria, Romania, Serbia, and Greece. Early in March the Great Powers informed the Balkan States that Turkey had asked for mediation. Bulgaria remained intransigent, but the others agreed to accept mediation by the Powers, though they insisted that Turkey must pay an indemnity. Peace talks began but were accompanied by a new incentive to war. On March 19th King George of Greece was killed while walking in the main street of Salonika without, on his own insistence, a bodyguard. It was feared that the assassination had been politically inspired and would bring renewed warfare, but the Greek government for once saved the situation by announcing that the murderer was a Greek "of feeble intellect, driven to desperation by sickness and want," and the spirit of the assembling peace conference was less adversely affected than had at first been feared. On March

22nd Sir Edward Grey assured the House of Commons that agreement had been reached on the future frontiers of Albania as a buffer state being created by the Powers; that further attacks on the Turkish city of Scutari would be "criminal folly," and that Europe had "weathered the storm." He added that the problem of Albania had almost brought about a general European conflagration.

But on the same day Austria-Hungary complicated the discussions by making strong demands on tiny but warlike Montenegro, which had laid siege to Scutari, and was believed to have done so with the approval of Russia. Austria was also determined that Serbia should not take possession of Albania, but Serbia, full of self-confidence after its recent successes, was equally set upon having it. If these differences brought armed conflict between Austria and Serbia or Montenegro, Russia would almost certainly support them, and the European fat would be in the fire. Montenegro replied to Austria's demands by declaring them to be a breach of neutrality, and Sir Edward Grey wrote later in his memoirs: "There was an acute crisis when Montenegro got hold of Scutari, which Austria was determined Montenegro should not have." The Montenegrins finally agreed to allow the civil population of Scutari to leave the city, and that situation was somewhat eased.

But the dangers were by no means ended. While the peace conference was still in session, hard fighting and atrocities were continuing. On March 27th the Bulgarians took Adrianople by storm, and though on April 2nd Turkey accepted the peace plan of the Powers, Montenegro refused to do so, and three days later Austria was reported to be determined to act independently against Montenegro if it did not raise its siege of Scutari. Montenegro did not desist, and on April 22nd its troops forced their way into the city against heroic Turkish resistance. It was feared in London, Vienna, and Rome that this might end all hopes for peace, and on May 2nd there was intense excitement in Vienna when Emperor Franz Joseph summoned his Crown Council. War feeling against Montenegro and Russia was high in Austria, though none of this news was thought important enough to appear on the front pages of most American newspapers.

The situation eased again when Austria said it would give Montenegro a reasonable time to get out of Scutari, and it was reported that Montenegro would probably withdraw after a face-saving interval. But rumors spread that as soon as the Balkan allies had got all they demanded collectively, Greece and Serbia would fight Bulgaria over the spoils, and that Italy and Austria-Hungary had a secret agreement to occupy Albania jointly within a few months.

These fears and uncertainties took their toll on the morale and business of Europe. The stock markets were nervous for months on end, and there were several black days of very heavy selling. Even when, on May 30th, the peace treaty was finally signed, the tension did not relax, for some of the most dangerous questions, such as exact Balkan frontiers, the future of Albania, and the ownership of certain Aegean islands were still unsettled, and while the treaty was being signed the Bulgarians and Greeks were fighting each other over territorial gains.

In June, Bulgaria was fighting Serbia as well as Greece, and on June 30th opened a major attack all along the Macedonian front. Brutal outrages on both sides shocked Americans more than the war itself, and on July 15th Sir Edward Grey told the Commons that it was impossible to exaggerate the horrors of the Balkan fighting. It would be difficult, he said, for the Concert of Europe to impose and enforce any peace on the belligerents, and their general exhaustion seemed the only hope.

Turkey, temporarily out of the fighting, had new troubles of its own. The grand vizier, who had headed the Young Turk regime, was assassinated in the streets of Constantinople, and the Turks suspected the Bulgarians of inspiring the act. Bulgaria, busy with the Greeks and Serbs, was suddenly struck hard on the flank by the Romanians, and 35,000 Bulgarians fell in ten days. The Sultan of Turkey then ordered his troops to join in the decimation of Bulgaria and regain the territory Turkey had lost in the last two wars. The Turks retook Adrianople, and the Greeks established control of Salonika and east of it.

On July 12th the Bulgarians said they were ready to talk peace, and five days later Austria-Hungary demanded that the Greeks and Serbians cease their hostilities against Bulgaria immediately, and warned that Austria would not allow Bulgaria to be too deeply humiliated either on the field or at the peace table. This curbed the belligerents, and the third peace conference in a year opened at Bucharest. It was on this occasion that Secretary of State Bryan made his sole official contribution to the Balkan affairs, and it was a curious one. Repressions of religious freedom in the Balkans had brought immigrants from those countries into America in larger numbers than Mr. Bryan and some other Americans thought desirable. He therefore sent a note to the peace conference asking the countries present to make a joint declaration in support of religious liberty. The prime minister of Romania, presiding, read Mr. Bryan's note to delegates who listened with straight faces. It was promptly suggested that since every country participating in the conference had its own laws declaring religious liberty, the declaration suggested by the United States would be superfluous. This was briskly, unanimously, and hypocritically voted, and the conference turned to its more immediate business and its normal disunity.

On August 10th Bulgaria signed a treaty that gave away territory and conquests on all sides. Each Balkan state tried to grab all the land it could, not only from Bulgaria but from its neighbors and allies, and the treaty seemed to have created more new causes for war than it solved old ones. Bulgaria began to demobilize immediately, but just a week later was on the verge of further war with Turkey, which had not been a party to the treaty. The Turks suddenly occupied Demotica, twenty-five miles from Adrianople, and threatened to advance against what was left of Bulgaria. Confused warfare continued through September, when Greece mobilized against both Turkey and Bulgaria, thus forcing those traditional and warring enemies into the same camp. The Paris and London exchanges became more "uneasy" than ever, but Bulgaria was in no position to continue war on any terms, and at the fourth peace conference within the year the Treaty of Constantinople gave back to Turkey most of the territory it had lost.

As the year drew toward its end, there was no assurance that the cessation of fighting was more than temporary. Sir Edward Grey may have secured a few nights of untroubled reading and perhaps a day or two of fly fishing, but he later wrote of the efforts of the Great Powers during 1913: "We had not settled anything, not even all the details of the Albanian boundaries [though] we had been a means of keeping all the six Powers in direct and friendly touch. . . . The settlement after the second Balkan war was not one of justice but of force. It stored up inevitable trouble for the time to come. To make peace secure for the future, it would have been necessary for the Great Powers to have intervened to make the settlement of Bucharest a just one. This they did not do. They dared not do it, being too afraid of trouble between themselves."

It was only a matter of months before Archduke Francis Ferdinand of Austria would be murdered at Sarajevo and all Europe would plunge into war, but not one American in a hundred would have believed that because of Balkan rivalries American armies would, in less than four years, be fighting in Europe.

VII

Internal Combustion

"Nothing has spread socialistic feeling in this country more than the automobile; to the country man they are a picture of arrogance and wealth with all its independence and carelessness."

That was the opinion of Woodrow Wilson in 1906. He must have changed his mind during the next seven years, since he was the first President-elect to be driven to the White House in an automobile—and of all Presidents he was the most constantly concerned to set good examples to his fellow citizens. Those who cheered him along the way probably did not consider the morality of the motorcar or the full implications of Mr. Wilson's modernity.

Most other Americans had also changed their minds about the horseless buggy by 1913. It was no longer an inventor's stunt, a transportation absurdity, or a millionaire's plaything. If in 1906 the automobile was stirring class resentment, by 1913 it was arousing only envy—a coveted phenomenon of America's progress. It would prove to be the nation's greatest social leveler and to affect American life more profoundly than its creators or Mr. Wilson guessed.

Enthusiasts predicted that automobiles would revolutionize transportation, though few of them would have believed that some forty years later a horse would be unique in most cities; that the American motor car industry would be producing over 5,000,000 new cars annually; that so many Americans would pay, or at least begin to pay, upward of $2,000 for one of the cheapest of them; that millions of workmen, low-salaried men, housewives, stenographers, and school children would daily drive their own cars to work, to market, and for pleasure.

In percentages the growth of the industry was already phenomenal. In 1908 the nation produced about 100,000 motorized vehicles, and in 1913 about 500,000, and several thousand men were engaged in making, selling, and servicing them. The value of the finished product was a quarter of a billion dollars, an increase of 82 per cent in ten years, in spite of the fact that cars were cheaper. In 1905 the lowest price for a "dependable" car was about $900, but in 1913 a better one cost only $500. The decrease in cost was largely due to the genius of one man whose name did not appear in *Who's Who* or among the directors of banks. Half a million Model-T Fords were rattling dependably over rutted country roads built for horse-drawn vehicles.

In spite of this expansion, few men were foolhardy enough to predict that the combustion engine would replace the horse. Although there were almost a million autos in the country, there were over twenty million horses, and their numbers too were increasing. New York City officials, concerned at the crush of traffic on Fifth Avenue, found it was caused chiefly by "heavy trucks drawn by four, six and eight horses" and by empty carriages, including eighty hansom cabs, lined up at the curb while their ladies shopped. Casualties from motorcar accidents were more dramatic than those caused by horses, but they were far fewer. Between 1907 and 1911, according to the American Museum of Safety, automobiles killed 456 persons while horse-drawn vehicles killed 1,147.

Nevertheless, the automobile industry was clearly fortune's favorite. According to *The World Almanac* it was making "a staggering investment in plant and materials." In 1913 there were over one hundred separate and independent manufacturers of passenger cars in the United States, and even the trust busters of the day could not criticize the free competition in the new industry—not yet.

The auto was improving its ability to hit pedestrians quicker and harder every year, even though the man in the street was learning to keep on his toes. Fast driving became a new problem of the courts, a favorite subject of journalists, and a source of revenue to small communities. Local constables and village budgets were profiting from fines collected from motorists who dashed through town at twenty or even thirty miles an hour, where the legal speed limit was five or ten. But not even nights in local jails could restrain motorists from driving faster and faster, and town councils were compelled to be realistic. In spite of all the complaints about speeders, New York State on January 7th raised its limit in populated districts from eight to fifteen miles per hour.

The 1913 New York auto show attracted larger crowds than ever before, and thousands gazed yearningly at every new car from "a little roadster at a bit less than $400 to a mighty limousine approaching the $10,000 mark." New features included wire wheels, electric headlights, and four-door models, but the most important development was the self-starter, sometimes operating on compressed air. The self-starter put American women literally in the driver's seat, and the results revolutionized family life, domestic budgets, and the amatory habits and opportunities of Americans from sixteen to seventy.

The prices of those 1913 models will give modern car owners nostalgia, and so will the fact that there were almost no "optional extras" at further cost. For $1,050 FOB Detroit, one could purchase a Hupmobile with four cylinders, selective gear transmission, electric horn, windshield, mohair top, jiffy side curtains, speedometer, Prestolite gas tank for the headlights and kerosene side lamps of heavy shining brass. If one had large funds and ideas, one could consider the Winton six with its long "yachtlike lines," long-stroke motor, left-hand drive, electric lights, eight-day clock, and demountable tire rims. Secondhand cars were available too. The advertising columns of the *Times* for January 1st offered a Cadillac toy tonneau "equipped like new" for $750, and the same company was prepared to "sacrifice" a Premier of unstated vintage for $900.

Public enthusiasm led to many prophecies that sober men thought extravagant if not fantastic. But no one thought that public purchasing power and the highways of the country could permit more than an ultimate maximum of two million cars on the roads, or that the automobile would ever replace the horse for farm and trucking work, and the United States Army was still purchasing Missouri mules in large numbers. The idea that motor trucks would ever seriously compete with railroads for heavy transport was not even suggested in the press. A few motoring madmen claimed that cars would soon be made that could do anything if given better roads, and America embarked on an era of unprecedented road building. The social and economic effects were profound. Good roads brought rural car owners closer to town, and brought city ways and city styles and luxuries back to remote farms. Railways had already created suburbs, but it was the auto and the smooth-paved road that made suburban living the American way of life. With the highways came the billboards, the buses, the ribbon developments, and later the roadhouses and motels.

The motorcar also gave women more freedom than they have ever derived from the ballot, and is even said to have motivated the startling changes in women's clothes. When the self-starter made it possible for women to become regular drivers, they found that long skirts, petticoats, veils, and other traditional female protections were inconvenient if not somewhat dangerous when it came to operating gear levers, hand brakes, and foot pedals. Mr. Kettering and Mr. Ford were unwittingly more responsible than any other men for the short skirt and the general reduction of women's clothes.

When women could drive their husbands to commuting trains and their children to school, and then be off again for marketing or community committees or bridge whist; when families could explore several states on a two-week holiday, or drive twenty miles and back for a Sunday visit; when young people could take the car to unchaperoned dances, movies, roadhouses, and midnight parking spots, a whole new set of habits and values came into American life. Parental oversight became almost impossible, and the conventions of Mrs. Grundy were simply disregarded.

Automobile enthusiasts of 1913 sometimes guessed wrong. They thought the use of automobiles would be restricted by the limited supply of gasoline, which had already reached a new high of fourteen cents a gallon. Optimists insisted that there could not be a shortage when the nation was producing the stupendous quantity of 9,000,000 barrels a year, with only 1/45 of that production being refined into naphtha, benzine, and gasoline, and with six times as much gasoline being used for illumination as for automobiles. Nevertheless there was a feeling of urgency to find new sources of oil and also to develop cars that would run on some other feel. The Stanley ran steadily, though somewhat lethargically, on steam; the little King roadster was running, more or less, on kerosene, and in Europe some cars were using alcohol, coal, and other fuels.

The prediction that the price of automobiles would continue to decrease also proved erroneous. Those who made it neglected to allow for financial inflations, increased wages to labor, and the American love of size, power, comfort, and speed. In 1913 Henry Ford announced that henceforth he would pay $5 per eight-hour day to workmen in his plant. This was startling not only because it was a fantastically high minimum wage but because he insisted that higher wages brought better work and more stable labor, and even said there should be a relationship between the profits of a manufacturer and the wages he paid his workmen. American manufacturers thought this principle highly dangerous, and the announcement of the Ford plan overshadowed the news from Mexico and the Balkans. "A bolt out of the sky . . . something unheard of in the history of business," said the New York *Sun.* "An epoch in the world's industrial history," pronounced the *World.*

Mr. Ford, it was said, could have got all the labor he wanted for an average of $2 a day. Was he mad or (worse) a socialist? He could not be a socialist, for he was a successful businessman, and what was more the socialists promptly called his plan a detestable trap. They must have seen more clearly than Mr. Ford's distraught competitors that, if his system worked, his employees would be too satisfied and prosperous to be attracted to socialism. An industrialist could not, of course, continue to pay such a high wage unless he could maintain constantly increasing production and sales. Mr. Ford did so by the ever-increasing efficiency of the assembly line he had pioneered. "Time and motion studies" became fashionable as a result, at first with the opposition of organized labor and later with its acquiescence. Other manufacturers, forced to offer wages and hours comparable to those of the Ford Company, found their profits did not suffer as their

efficiency and production mounted. Henry Ford had put into successful operation the new theory of an ever-expanding economy, and he
had chosen the right country, the right time, and the right industry
to make that theory successful. The results made the American motorcar industry the envy of the world, but it had two effects Mr. Ford
did not foresee and did not like. It made it more difficult for small
companies with limited capital resources to survive competition, and
one by one they fell by the wayside or were absorbed through mergers.
Thus Mr. Ford, who strongly favored private enterprise and disliked
dependence on big banks, initiated practices that drove the industry
to the lenders of capital and turned a hundred independent pleasure-
car manufacturers into less than ten.

In spite of their striking success, American auto manufacturers
wanted government protection from foreign competition. Representatives of this new and thriving industry told the tariff committees in
Washington that to reduce the existing duty of European motorcars
to a mere 45 per cent would flood the American market with foreign
cars and drive American manufacturers bankrupt. They are far from
bankrupt today, but there is still a duty, and more than a nominal one,
on foreign-built cars.

When railroad trains had begun running at unprecedented speeds,
it had been seriously questioned whether the human biological system could long survive traveling at fifty miles an hour. A century later
alarmists raised the same alarm over the speed of motorcars. Physi-
ologists predicted that constant riding and lack of exercise would
weaken human muscles, a prophecy yet to be disproved. The *Times*
regretted that "the motor car, which has wrought so many changes in
our social life, has done much to abolish walking for health and pleasure." Commentators of the day were half convinced that American
legs might ultimately become atrophied if not vestigial, though this
did not induce many citizens to walk anywhere if they could ride.

These were mere speculations compared with the practical issues
raised by the new industry. Anyone could drive a horse without becoming much of a public menace, but it soon became apparent that
society could not in self-defense allow every man, woman, and child

to drive an automobile. Some states had begun to require licenses for automobile drivers, but the requirements were usually nominal and sporadically enforced. Few holders of licenses had taken drivers' tests or had their eyes examined, and even in the most populous states only about half of those who drove cars possessed any kind of permit. Early in 1913 the Secretary of State of the State of New York reported that some 300,000 persons were driving cars in the state without licenses, and the *Times* urged that every driver be compelled to have one. Most states soon established qualifications, but in many states tests of vision and driving ability were not even offered until after World War I.

Though the motorcar was the most popular use of the combustion engine, it was by no means the only one. Farmers living many miles from electric lines were beginning to light their homes and run their new milking machines with power generated from gasoline engines. The reapers and cultivators on the great central plains would soon be pulled by gasoline tractors. Fishermen began to install motors in boats too small for steam power, and the combustion engine began the first great boom in small pleasure craft of all sorts. Small and medium-sized factories could install motors that ran their machinery as well as coal or steam, took up less space, were more convenient, and could be turned off when not in use. The steam engine had been the great economic invention of the nineteenth century; the combustion engine of the twentieth century was equally revolutionary, and far more ubiquitous.

By 1913 the automobile was a familiar sight except in the back country, but men still stopped to crane their necks at an airplane, and not one in a thousand had ever flown in one. Most men did not think that human flight would ever become general, or that flying machines would have uses beyond military reconnaissance and civilian sport. The gas-inflated dirigible seemed more practical; its capacity to stay in the air when moving slowly, and to hover before landing, made it seem infinitely safer. How could a heavier-than-air machine, which after all had no more air buoyancy than a thrown stone, ever become a practical flying device? The Wright brothers and other pioneers had demonstrated that planes could fly faster than dirigibles, but the public regarded sustained and safe airplane flight much as it now regards a trip to the moon. There were a few emphatic dissenters from these reservations, but no one paid much attention to them, and in 1913 airplane development was almost entirely sponsored in Europe, and by military men. Even they did not think the heavier-than-air machine could be more than a supplement to artillery and ground troops—certainly not a potential rival of train and ship as a common carrier.

The American public and American military leaders were less airminded than their European counterparts. Not a single large private company in the United States had seriously taken up the development of the airplane, and while the citizens of Paris and Berlin spent their Sunday afternoons gaping at biplanes and balloons at nearby flying fields, Americans flocked to watch Ralph dePalma and Barney Oldfield slither their underslung racing roadsters around the narrow high-crowned turns of Long Island in the Vanderbilt Cup Races. General Benjamin D. Foulois, "the senior military aviator in the United States," deplored in January the lack of interest in aviation in America, and said that the "United States stands at the foot of all the great powers in the development of military aviation."

The figures indicated how right he was. In 1913 the total dollar amounts spent by the various governments as "aeronautical outlay" were: Germany, 28 million; France, 23 million; Russia, 12 million, Britain, 3¼ million; and the United States, ½ million. On May 1, 1913, France had 968 licensed aviators; Britain, 376; Germany, 335; and the United States, 193. Airplanes of all types built or on order toward the end of 1913 were: France, 550; Germany, 375; Russia, 315; Italy, 270; Great Britain, 180; Belgium, 150; Japan, 100; Spain, 75; and the United States, 70. Germany had 40 dirigibles; the United States had one. The Germans were the leaders in the development of the Zeppelin and the French of the monoplane, which seemed to the average American even less likely than the biplane to be stable and manageable, though in races at Rheims in September a French monoplane flew 84 miles per hour, faster than any biplane.

Attempts to fly long distances were beginning, stimulated by an offer from the London *Daily Mail* of $50,000 to the first plane that flew the Atlantic. By May three aviators, one British, one French, and one German, had announced that they would compete for the prize, but the United States military experts said that although some day a heavier-than-air machine would fly across the ocean, such a flight was impossible at present. But before 1913 ended, De Moulanis flew 1,300 miles from Paris to Warsaw and claimed that the only limitation on distance flight was a plane's capacity to carry fuel. Americans were impressed by the stunting of another Frenchman, Adolphe Pégoud, who for the first time looped the loop and flew his plane upside down.

Aeronautical progress seemed a race between the airplane and the dirigible, and many Americans were betting on the gas-inflated bag, particularly after Count Zeppelin flew from Baden-Baden to Vienna in four hours one day in early June. Another German group announced that it would attempt a flight across the Atlantic that very summer in a balloon 325 feet long, with a 1,000-horsepower engine. Americans began to inquire why their own country, which had taken the lead in inventing the airplane, was doing so little to develop it. They were entering into the spirit of the game, though not yet into the competition. That would come with World War I, when the airplane would develop more in four years than in all its previous history, and the United States would suddenly outproduce Europe.

The war would also prove the plane far more effective than the balloon or dirigible for military fighting. It would disprove the 1913 statements of experts like Brigadier General James N. Allison who, after observing the use of planes in the Balkan fighting, concluded that their military values were limited to observation. This was a widespread opinion, and the science expert of American journalism, Waldemar Kaempffert, shared it.

Yet at the end of 1913 there were youths in American colleges who in two years, even before America was at war, would be piloting planes in dogfights over France. There were others who in seven years would be comfortable passengers on regular commercial flights from Paris to London. Did the thousands of mechanics who were incrementally perfecting the combustion engine ever think, as they wiped their greasy hands on greasier cotton waste, that the noisy machines they were nursing would turn half the circumference of the world into an overnight flight within forty years? Did they stop to imagine that in their lifetimes the possession of his own motorcar would seem to many a Yale senior almost as essential as the possession of a toothbrush?

VIII

The Weaker Sex

The year provided American men with many things to talk about, but what they discussed most vigorously was the New Woman. It was a year of female self-assertion when women displayed their abilities and their attributes in a fury of exhibitionism. Their spectacular innovations, from suffrage to slit skirts, shook the very foundations of society. In women's rights it was the year of demonstrations; in women's clothes the year of revelations. As they increased their economic and political activities, they diminished their conventional and sartorial modesties.

These developments seemed sudden, but they were merely drastic escapes from long-endured suppressions. Women's demands for decent jobs at decent wages were simply the latest chapter in their long fight for economic recognition and justice. Their insistence on the ballot was the climax of earlier efforts, and their elimination of hampering garments was a symbol of long-repressed yearnings for freedom. Though women's suffrage and women's styles filled more columns in the daily press, it was women's economic advance that changed them and society most fundamentally. The independence they won by earning wages was far greater than any freedoms derived from the ballot or the boyish bob.

More and more women, including wives and mothers, were demonstrating their capacity to hold jobs outside their homes above the level of domestic servant or file clerk. Refusing to be merely marginal or wage-slave labor they were beginning to compete with men as skilled operators of machinery, typewriters, and double-entry bookkeeping. Men as husbands and fathers might deplore this departure from female dependence, but men as employers were making the most of women as cheap assets in office and factory. Even some daughters of prosperous parents were insisting on taking jobs and—what was even more disturbing—on living independently of their parents, spending their earnings as they liked and meeting and marrying men of their own choice.

By 1913 the industrial possibilities of women were beginning to be recognized, but their industrial equality was not. Few women were being paid what men were paid for the same work, and in some industries their wages were only pittances. They had been forced to accept this discrimination to get jobs at all, but once established in them they were beginning to demand a little less injustice. Most women did not ask for wages equal to men, but for working hours and conditions a little less reminiscent of the English factory system in 1800.

It was not the women of the suffrage movement who led the campaign for economic justice. To the suffragettes the paramount issue was the vote; given that, they believed they could use it to improve women's economic status. Women not in employment but in traditional work at home—and they still constituted the vast majority—were sympathetic with the efforts of their wage-earning sisters but did little to help them. The agitation for women's economic and industrial rights came from employed women, social workers, and a few men shocked by the wages and working conditions of many women and young girls.

One might think that the leaders of organized labor would have supported the women's cause of decent hours, conditions, and wages in industry, since it was their own. But, generally speaking, women did not get much help, or sometimes much sympathy, from the labor unions. Some labor leaders even opposed improved conditions for women in industry for fear they would bring too many women into the labor market to compete with men. Most labor unions did not admit, or did not welcome, women into membership, and few working women joined or organized unions.

It was World War I, with its stimulus to industry and employment, that brought about the real advance in the standing of the workingwoman, but 1913 contributed to that advance by making the facts known to the public. Ironically enough, the question of economic justice for women came to public attention partly through public interest in what was called the Social Evil.

Investigations of vice are standard public entertainment at least once in every decade. The year 1913 was an appropriate time for another public plunge into the unsavory but interesting facts of life, for some years had passed since the muckrakers had titivated the public pleasure in other people's sin by uncovering the slime of urban underworlds. With Congress investigating almost everything, state and city officials took the cue from Washington and set up their own commissions for local research into whatever troubled or entertained their constituents. Such investigations frequently brought revelations quite different from those intended, and sometimes embarrassing to their sponsors. Research into local vice, a relatively innocuous avocation, produced newsworthy information about the wages and working conditions of many women.

The activities of the Vice Commission of the State of Illinois were a good example. Probing prostitution with dignified enthusiasm and an excellent press, the commission was incidentally informed that there might be a causal relation between the working girl's low wages and her morals. This was treading upon ground that might prove politically dangerous, but so startling a suggestion as an alliance between poverty and sin inspired reporters and brought headlines, and the commission decided to take further evidence in the matter.

Social workers insisted there was a connection between a low wage and a low life, but other authorities questioned that conclusion. Mr. Julius Rosenwald, head of Sears, Roebuck & Company, and naturally a philanthropist, defended the morals of his women employees and his own wage scale. He told the commissioners that the average wage Sears, Roebuck paid its 4,372 women employees was well above the national scale, and indeed soared from $9 to $12 a week, and that they were unskilled workers whose moral security was presumed by the fact that they were supposed to live at home.

His testimony was given ample space even in the columns of the New York *Times,* and the wages of industry were compared with the wages of sin in public discussion across the nation. Twelve other states and a number of cities climbed on this interesting bandwagon by appointing committees to join in the "vice fight." The results added little to the public's knowledge of vice but much to its knowledge of women's wages.

It soon appeared that Mr. Rosenwald was correct in saying that his company was paying its women better wages than many others. In the silk mills of Paterson, New Jersey, 8.7 per cent of the women over sixteen and 40 per cent of those under sixteen received less than $4 a week. In certain factories in Pennsylvania women's wages were still lower. There 57 per cent of the women over sixteen and 91 per cent of the girls under sixteen got less than $4 a week.

The New York State Investigation Committee reported that despite child-labor laws many girls, the oldest fourteen and youngest three years of age, were working in thirty-three canning plants in the state. Wages for the younger girls were infinitesimal, and the average canning-factory wage for women, working as many as fourteen hours a day, was $4.53 a week. That commission was headed by Robert F. Wagner, who later, as a Senator of New York, was the author of the Wagner Labor Act, and by Alfred E. Smith, then speaker of the Assembly.

Theodore Roosevelt, that irrepressible explorer, had already made his personal investigation of the clothing trades of New York City, and on January 24th had written to Michael Sharp:

I visited bodies of girl strikers in the dress trades in Henry Street and St. Mark's Place. In Henry Street the girls were mostly recent immigrants from southern Spain and from the Turkish empire. Those from the Turkish empire could not speak English (or Yiddish) so that they were peculiarly helpless under our conditions here. Some of the girls were fourteen and fifteen years old . . . The wages in one or two cases were as low as $3.00 a week . . . I was informed that there were girls who worked for $2.50 a week. Some of the girls out of the miserable pittance paid them, have themselves to pay for repairs to the machines, and for thread and needles . . . . Another, who had paid $32. for a machine [on which she worked] worked from 8.0 A.M to 8.0 P.M. and mentioned that in summer she was charged ten cents a week for ice water.

These disclosures shocked Congress into discussion of a minimum wage for women of $8 a week. Nothing came of it at the time, and public interest was soon deflected to other issues and headlines, but the facts had been aired and action was inevitable in time. In women's struggle for economic equality, the developments of 1913 were a significant chapter, though it was surprising that the women's suffrage movement did not make more capital out of the current situation of women wage earners.

But women's economic status interested most men less than other forms of female self-expression. Nearly every wife and daughter was asserting herself in some alarming way. Conventions in manners, dress, and amusements were being casually and sometimes brazenly disregarded. The female revolt against whatever men had thought proper was especially annoying to husbands and fathers, because their womenfolk did not seem to care at all what they thought of it.

More and more "nice" women were taking up smoking and, what was worse, smoking in public. The Women's University Club of New York was including in its plans for a new club a smoking room for members, and this was startling enough to be reported at length in the *Times*. Women of the kind previously called "virtuous" were drinking the new cocktails in public and even invading men's saloons. They were dressing as no well-brought-up woman had previously dressed, acting as no modest women had previously acted, and talking as no decent woman had previously talked, at least in public. Would this discard of modesty and restraint lead women to discard sexual virtue as well? Some men feared so, others hoped so. Women said they were only casting off the ancient shackles of tradition and inhibition, but were they not also undermining social and domestic morality? What would be the effect on children of these irresponsible mothers? What would happen to the American Home? Opinions differed emphatically, but every man had one.

The changes in women's dress were so drastic that by May they had become the subject of sermons, jokes, cartoons, and headlines. Women were discarding corsets, camisoles, petticoats, ankle-length skirts, and only heaven perhaps knew what else. Shirtwaists and blouses had become "peekaboo," and knees were openly exposed to public censure or approval. By June the "hobble skirt" was being generally if not widely worn in the suburbs as well as the cities, and sanctioned by Paris styles the experts pronounced as "the most daring in a hundred years." The new skirt led to other adjustments. Its tightness revealed any unbecoming lumps, human or artificial, beneath, and underclothes were therefore reduced in yardage or eliminated altogether. For women in tight skirts to walk at all, a slit or slash nearly to the knee was required.

As summer came the furor mounted, for women appeared in bathing suits their mothers would have called scandalous. Shopgirls at Rockaway Beach, middle-class teen-agers at Asbury Park, and socialites at Newport were all discarding the voluminous black bloomers and cotton stockings hitherto regarded as essentials of bathing propriety. The one-piece black neck-to-toe bathing suit featured by the expert swimmer Annette Kellerman in the popular movie *Neptune's Daughter* would obviously be the next step.

Press photographers had a field day; harried police chiefs and town councils from Maine to Florida were faced with problems of morality and law enforcement they had never anticipated. If they wanted to follow public opinion it was difficult to find out just what majority opinion really was on slit skirts and bathing suits; yet if they did not guess correctly they might fail of reelection. One section of their constituents insisted loudly that public morals should be strictly enforced by public officers; others approved the disrobings, or at least said they should not be curbed by ordinances and arrests.

Official and volunteer guardians of public morals took every possible position. Some police officers pretended indifference or incapacity, while others arrested women on beaches and city streets;

preachers thundered from pulpits; citizens wrote strong letters to the newspapers; delegations marched on city halls—and women continued to wear or not wear whatever they saw fit on the Main Streets, the Fifth Avenues, the Bailey's Beaches and the Coney Islands of the nation. Each skirmish in the battle was national news, and Americans read with every reaction from anger to amusement that in Sag Harbor, Long Island, the village trustees had announced that all girls found on the single street after 9:00 P.M. without a parent or guardian would be arrested; that in Louisville, Kentucky, the chief of police had ordered the arrest of all women in slit skirts without "protecting undergarments," that in Richmond, Virginia, Blossom Browning was arrested for wearing a slit skirt while scrubbing down her mistress's front steps, or that in Chicago the City Council, after long debate, decided not to pass an ordinance making the wearing of tight skirts illegal, because the police insisted that they could not enforce it.

Most religious societies attacked the new clothes and customs as immoral, but even pillars of the churches differed as to what constituted immorality in a skirt, shirtwaist, or bathing suit. The Reverend H. T. Walsh, of New Britain, Connecticut, was confident in defining sin: He announced that he would refuse communion to any woman who approached the altar, or his home, in a slit skirt. The Y.W.C.A. was so concerned that it issued a booklet of "Don'ts for Young Girls Away from Home," which included the following precautionary admonitions:

Girls should never stay to help a woman who apparently falls at their feet in the street, but should immediately call a policeman to her aid.

Don't accept invitations from strangers to join Sunday Schools or Bible Classes, even if the strangers wear the crosses of Nuns or Sisters.

Even the Pennsylvania Railroad, which had seldom shown concern for the dress or morals of its paying passengers, supported the forces of virtue. It announced on August 16th that if a woman slipped or fell on railroad property, the company "will take note of the style of her skirt and heels, of her age, and of the circumstances of her life, and will publish them." The record does not show how often the company made good its threat, and whether the results decreased liability claims against the railroad or increased women's clothing, but no great change in the latter was noted. Other self-appointed censors defended their special interests, like the Chicago dressmakers, who in vehement assembly condemned the new fashions as a "fraud, cheat, and atrocity, perpetrated on an intelligent public by foreigners."

As part of the new deal in freedom, American men as well as women were indulging the greatest craze for dancing the country had ever known, and the new dances seemed invented to encourage immodesty. To those conservative oldsters to whom the waltz had been the closest and most intimate physical contact on the dance floor, the Turkey Trot and even the One Step seemed inciting and abandoned. Mayor William J. Gaynor of New York, certainly no Puritan, called the Turkey Trot and the dance-floor doings of the city's new night clubs "lascivious orgies," and threw the full weight of his office into a campaign to prevent them throughout the city. But at the end of the year they were as popular as ever, except that the Turkey Trot was giving way to an even more all-embracing dance called the bunny hug.

An editorial in the *Times* said the Turkey Trot was a "phenomenon closely analogous to those dancing manias of the Middle Ages . . . to which victims of a neurotic diathasis are susceptible." Many a pillar of suburbia probably read this diagnosis on the home-bound commuters' express, and then hurried off to the country club to indulge in a little middle-aged neurotic diathasis. The dancing craze so swept the country that the evenings were not long enough to gratify it, and afternoon thé dansants were popular supplements. Yale's 1913 Junior Prom was "the greatest in history," and more than a thousand "dowagers and chaperones," luxuriously installed in boxes fenced off from their field of duty, found themselves inadequate when the five thousand light bulbs were turned off during most of the dances, and when many young couples went on to the Taft Hotel and "danced until the following noon." The Yale faculty had sternly forbidden "moonlight dances and the Turkey Trot," but both were generously indulged.

In only a few places did authoritarian controls still operate successfully. One of these was the United States Naval Academy, where
the superintendent issued a formal "Regulations for Dancing at
Annapolis," which included these orders to midshipmen:

None of the modern dances are to be performed at the USNA under
any circumstances.
Midshipmen must keep their left arms straight during all dances.
A space of at least three inches must be kept between the dancing couples at all times.
Midshipmen must not take the arm of their partners under any circumstances.

In spite of these attempts at restraint, most Americans were on
the loose, and like naughty children curious to know how much their
conduct shocked others. Foreign visitors were invariably quizzed by
reporters on American manners and mores, and were not silent. Mrs.
Alec Tweedie of England's upper set, in a series of feature articles,
blamed all she did not like or understand in America on its women.
Home life and responsibility, she said, were disappearing in America,
largely because American women "lunch and dine out in bunches"
and "have learned to amuse themselves."

The opinions of Miss Pellisser were read with special interest
because she had taught the children of Britain's royal family "how
to behave." American girls, she said, with the authority of one who
had spanked princesses, were "clever, pretty, well-dressed, and sweet,
but they don't know how to behave. . . . They wriggle into a room
like snakes, cross their knees, stare at callers, and drop the sugar
tongs. . . . They are brusque, jerky, and full of nervous energy, without grace, poise or repose." The American young woman "is possessed
of a craze to do just what everyone else does. . . . She needs to be
taught deportment very badly indeed. . . . The American parent leaves
the daughter's education almost entirely to the school." Thus badly
brought up, what could be expected of an American young woman
but that she would bathe without bloomers, dance without petticoats,
and incidentally captivate and marry Englishmen with titles? Miss

Pellisser did not answer that, or explain how the well-born Mrs. Pankhurst, and even some titled English ladies, came to be setting off bombs and burning up country houses.

The French were also heard from, though the famous Pierre Loti's comments disappointingly exemplified French tact more than Gallic venery. He discussed the conversation of American women rather than their more obvious charms. "Passing quickly from one subject to another, they said things that were incoherent yet profound. . . . They differed from our women in being . . . freer in conversation, but never allowing any room for the equivocal."

Abdul-Hamid II, Turkey's deposed leader, was read with attention as a man of considerable harem experience. He professed grave doubt that Western women were as faithful or as beautiful as those of the Orient, and he joined Mrs. Tweedie in urging them back to the domestic hearth. "Our women belong in the home," he said, conjuring up in the minds of male Americans a home life rather more varied than their own. But Abdul-Hamid surprised as well as discouraged American men by adding that an Oriental woman is "absolute mistress of her own home."

Foreign opinions of American women were rounded out by Hiseini Seno, a scientist passing through New York. He found American women far less self-effacing and therefore less wise and charming than the women of his native Japan. American women were "trying to be just like men along all lines. They want to become lawyers because there are men lawyers. . . . They go still further in studies which they themselves know they cannot make use of. . . . Most of the [American] women with whom I have come in contact think they are always the center of every problem. They are too individualistic, or, rather, too selfish."

American men were probably most in agreement with Jean Finot, editor of *La Revue*, who insisted that only by remaining different from men could women compete equally with them, and encouraged every male wag to repeat the old cry of "Vive la différence!" Theodore Roosevelt, noted for the courage of his intellectual indiscretions, had taken a similar line back in 1908, when he had written to a friend: "I believe men and women should stand on an equality of rights, but I do not believe the equality of rights means equality of functions." Dr. Dudley Sargent, head of the Department of Physical Education at Harvard, disposed of the whole topic in a pseudopsychological nutshell: "The woman who stands on the street corner shouting 'Votes for women' is simply seeking an outlet for a perfectly normal amount of emotion which fifty years ago would have been properly expended in the care of a household."

Women differed among themselves as to the merits and uses of their new freedom, and generalizations about women of 1913 are as dangerous as generalities about any other women. One thing was clear: though the women of 1913 were asserting their own freedom they were not happy when their daughters did so even more flamboyantly. Mothers thought their daughters were disobeying them more flagrantly than in previous generations, and complained about it in magazine articles. Daughters thought their mothers wanted to regiment them beyond all reason, and complained about it in their school magazines. Mother-daughter relationships were therefore approximately normal.

The domestic scene was further complicated by the emergence of that modern insolubility, the Servant Problem, and many of the changes in middle-class habits and values resulted partly from the difficulties of adjusting to the new independence of cooks and maids. Girls of the servant class were also feeling their oats, and acting upon the same impulses as the lady of the house, and in the same ways. They too were asserting their independence and pursuing their personal versions of their rights and duties. The fact that the domestic servant and the working girl were expressing themselves as firmly and unconventionally as their mistresses and the wives of their employers was the greatest social change of all. If the women of 1913 were revolting, they were no longer revolting by social layers, but with a democratic, though class-conscious, unity.

IX

Crusaders

No one in 1913 knew, and no one knows now, how many women in America ardently wanted the right to vote. A few were emphatic in their demand for suffrage; some opposed it; but most women probably favored it as a matter of principle but with no strong desire to make use of the ballot. It was a vocal minority that won women the vote, and a vocal minority of men that vehemently opposed it.

The methods of English and American suffragettes were in striking contrast and there is a curious paradox in the comparison. English men have been famous for deference to law and orderly change, but English suffragettes did not show a similar restraint. American men, on the other hand, have been more ready to take the law into their own hands, yet American women seeking the vote kept within the law and openly deplored the illegal activities of Mrs. Pankhurst and her British suffragettes. The American suffragette leader, Anna Howard Shaw, told British women that their militant conduct was hurting the cause in America. American men probably accepted women's suffrage more readily because their wives and sisters did not use arson and high explosives to gain it.

There seemed no limit to which English militant suffragettes would not go in their pursuit of the right to vote. Britain in 1913 was shaken by the explosions they admittedly set off; by arson, jailings, hunger strikes, and even threats of murder. In February, a country house at Walton Heath, intended as the new home of Chancellor of the Exchequer Lloyd George, was largely destroyed by a bomb for which Mrs. Pankhurst announced she accepted full responsibility. Jailed without bail, she went on a hunger strike. Not even British law could withstand British sentiment against letting a woman starve herself to death. Forcible feeding did not prove an acceptable solution, and Mrs. Pankhurst was soon free to burn again.

On the night of May 1st, immediatedly following the defeat of a Woman's Suffrage bill in the House of Commons by only 47 votes, a church was burned, a fine new building in London destroyed, and a bomb with lighted fuse found outside the Grand Hotel in London. Suffragettes mutilated three hundred precious old books in the library of St. John's College, Cambridge; they destroyed railway stations; they burned to the ground a modern castle that had cost over $2,500,000; they fired the big recreation pier at Southport and the mansion of Sir William Lever with its valuable old paintings. They attacked with dog whips Prime Minister Asquith and a vigorous young statesman named Winston Churchill, neither of whom attempted to defend himself against the women. Mrs. Pankhurst, alternately in and out of jail, announced to the British government: "You must give us political freedom or death. You must give us the right to vote or kill us," and later served notice: "Human life now will, we have resolved, be respected no longer." Burning libraries and public recreation piers seemed curious ways to demonstrate one's qualifications to be a responsible voting citizen.

American reporters consequently looked forward to lively assignments when Mrs. Pankhurst announced her intention of visiting America. They were not disappointed. When the French liner *Provence* reached New York on October 18th, Mrs. Pankhurst was refused entry on grounds of moral turpitude, and interned at Ellis Island. After a hearing by a special board of inquiry, she was ordered deported as an undesirable alien. The consequent publicity was nation-wide, and many who thoroughly disapproved of Mrs. Pankhurst wondered whether the immigration officials had acted wisely. She countered with defiance mixed ingeniously with an appeal based on the frailty of her sex, threatening a hunger strike if barred from entry and then adding: "If I am deported from this city I shall be dead twenty-four hours after sailing, because I am too weak to stand the strain."

The authorities found themselves in the same dilemma that had seemed so amusing when it was the British government that had been baffled. American public opinion, like that of England, would not approve letting a woman starve even if she insisted on doing so, and no one wanted to let Mrs. Pankhurst make herself a martyr. Yet if she were admitted to this country, who knew what trouble she might stir up among American women, who had not thus far taken a dog whip to President Wilson or put bombs in the mansion of Andrew Carnegie?

It was left to the President to cut the Gordian knot, and on October 21st he personally ordered that Mrs. Pankhurst be released from custody. She proved not "too weak to stand the strain" of dining that night in the home of Mrs. O. H. P. Belmont and then addressing a meeting of the Women's Political Union amid the applause and cat-calls of some three hundred men and women. The next night she spoke in Madison Square Garden, where she denied that while on Ellis Island she had threatened to go on a hunger strike. After that lively beginning, however, her news value diminished rapidly, since her American following was very small and public curiosity was soon gratified.

Most American men regarded their women crusaders with toler-ance, amusement, or sympathy rather than with stronger emotions one way or another. The attitude of many men was expressed by Theodore Roosevelt in a letter of 1908 to Lyman Abbott: "Personally I believe in women's suffrage but I am not enthusiastic about it be-cause I do not regard it as a very important matter," but in 1912 his Progressive party had rapidly leaped on the suffragette bandwagon with a resolution favoring suffrage for women.

President Wilson was believed to be sympathetic with the cause, but he had not urged votes for women in his campaign or to Congress. The *Times* spoke for many men when it said editorially: ". . . it is clear that the day when women will generally be privileged to vote is a long way off, on both sides of the ocean, and for that we may well be thankful." The *Times* was seldom more wrong, for the hand-writing on the wall was clear; Illinois and Alaska had already given women the vote, and the issue was before the authorities in ten other states.

American suffragists were at their most active and vocal in 1913. In addition to local meetings, articles, soapbox orations, parades, and home curtain lectures, they staged a number of major events. In New York some ten thousand women and a considerable number of male sympathizers paraded on May 10th. The temperature was 87 degrees in the shade, and some of the spectators who lined the streets were unpleasant, but most of the women finished the long hard course. A similar parade in Brooklyn in November was moderately successful, though there the ladies encountered a knotty problem that defied their claims of political acumen. A nonunion band they had hired for the parade was forced to drop out of line by union musicians in other bands.

The suffragettes planned their most impressive demonstration in Washington at the time of President Wilson's inaugural, but this proved a disappointment. Police protection was needed and was not supplied; the marching women were frequently harassed and insulted by men and boys. No woman was seriously injured, but the parade was disorganized and the affair did the women more credit than it did the Washington police force and public. It was the suffragette hike from New York preceding the inauguration that held the public interest for three weeks. Volunteer women announced their intention to march on foot from New York to Washington, carrying a message from the national suffrage organization to the new President. The expedition was reported in inaccurate detail by the leading newspapers, and on the whole it probably won new friends to the women's cause. Even the bitterest opponents had the disarming satisfaction of seeing that these alarming Amazons were just as feminine and fallible as the conservatives wanted all women to be. The crusading hike had no importance in itself, but it revealed in interesting ways the temper of the times.

The marchers left New York on February 12th in somewhat smaller numbers than had been expected, for only some fifty women set out, and not all of these intended to stay the course. They were to have been accompanied by a "megaphone band," three wagons to carry spare clothes, medical supplies, and suffrage pamphlets, and two autos as couriers and emergency aids. For various reasons some of these vehicles failed to appear at the starting line. The marchers were all supposed to wear long brown cloaks, supplied for one dollar each, but the whole movement was endangered when the women saw how they looked in these monastic garments. They were only with difficulty persuaded to wear them, and before the end of the first day many irregularities of uniform appeared.

The crusaders did not actually start on foot as planned. There were snow patches on the ground, and at the last moment it was decided that the road over the meadows to Newark could not be negotiated without great loss of time and energy. So the gallant troop mounted the cars of the Hudson and Manhattan Railroad and rode them, somewhat ingloriously, to Newark. Colonel Ida Craft, second in command to General Rosalie Jones, strongly protested this initial compromise with the elements and elected to walk continuously up and down the aisles of the cars so that no one could say that she, at least, had not walked to Newark. Her intentions were better than her mathematics, for no one managed to make clear to her that even if she walked all the time the train was in motion she would not be covering a distance equivalent to that from Manhattan to Newark. Since she insisted on leaving the car doors open as she passed her Spartan way from coach to coach, and since the train was crowded with ordinary passengers not infected with the crusading spirit, Colonel Craft's private pilgrimage was not popular. After three round trips from stem to stern she was compelled to yield to public protests and abandon her demonstration. "It isn't fair," she said, weeping copiously, or so recorded the reporters who accompanied the marchers.

At Newark, General Jones solved a logistical problem with the quick decision worthy of a skilled military leader. To make up for the nonappearance of an expected horse, she bought on the streets for $59.98 what the reporters called a prancing steed, the surprised seller with some optimism called a good nag, and the crusaders promptly christened Lausanne. It was, by ironic chance, a stallion, with weak legs and a surprising lack of endurance. It never seemed to enter into the spirit of the crusade, but with considerable urging and assistance it survived the long hike and was the only male to go all the way.

Other episodes that first day caused further delays and excitements. As the strangely garbed procession passed an express wagon, the white mare drawing it fell down in apparent fright and would not get up. General Jones called a halt, and the more equinely experienced of the ladies, assisted by male aborigines of Newark, assisted the mare to her feet. Then, at the corner of Bigelow and Frelinghuysen avenues another horse, this one drawing a lumber wagon, bolted, but was caught two blocks away by a passing native. These sobering tributes to their unique appearance brought home to the crusaders the problems of armies marching through unfriendly territory, but by adroit evasive tactics the irregular column traversed the northern countries without further misadventures. As the procession neared Lyons a motherly-looking woman rushed from a farmhouse and handed the marchers a dozen hot boiled eggs. "Carry one in each hand," she instructed the ladies. "They will keep you warm." Most of the eggs were gratefully eaten before the column reached camp that night.

The army did not often march without its camp followers. It accumulated peripatetic adherents, local reporters, rude commentators, small boys, and dogs. This made it doubly difficult for General Jones to keep order, prevent straggling and fraternization, and protect her troops from constant distractions. One unexpected young man intermittently marched with the vanguard all day, carrying a large home-made blue and white banner with stars, which he insisted would, if planted in the grounds of the Capitol, secure women the vote. He said his name was Percy Passmore and that he was a clerk living in Newark, with no money but great faith. The procession was also joined as it left Elizabeth by Ernest Stevens and E. Lemmon, members, they said, of the Wanderlust Club. They promised to return to guide the army into Philadelphia.

After a night in Metuchen the frailer members of the crusade looked forward with misgivings to their reception by the students of Rutgers College, but New Brunswick was negotiated without casualties. At Princeton the army called on President-elect Wilson, but he was reported not at home. The Princeton students were mostly friendly, and the Lawrenceville schoolboys turned out a hundred strong with a large banner reading "Votes for Women." General Jones led her expeditionary force into Trenton ahead of schedule and with high morale, but in a very thin brown line, and with Corporal Martha Klutschen so exhausted that she had to be helped into the hotel.

The next day the ladies paraded through Camden singing, "Tramp, tramp, tramp, the girls are marching," preceded by welcoming delegates from the local suffrage unit. Colonel Craft, the indefatigable marcher of the Hudson tubes, lost eight hairpins, and her hair came down in the middle of the city. With rare presence of mind General Jones halted the column and called for volunteers to share their emergency supplies. Eight privates contributed one hairpin each and the march was resumed. The army crossed the Delaware by the Camden ferry, very conscious of historic parallels as General Jones stood in the bow holding the American flag in emulation of General Washington.

Most Philadelphia men and boys were good-natured though curious, but an unruly few tried to take away the crusaders' yellow banner, and the army had to call on friendly bystanders to keep from losing it. Police cleared a path up Walnut Street to the Hotel Walton where the local suffragette turnout to greet the crusaders proved disappointingly small until it was explained that "Philadelphia ladies do not like to go out on a Sunday afternoon." This discouragement was ameliorated by other conquests. There was a dinner in honor of the marchers, and General Rosalie Jones received her third offer of marriage since the march began. Her amorous swain this time was a veteran who "had lost his leg at Chancellorsville in another great cause" who said he knew "how tired your little feet must be. . . . I may only have one leg but my heart is bigger than the hearts of any two men. Why don't you rest your tired little head upon it? Just

say the word and I am yours!" General Jones decided to put the
Cause before restful romance.

At Wilmington the army was welcomed by the mayor and a large
crowd, but its commissary received a dire logistical blow. A large
box of hardtack and army rations, donated by Mrs. O. H. P. Belmont
to support the expeditionary force through the back country of Delaware and Maryland had, it developed, gone by mistake to General
Jones's home on Long Island. General Jones was partly consoled by
the gift of a manx kitten, and the army continued to live off the country. The troops rested, except for minor foraging expeditions to
friendly country estates, all the next day in Wilmington. Several
southern gentlemen called on the general to inquire "how the army
stood on the question for Negro women." With the evasive skill of a
presidential candidate, Miss Jones replied that the men and women
of each state must decide that matter for themselves, and the nation
was preserved.

The following day a slightly decimated army picked its way over
"indifferent roads" to Elkton, Maryland. At Newark, Delaware, 175
cadets of the university presented arms to the passing battalion, and
church bells pealed in some small towns as it passed through. When
General Jones invited members of a gathering at Newport to ask
questions, a small girl piped up shrilly, "Ain't there enough men to
vote?"

Samuel J. Taylor had joined the marchers outside Philadelphia,
and led the column playing on his harmonica, while Ernest Stevens,
sporadically in attendance all the way from Elizabeth, read the army
an original poem that began:

> The suffragette is at the door,
>   Maryland, my Maryland;
> On foot she hikes to Baltimore;
>   Maryland, my Maryland.

Thus inspired, the marchers continued, even though the single scout
car broke down and had to be towed by two horses to the nearest
blacksmith's shop "where a lost pin was replaced."

The following day the army labored along "the worst stretch of road between Boston and Atlanta" but arrived at Havre de Grace as planned. A local band led it into town, and Mayor Weber made a speech of welcome. The ladies made their way forward to Bel Air, trailing the last two miles through muddy roads in a heavy rain. Colonel Craft was now last in line. General Jones begged her to give up the march, but the colonel refused, though "her feet were bleeding and so swollen that she could not take off her shoes." But the next day she had recovered her spirits sufficiently to refuse to speak to General Jones, who had led the army directly into Baltimore when it had been expected to remain overnight in Overlea, five miles out. "We cannot slight southern hospitality," complained the colonel. "I can see no reason for rushing ahead." Faced with mutiny as well as blisters by her second in command, and unable to reply except through intermediaries, General Jones pulled rank and relayed a tart message that "a general expects obedience and anyhow this march is not a social affair."

The gallant survivors arrived in Bladensburg, just outside Washington, on February 27th, only fifteen days after entraining in New York. There they were greatly upset to learn that the National Women's Suffrage Association was in effect repudiating their heroism by refusing to let General Jones deliver personally to President Wilson the message that she had carried all the way from New York. The suffrage authorities, after the manner of Washington bureaucrats, insisted that the historic scroll must be delivered "through channels." This brought the general, for the first time, near tears. To add to the gloom, the marchers met more insults and rowdyism that day than at any time since leaving New York. The chief offenders appeared to be students of the University of Maryland, and the police did nothing to discourage them. But such adversities had their compensation; they brought a reconciliation between the general and the colonel, who spoke again.

On March 1st "The Army of the Hudson," with as much spit and polish as conditions permitted, entered the Capital City, still on foot, with all disagreements postponed if not forgiven. It was true that the army approached the the city by one route while its reception committee awaited it on another, but this was only a regrettable incident in the victorious progress. Dr. Stevens carried a large American flag; the yellow suffrage banner was proudly flaunted, and General Jones, faithfully wrapped in her long brown cloak, led the column with a bugler beside her. The crowd was more entertained than converted, but the mission had been accomplished.

X
Heroes and Villains

Most current problems of 1913 were growing pains, the expression of inward confusion. Americans were developing a society and a way of life very different from the one they had inherited and been conditioned to cope with. They were pressing forward with outward enthusiasm but occasional inward doubts, for they felt contradictions within themselves as well as all around them. Their conscience troubled them about some of the aspects and values of their new society, and they had moments of nostalgia for the simpler ways and discarded virtues of their earlier days. No man seemed to himself less a split personality than the typical American of 1913, but his uncertainties were revealed in his eagerness to know what others thought of him. One English visitor of the time commented, "Never has there been such an example of a nation sitting in judgment on itself." But that was only half the story; Americans sought opinions outside themselves, because they were dubious of their own criteria.

The more thoughtful citizens were seeking principles and abstract truths that would guide them through their cultural confusions. Congressional investigations, municipal probings, public debates, and social analysis provided them with masses of facts but very few orientations. Life and science were hurling change at them faster than they could assimilate it. Reform was in the air, but it was scattered and sporadic because it was not based on consistent values or agreed goals. Americans were searching for certainties but without a compass.

Since getting and spending had become the chief preoccupation of most Americans, their debates and reforms centered on economic issues. The public was uncertain what ground rules they should apply to regulate the excesses of corporations and labor unions, and what part the federal government should play in making and enforcing those rules. Legislation and court decisions, national and local, did not provide a clearcut and comprehensive guide to economic equity. When should a man or a company or a union be condemned for lack of social responsibility, and when approved for skill and success? Sometimes the public admired the man even while it deplored his actions or his aims. The law could not cover all aspects of human conduct, for there would always be things that were not illegal but nevertheless against the interests of society. Even in matters appropriate to legislation there was judicial confusion, and legal interpretations sometimes needed their own interpreters.

A recent ruling of the Supreme Court was a case in point. Interpreting the Sherman Antitrust Act, which had been invoked in the Standard Oil case, the Justices had said that in determining whether a corporation was acting in restraint of trade the courts should be governed by the "standard of reason." But they did not define that standard, and people often disagreed about what was reasonable. A few days before Mr. Wilson's inauguration the Senate Committee on Interstate Commerce attempted to define the "standard of reason" but the committee's interpretation added up to the fact that the standard of reason was whatever the last Court decision said it was. That gave no solid foundation for future conduct of judgment, and left economic ethics in a worse tangle than ever. Somewhere along the line the simple question of right and wrong had got lost in legal debate and precedent. The real trouble, of course, was that the people were asking law to give them ethical guidance, and law was no substitute for an established code of social morality. The old code had broken down, and no new one had been generally accepted.

The values of any society are indicated by the men it selects to admire and to condemn. Americans of 1913 had, collectively, no guides except their own emotional reactions and their fluid standards to tell them what they should admire and what they should not. If a man cut the Gordian knots that stood in his way he was a hero, but if he cut them a little too unscrupulously he was a villain, and there was disagreement where the lines of demarcation should lie. No man could be certain in advance whether he would emerge a saint or sinner.

It was as difficult to judge corporations and labor unions as it was to judge men. Most of the business experts said that the big banks and corporations were advancing the prosperity and stability of the nation and that most of the men who directed them were good and responsible citizens. But business experts were part of business, and that made their opinions subject to doubt. Liberals, labor leaders, and many journalists differed with them, and said big business ignored the public welfare. Certainly some business sahibs seemed to regard themselves as above the law, or at least to be indifferent to the general interests of society. Most men thought the concentration of wealth and power had gone too far when it was disclosed that the Morgan and Rockefeller groups together held directorships in 112 banks, railroads, insurance companies, and other corporations, with aggregate resources of over twenty-two billion dollars.

Congressional committees during the Taft administration had sought the facts about corporate conduct, and William E. Corey, former president of United States Steel, had "admitted the existence of an international pool in steel rails." This shocked only the naïve and those determined to be shocked, and it did not throw much light on the existence and practices of a steel monopoly within the United States. The committees continued to probe.

The House committee headed by Representative Arsène Pujo had begun in 1912 to inquire into the "money trust," and secured a mass of information about the methods and management of the New York Stock Exchange, the Clearing House and the marketing of securities, but most of this was too technical for the average man to understand. The public wanted personalities, and in 1913 Mr. Pujo and his associates provided them. They called the dominant figure in Wall Street, Mr. Pierpont Morgan, to the committee's stage.

Mr. Morgan, in spite of his national reputation, was an unknown personality to the public, for he disliked public appearances and had kept out of the limelight. That made him seem even more sinister, and a few cartoonists had pictured him as a grim and unscrupulous tyrant seated on a throne surrounded by bags of gold—the very quintessence of entrenched greed. Men who knew Mr. Morgan personally were angered by that concept; they said he was a man of solid character and good influence, with a high sense of public responsibility. Financial experts said his initiative and leadership had saved the panic of 1907 from being far worse, but liberals insisted that although he might have saved the sinking ship in 1907, the system of which he was captain had led society's ship into the financial storm.

Mr. Morgan's manner and disclosures before the committee were far less dramatic than the public had hoped. He proved to be a firm but mild-mannered old gentleman of obviously high personal integrity, and his testimony was generally regarded as giving the lie to those who had called him indifferent to the public interests. There was nothing belligerent, domineering, or devious in his performance; indeed it seemed that he was trying so hard to be cooperative under the committee's questioning and the harrying of the press that he was under great nervous tension. When he died in Italy a few months later, his physician was reported to have said that the chief immediate cause of his death had been the nervous strain engendered by the ordeals of his appearance before the Pujo Committee. The public, which had first made Mr. Morgan something of a villain, began to wonder if he had not been something of a hero instead. In business and financial circles of the day his memory was held in high respect.

Other Wall Street leaders gave testimony more fluent and newsworthy, though not more trustworthy, than Mr. Morgan's. James Stillman of the National City Bank was more adroit as a witness, and presented a more detailed picture of the inner mechanics of the financial system, but no one could put a finger on anything to condemn in his own activities. George F. Baker, the "grand old man of Wall Street," impressed and disarmed the committee and the public by his frankness, breadth of view, and judicial quality. He agreed that the nation's private financial system was highly centralized, but defended that centralization as an asset to the nation under its current leadership. When asked by the committee whether the concentration of credit control he described was not dangerous to the nation's welfare, Mr. Baker replied: "It might not be dangerous, but still it has gone far enough. In good hands, I do not see that it would do any harm. If it got into bad hands it would be very bad." Most American citizens had by that time reached about the same conclusion.

The final reports of the committee followed party lines. The majority report, signed by all six of the Democratic members, stated that there was "no testimony from any source to support the allegation of an organized trust in money and credits." That statement, from the members of the party that had long made and would long continue to make a villain of Wall Street, represented a victory for big business and banking. The strongest criticism the Democrats of the committee offered was that there was "an established and well-defined identity of community interest between a few leaders of finance . . . through stock ownership, interlocking directorates, partnership and joint-account transactions . . . which have resulted in a great and rapidly growing concentration of control of money and credit." As a statement of fact this was reasonable enough; the witnesses had said as much.

The principal minority report, signed by three of the four Republican members, granted that the testimony had "disclosed a dangerous concentration of credit in New York City, and to some extent in Boston and Chicago," but denied that the committee's inquiries had "disclosed the existence of any so-called 'money trust.'" A third report, filed in splendid isolation by Republican Congressman Henry McMorran, of Michigan, held that a "sinister light has been thrown over many banking processes which was not justified by the facts, that no report had been made to show the remarkable and commendable explanation of these practices, and that in many cases an impression has been given to the country as to the character and motives of leading bankers which is altogether unfair."

The committee's long inquiries brought no legislative results. Later in the year the Democrats drafted two bills proposing certain regulations of financial operations, but no action was taken on either of these. The banking and currency studies of Senator Carter Glass and his committee, though less dramatic, were far more profound and influential in the drafting and adoption of currency control through the Federal Reserve Act. It was another representative of big finance who gave the Pujo Committee its greatest human-interest story, though the episode contributed nothing to the financial knowledge of the legislation of Congress.

For the purpose of the drama there could have been no better name than that of Rockefeller for one of its actors, even though he was not the fabulous John D. In late 1912 the Pujo Committee asked Mr. William Rockefeller to testify concerning certain financial transactions to which he was believed a party. Mr. Rockefeller declined the invitation. Whatever his motives, the public assumed his reluctance was due to a fear of being forced to unsavory revelations, and initially cast him in the role of villain.

The committee repeated its request. Mr. Rockefeller did not invoke the Fifth Amendment (it was forty years too early for that): he simply refused to see the committee or anyone else. Not even the press could find out whether he was ensconced in his town mansion at 689 Fifth Avenue or in his country estate near Tarrytown. Both were as strongly built and as carefully guarded as medieval fortresses, and even the most enterprising reporters were politely but firmly turned away at the entrance gates or front doors.

The prestige of the committee was clearly at stake, for the situation seemed to have become a test between the power of government and the power of private capital. The committee tried to subpoena Mr. Rockefeller, but to be valid a subpoena must be served on the man himself, and process servers failed to gain admission to either stronghold or to set eyes on their man. All the tricks of the journalistic trade did not even locate the reluctant witness. The public enjoyed its daily headlines and this cat-and-mouse game; human nature, being what it is, took increasing delight in the evasive tactics of the well-entrenched mouse.

The pace quickened in January. The Sergeant-at-Arms of the House of Representatives, forty members of his staff, and a number of Burns and Pinkerton detectives, took turns in the siege and kept vigils in substantial squads at the town and country houses of their quarry. The Sergeant-at-Arms, obviously angered by loss of face, finally announced that he would ask Congress to authorize him to force an entrance. The public was entranced, and its members divided between those who applauded Mr. Rockefeller's sturdy defense of the principle that a man's house is his castle, and those who thought that if necessary Sergeant-at-Arms Riddle should call in the Marines.

Before battering rams were brought into play, Dr. Walter Campbell of 7 East Fifty-fifth Street, a physician of impeccable medical standing, informed the Sergeant-at-Arms that as Mr. Rockefeller's personal physician he had advised him that his throat infection would make it dangerous to testify. Then, to the chagrin of the government and the press, it was discovered that the reluctant witness was not in either of his beleaguered homes but in Nassau in the Bahamas. Messages were sent to him to return, but since Nassau was British territory he could not be forced back except by the long and complicated process of extradition. The committee threatened the fugitive with contempt of court, when he did return to the United States, unless he appeared immediately before the committee. The unsubpoenaed witness sent back the message that he would return and testify when his physician approved his doing so. Another round had been won by the defending champion.

Early in February Mr. Rockefeller agreed to be questioned by representatives of the committee if they would come to him. Congressman Pujo and the committee's counsel, Samuel Untermyer, went to Jekyll Island and met their quarry there, while the public held its breath for the climax of the third act. But the denouement provided more pathos than drama. Mr. Pujo and Mr. Untermyer reported they had been shocked when they discovered how ill a man Mr. Rockefeller was. His throat ailment was obviously very serious and probably incurable, and he could hardly speak. They asked him only a few questions before the doctor intervened, but Mr. Pujo said that he would in any case not have continued his questioning. There was no talk of taking any further testimony, especially since Mr. Rockefeller was probably unable to throw any important light on matters of real importance to the committee. The headline drama ended on a note of pathos and contrition. Another reputed villain had proved to be something far from fearsome, and the public had to turn elsewhere for its daily ration of vicarious villainy.

One figure in American life was, however, dependably heroic, and that was Theodore Roosevelt. Even those who opposed him politically could not help feeling the appeal of his vigorous and indomitable personality. The range of his interests and talents, his courage, resilience, and ebullient enjoyment of everything from conversations with cattlemen and kings to knockdown fights with Democrats or "malefactors of great wealth"—all these epitomized the Paul Bunyanesque vitality that Americans like to think uniquely American. It seemed that no other country could produce such a character, for Winston Churchill had not yet come fully into his own. T. R.'s favorite words became the popular idioms of the day; when he shook hands he was "dee-lighted," and no man could help believing him; anything he liked was "bully"; and when he was shot and wounded while making a political address he finished his speech and then announced he felt "like a bull moose," and the name was promptly assigned to his new Progressive party. Inimitable and unconquerable, he was almost a national monument.

By 1913 T. R. had passed the peak of national admiration, but his energy seemed unabated and his doings were still national news. The public consequently followed, as it might follow the last fights of a heavyweight world's champion, every detail of the libel suit he brought against George A. Newell, Wisconsin, editor of the *Iron Age*. In the heat of the 1912 campaign, Mr. Newell had published the statement that "Roosevelt gets drunk and that not infrequently, and all his associates know it." T. R. sued him for libel. After much testimony, nearly all convincingly scouting the statement, Mr. Newell asked to be permitted to address the court, and said to it:

"Up to the time of this trial I had believed that the statements made in the article which I published were entirely warranted. But in the face of the unqualified testimony of so many distinguished men who have been in a position for years to know the truth, I am forced to the conclusion that I was mistaken, I am unwilling to continue to assert that Mr. Roosevelt actually and in fact drank to excess."

T. R. promptly asked the court's permission to make his own statement, and said in part: "In view of the statement of the defendant, I shall ask the court to instruct the jury that I desire only nominal damages. I did not go into this suit for money [but] to deal with all these slanders. . . . I have achieved my purpose and I am content."

Since under Michigan law nominal damages were fixed at six cents, the judge directed the jury to "render a verdict in favor of the plaintiff for that amount," and it was done. The case ended, as T. R.'s admirers had hoped it would, in one more victory in principle for their hero, and one more demonstration of his good sportsmanship. The public was "dee-lighted" at the humor of the verdict, since the only thing in America that cost exactly six cents was a glass of buttermilk.

There were other figures, heroic, villainous, or merely inflated by circumstance, to divert the American public and reveal the uncertainties of its admirations. One of these proved to be no more than a miscast understudy, called by the irony of events to brief theatrical prominence. But the story of that little man, raised to large proportions by attack and defiance, has more political significance than the pathetic drama of William Rockefeller or the legal adventures of T. R.

The Democratic party in New York City was dominated by Charles F. Murphy, the head of Tammany Hall. In 1912 he chose and elected as Governor of the State of New York a Tammany lieutenant named William Sulzer. Mr. Sulzer had been a member of the New York State Assembly and then served in Congress as a respectable nonentity from 1895 to 1913. Soon after his installation as governor, however, he broke with Tammany over political patronage, and by mid-March he was at open war with Mr. Murphy. Mr. Sulzer's revolt won him wide sympathy, since Tammany was regarded by most good citizens of both parties as a corrupting force. When Tammany men began to make serious charges against him, few believed them.

On April 8th Governor Sulzer urged the passage of a direct primary law that would weaken machine control over nominating conventions. This was a blow to Tammany, and it soon became obvious that Charles Murphy was out to "get" the governor. The legislature, considerably under Tammany control, refused to confirm the governor's appointments, and on May 3rd it defeated the direct primary bill. The governor then arbitrarily summoned the legislature to a special session on June 16th to reconsider the bill. The bill was again rejected, and in counterattack the legislature appointed the Frawley Legislative Committee of Inquiry to investigate the conduct of the various departments of the state government and the governor's use of patronage and the veto power.

After a month's fruitless search for evidence of any misconduct in those areas, the committee turned to quite another matter—the governor's personal financial affairs. On July 16th Mr. Sulzer defied the committee by refusing to obey its subpoena to produce certain documents bearing on the reporting and use of his campaign contributions. On July 20th the committee announced that in his sworn statement of campaign receipts under the Corrupt Practices Act, Mr. Sulzer had failed to report certain checks he had received.

In mid-August impeachment proceedings were under way, and September 18th was the date set for the impeachment trial. Governor Sulzer denied the right of the Assembly to suspend or impeach him during a special session, and refused to relinquish his office to Lieutenant Governor Martin H. Glynn until after the impeachment trial. As a result two men claimed the right and functions of governor, and for several days competed in doing state business and directing state officers. On August 27th the legislature voted to recognize Mr. Glynn as acting governor, and on September 11th the State Supreme Court denied Mr. Sulzer's right to exercise the functions of governor pending the results of the impeachment trial.

Until September most men had thought the charges against Mr. Sulzer had been trumped up by Tammany Hall to discredit a rebellious member. Theodore Roosevelt wrote to the impeached governor on September 2nd: "I have yet to meet a single person who believes, or even pretends to believe, that a single honest motive has animated the proceedings of your antagonists." But as the evidence came in, it forced many men to conclude that Mr. Sulzer had been loose in his ethical judgments, careless in handling money, and perhaps guilty of perjury in his sworn statement. Newspapers like the *Times*, which had previously supported Mr. Sulzer against Tammany, began to turn against him.

On October 16th the impeachment court found the governor guilty of filing a false campaign statement, of committing perjury in swearing to that statement, and of attempting to suppress evidence by threatening witnesses. To the detached observer there seemed little question of his serious indiscretions if nothing more, but many opponents of Tammany Hall suggested that Mr. Sulzer had probably been no more careless than previous Tammany henchmen who had not been caught. In some sections of New York the impeached governor continued to be greeted by cheering crowds, and announced that he would continue in politics to fight Tammany. The Progressives of the Sixth New York District nominated him on an independent ticket for assemblyman, and he made a vigorous campaign, with violent speeches against Charles F. Murphy. Toward the end of the campaign he announced he had been threatened with assassination if he made his usual attack on Tammany in certain areas of the city. On November 3rd he won election to the Assembly with twice the number of votes secured by his Democratic and Republican opponents together.

Mr. Sulzer's later career was undistinguished, and his name vanished so rapidly from the headlines that it was almost as though he had left the country. In 1916 a small minority splinter group called the American party nominated him for the Presidency, but he refused to accept the nomination. He died on November 6, 1941, and few men or periodicals even took notice of his end.

There were those in America, though their numbers had diminished, to whom William Jennings Bryan was still a hero. Ever since his original advocacy of free silver and his eloquent denunciation of the money powers of the East, the golden-throated Nebraskan had maintained a devoted following among the liberals and the discontented. To frightened conservatives he had once been a villain, but his defeats as a perennial presidential candidate had made him less fearsome. Now his activities as the new Secretary of State tested the devotion of even his most loyal adherents.

In a public address in March Mr. Bryan congratulated the Irish Nationalists on their success in the Home Rule bill and called it "the virtual end of hereditary rule" in the British Empire. From a Secretary of State this was something less than diplomatic; the American government had once dismissed a French ambassador for no more. The London *Post* called his remarks "a blazing indiscretion" and "a gratuitous and unwarrantable interference in the domestic affairs of the United Kingdom," and those words were no stronger than the reactions of most Englishmen. In view of current tensions over Mexico and the Panama Canal tolls, the Secretary could not have timed his infelicities worse, or made a less auspicious contribution to the world peace he was advocating with more sincerity than skill. Nor did he increase his popularity with other nations when, at his first formal state dinner to forty foreign diplomats, he broke all precedent by serving only grapejuice.

In May he was again in the headlines in a way that did not add to his heroic stature. Previous to his appointment to the Cabinet Mr. Bryan had been one of the chief attractions on the Chautauqua lecture and entertainment circuit, and the experience had been remunerative. The President, the Congress, and most of the public were surprised to find that as Secretary of State Mr. Bryan was continuing this cultural barnstorming, possibly at augmented honoraria. Protests were voiced in Congress as well as in the press, and the President was urged to order his Secretary of State to withdraw from an undignified and time-consuming commercial sideline. Mr. Bryan was firm, and in his first paid lecture after the criticisms had appeared nationally in the press, he said, "I find it necessary to lecture in order to supplement the salary I receive from the government, the salary not being sufficient to cover my expenses."

Since the Secretary's salary was the highest in the Cabinet, and regarded as enviably large by ninety-nine out of a hundred Americans of the time, this was not convincing. Senator Joseph Bristow, of

Kansas, introduced a scathing resolution in the Senate, but the Secretary continued to leave his Department desk for lectures in far places at a net profit estimated to be considerable. He repeated that he would continue to lecture as long as he should "deem it necessary to do so." Those who remembered his famous "cross of gold" speech were beginning to appreciate the depth of his devotion to silver.

In June it was reported that the President had asked Mr. Bryan to reduce his speaking travels and devote more time to his work in Washington, though irreverent souls suggested that the President might be more pleased if Mr. Bryan stayed away from Washington altogether. There was no apparent diminution of the Secretary's profitable safaris, and in July the criticism was stronger than ever. On the day he was accused in the Senate of neglect of duty, he calmly left to lecture in Winona, Indiana. In September English newspapers called him a "mountebank," and the German press referred to him as a "variety star" and a "clown" in his "Chautauqua circus antics." About that time Theodore Roosevelt was writing to Henry Cabot Lodge: "Bryan is, I believe, the most contemptible figure we have ever had as Secretary of State." But Mr. Bryan, durable as well as unique, weathered the storm.

Other American idols grew somewhat tarnished from exposure during the year. Jim Thorpe, American Indian and international athletic hero, confessed that, although a professed amateur and a hero of the 1912 Olympic Games at Stockholm, he had played professional baseball under false names in 1909 and 1910. The American public was less used to such foibles by its amateur heroes in 1913 than in 1958, and the Thorpe case was an international embarrassment. The United States returned to the Swedish Olympic Committee the medals Mr. Thorpe had received from the hands of the King of Sweden, and the Olympic Decathlon cup he had been presented by the Czar of Russia. Though Mr. Thorpe ceased to be an impeccable hero, he remained a popular commercial one, and was promptly signed up by the New York Giants at a salary considerably more than the $5,000 that Yale was paying former President Taft (whose dimensions were certainly heroic and whose honesty was untarnished) as its Kent Professor of Law. Jack Johnson, Negro heavyweight champion, also descended from his pedestal into evil days and evil ways, and British authorities were expressing grave doubts about letting a man with his moral record appear on the London stage.

Another spectacular hero came a literal cropper before the year was out. Rodman Laws had jumped with a crude parachute from the highest section of Brooklyn Bridge and landed without injury in the river, to the ardent admiration of the adolescent of all ages. But he ended his public career on a diminishing note when in March he announced he would ride a steel rocket of his own design from Jersey City to Elizabeth. Strapped to the rocket and surrounded by invited reporters and uninvited dogs and small boys, he gallantly took off. But, like some more modern rockets, his burst as it left the scaffold, and Laws landed in a clump of alders some thirty feet away. Even his injuries were unheroic; he got off with a few bruises and a very grimy face. History and science thereafter ignored Mr. Laws, but 1960 should credit him as America's first human satellite.

In contrast to that unsuccessful quest for fame, one John Henry Mears, doutless inspired by Jules Verne, made his name profitably known by circling the world in the record time of thirty days. His adventures in ocean liners and *wagons-lits* were by no means so varied and romantic as those of Phileas Fogg, and the limitations of his literary style made his achievement less rewarding. But since the cost of his transportation, he said, totaled only $836.41, he could hardly have been expected to buy balloons, elephants, and Chinese junks for emergency travel, and Lloyd's of London proved remarkably uninterested in his progress.

Other achievements were more impressive to the average American. Hannes Kolehmainen of Finland began his unparalleled career as a distance runner by breaking the world's records for the indoor five- and three-mile runs on successive days in Brooklyn and New York. Billy Sunday drew crowds worthy of Billy Graham at his revival meetings, and inspired hundreds nightly to "hit the sawdust trail" up the aisle to religious conversion. It is difficult to say whether the public most admired his sermons, his platform athletics, or his record as a professional baseball player, but the combination was irresistible. An emotionalist of a different kind, Dr. Maria Montessori, told large audiences of gullible teachers and parents that children should be freed from discipline and convention in education and allowed to develop through "self-activity." This was a more startling unorthodoxy then than now, and her doctrines were enthusiastically adopted by many American educationists, especially those who were themselves a little weak in grammar, mathematics, or the capacity to discipline wisely. Future American heroes, if discipline is part of heroism, would have to be born, not made.

In 1913 Americans were just discovering the charms of popularity polls to measure their collective admirations. The seniors of Wesleyan College were probably sincere when they voted Miss Billie Burke their favorite actress, Kipling their favorite contemporary author, and Robert Louis Stevenson their favorite "standard author." But it seems doubtful that Cornell seniors really preferred Scott to all other writers and liked water as much as beer.

The *Independent* magazine polled its rather effortfully intellectual readers for their selection of the ten "most useful living Americans." In order of preference the heroes and heroines proved to be Thomas A. Edison, Jane Addams, Andrew Carnegie, Theodore Roosevelt, Helen Gould Shepard, Alexis Carrel, General George Goethals, William J. Bryan, Woodrow Wilson, and Luther Burbank. One wonders why the President seemed less useful than Mr. Roosevelt and Mr. Bryan, whom he had defeated in the last election, and why Henry Ford was not included. The editors themselves drew inferences on American values by pointing out that philosophy, religion, literature, and the arts were not represented in the top ten. But the *Independent* had itself reflected national values in asking for the "most useful" citizens, and could hardly expect what the public called "culture" to be considered useful.

If the poll had sought a rating of the true popular heroes of 1913, it would certainly have included Christy Mathewson of the New York Giants, George M. Cohan of the Broadway stage, Jim Thorpe of athletic fame, and Mary Pickford and William S. Hart of the silent screen. The *Independent*'s own list of the "great interests of the average American" was disillusioning to the idealists. America's chief interests were, its editors said, the stock market, female apparel, baseball, the movies, bridge whist, the turkey trot, headlines, "funny pages," and the prizefight. Perhaps Ambrose Bierce was right in calling prewar America "the weak and fluffy decade."

One measure of any society is the type and character of its heroes, the qualities it admires, the performers it awards most highly. By that measure 1913 was like the later years in the immaturity of its popular enthusiasms. Americans were content to seek an undemanding El Dorado of perennial adolescence.

XI

The Shame of the Cities

The people of the United States would always be chiefly rural and therefore good. That was the aim and hope of men like Thomas Jefferson, who wrote to James Madison in 1787: "I think our governments will remain virtuous as long as they are chiefly agricultural," but when our people "get piled up on one another as in Europe, they will become corrupt, as in Europe."

There would be cities, of course, but they should be seaports and trading centers, serving the smaller towns and countryside, but never dominating them. American free men would naturally prefer country to city life, and there was land enough for all. Until after the Civil War Jefferson's hope seemed on the way to realization, for though cities were growing, the attitudes and economy of the farm and the village set the tone of American society.

Forces were at work that changed all that, but they did not reveal their full power until the turn of the century. One of those forces was the development of factory industry; another was immigration. They were separate forces but they supported each other. The cheap labor that immigration poured into industry helped it to expand, and its expansion brought the call for more cheap labor. It seemed at first an excellent arrangement for all concerned. Industry gave immigrants jobs, and by increasing the wealth and population of the cities gave farmers greater markets, pushed up the values of land, and made the national economy stronger and more prosperous.

Since everyone seemed to benefit from the growth of the cities, the hopes and fears of Jefferson were increasingly ignored. The men of the towns had never shared them, and critics of urbanism like

Thoreau were regarded as anachronistic romanticists. In any case no verbal protest or cultural concern could have stopped the tide of the Industrial Revolution from sweeping over a land that offered infinite material resources, a free field for private enterprise, expanding labor and expanding markets. After all, few men of any age or clime have let abstract considerations of social or cultural values divert them from the pursuit of prosperity when it lay so temptingly before them. Men are usually slower to see the adverse effects of some great innovation than its advantages. The ultimate effects of an infinitude of small cultural compromises are hard to foresee, especially if no one wants to see them.

A few men did interrupt their pursuit of private gain long enough to consider the effects of unregulated urban growth, but they were not so much concerned about what cities might do to national culture and national ethics as about what cities were doing to good government and the profits of agriculture. Andrew D. White had written in the *Forum* that "with very few exceptions the city governments of the United States are the worst in the world—the most expensive, the most corrupt," and Lord Bryce had concluded that city government was "the one conspicuous failure of the United States."

That was true enough, and becoming painfully apparent, but it missed the chief danger, which went beyond municipal inefficiency and corruption. Perhaps that was because the mountain of civic misgovernment was so high that men could not see the social morasses that lay behind it. Men made shortsighted by their own comforts and securities assumed the permanence of their culture and way of life. They did not often visit or visualize what kind of a society might rise like miasma from the slums of New York, the stockyards of Chicago, or the sweatshops of Paterson and lower Broadway. They did not realize what went on in the minds and spirits of the men, women, and children who lived there—what values and habits of thought such conditions were developing in the millions who would become voting citizens—what the effects of industrial concentration and immigration would be on future democratic ideals and a culture derived from the Anglo-Saxon tradition. Until the 1910 census produced the startling figures, very few good citizens had realized even the numerical results of massive immigration and industrialization upon the social composition of the great cities, or the implication of the numerical domination of city dwellers over the rest of society. In 1913 nearly 50,000,000 first- or second-generation foreign-born were living in the United States, most of them in a few large cities. By 1900 New York was more populous than Paris; Chicago and Philadelphia were larger than all but five cities in Europe. The population of Los Angeles rose from 5,000 in 1860 to 100,000 in 1900, and that of Denver from almost zero to 134,000. Rural population did not increase proportionally; indeed, between 1880 and 1890 the rural districts of seven states decreased in population by some 200,000—while the cities of those states increased by 2,500,000.

People still thought of New York as an American city, but in fact it had become a polyglot city. In 1910 only 21.4 per cent of New York's population was of American-born stock; it was the largest Jewish city and the second largest Italian city in the world. They thought of Boston as Yankee, though its popular culture and political control were more Irish than Puritan. Chicago was already an olio of several small cities: Greek, Slovak, Hungarian, Sicilian, Lithuanian, and Russian.

Most descendants of the early settlers, even if they knew these facts, would have assumed that they and their kind, even if ultimately outnumbered, could continue to set the tone of politics and culture. Nothing was further from the truth. What was more, the immigrant culture was not derived from the traditions of northern Europe. Between 1900 and 1910 nearly 77 per cent of the immigrants were Latin, Slav, or Mediterranean in origin, and 90 per cent of them had come from the less-educated elements in their native lands. Even the city dwellers officially recorded as native-born American included many children of the foreign-born, with social mores very different from those of Jefferson and Franklin. "Manhattan," said Hamlin Garland, "is a city of aliens—who know little and care less for American traditions. After a lecture trip in the interior I return each time to New York as to a foreign seaport."

Many of the new Americans were unable to read or speak English, and so drew together in defensive clans. Some became disillusioned about an America that did not meet their expectations of equality, virtue, and easy riches. A large number of them were used to being dependent on authority, and sought it here from unfortunate sources; others resented authority in any form, even democratic authority. Some retained their European ways; others discarded them so quickly that they left cultural vacuums that the cheapest of American mores rushed in to fill. Most of the later immigrants cared less for abstract principles of freedom than for immediate economic security and material improvement. There were exceptions, but not enough of them to prevent immigrant culture from becoming a confused mixture of the less good from their old and new environments.

Americans of 1913 viewed the resultant degeneration of their politics with more concern than the accompanying degeneration of their culture. Politically, the immigrant supported the city bosses and was vulnerable to the seductions of the city slickers, the cheap labor recruiters, and the more radical unions and the ward heelers. It was often the local political machine that gave the immigrant the only kindnesses and human interest he received, and it followed that the immigrant gave the boss his vote. As one authority put it, "The loyalty of immigrant voters to the bosses was one of the reasons why local reform was short-lived." Francis Parkman had written, "Where the carcass is, the vultures gather."

Though Americans were waking up to these realities in 1913, few of them recognized the scope of the problem or attacked it in other than local and sporadic ways. One man who did see it clearly was Professor Edward A. Ross, of Wisconsin, who warned that immigration had expanded illiteracy, industrial peonage, juvenile delinquency, pauperism, slums, drunkenness, insanity, vice, class consciousness, political corruption, and low standards in education. This was an overwhelming indictment, but it was true.

But though the immigrants augmented political and social problems, they cannot be blamed for all the flaws that were developing in

American life and culture. There were other causes of American ills, and a small but vociferous group of journalists had begun to point them out. This handful of men and women, who would have disagreed on most subjects among themselves, had a common general purpose and common method. They turned their microscopes on some aspect of the American scene and tried to make accurate pictures of what they saw. Because S. S. McClure gave them encouragement and a place to publish, their chief vehicle of expression was *McClure's Magazine.*

In 1906 Theodore Roosevelt had compared the journalists who featured only the seamy sides of American life and politics to the man in *The Pilgrim's Progress* who "could look no way but downward, with a muckrake in his hands." He did not mean to apply that term to the more high-minded of exposers of corruption, but to their imitators who sought headlines and profits more than truth and improvement. But the public liked the term, and applied it indiscriminately to the best as well as to the worst of the journalist exposers.

The good "muckrakers," by whatever name, did a great service to American society. They made citizens take off their blinders and see their society as it really was. They were the destroyers of complacent myths, the first fighting realists in American social thought. They worked their way into the back rooms of city halls where the deals were being made, and into saloons where those deals were being implemented at the working level. They traced and reported the devious operations of city bosses, street-railway magnates, building contractors, legal hatchet men and the leg-men of the big trusts. They loitered in carbarns, slums, and stockyards, using their eyes and their noses. They followed threads that led from firetrap tenements to municipal offices, and from houses of prostitution to the bank accounts of respected citizens. They uncovered nothing that someone had not already known, but the mosaic they collectively assembled from the fragments of corruption gave Americans a picture of their society very different from the myth. The muckrakers contributed as much as anyone to what Edward Bellamy had called, with some exaggeration, "the present universal ferment of men's minds as to the imperfections of present social arrangements."

The muckraker was not usually a radical in politics, but an able American with a strong sense of curiosity and justice who had found his special vocation. He was impatient with the virtuous posings, the oversimple panaceas, the ignorances and the ineptitudes of the table pounders for reform. His job, as he saw it, was to diagnose the illness of American society, not to specify precise remedies; to point out the cause-and-effect relationships between boss rule and gangsters, between business profits and graft, between public indifference and urban corruption.

To many an honest conservative citizen the muckrakers were indecently scurrilous and destructive, featuring only the excrescences of American life. No businessman or politician, no matter how decent, seemed immune from their attacks and, he feared, their misrepresentation. There was something to be said for his attitude, for many journalists were better at finding dirt underneath the carpet than accurate in saying how it got there. Not all corporations were social evils, not all rich men were selfish or crooked, not all men in public office were weak or corrupt—yet that was almost the cumulative impression made by the muckrakers and their cheaper imitators.

Too much muckraking could, indeed, impair its own objective. By 1913 many citizens had become so inured to reading exposés of urban corruption that they accepted bosses and graft as almost inevitable camp followers of democracy. George W. Alger said of the spate of journalistic revelations, "Exposure forms the typical literature of our daily life," and many good citizens read of local scandals with the same detachment that they read realistic fiction: the situation had nothing to do with them except as entertainment. As Mr. Alger put it: "The advancement of the constructive elements of society has been neglected to give space to these spicy stories of graft and greed." That was only a half-truth, but it was the other side of the muckraking medal. Finley Peter Dunne delighted nearly everyone when his Mr. Dooley satirized the exposures of the "McClure gang":

When I pick me a fav-rite magazine off the floor, what do I find? Ivry-thing has gone wrong. Th' wurruld is little betther thin a convict's camp. . . . And so it goes. . . . It's a wicked, wicked horrible place, an' this here counthry is about th' toughest spot in it. I don't thrust anny man anny more . . . if I hear th' stealthy step iv me dearest frind at th' dure I lock the cash drawer. . . . We're wan iv th' gr-reatest people in the wurruld to clean house, an' th' way we like best to clean house is to burn it down. . . . Th' noise ye hear is not th' firrst gun iv a rivolution. It's only the people iv th' United States batin' a carpet. . . . Who is that yellin'? That's our ol' frind High Fi-nance bein' compelled to take his annual bath.

Such reactions were inevitable, and they were of course partly the defense of Americans unwilling to face the facts of their own weaknesses. But though they might laugh with Mr. Dooley, they began to see that the trouble went deeper than the corruptions of city politicians. The problems of the cities were derived from forces nearly every citizen approved: rapid industrial growth, big profits, real-estate bonanzas, unhampered free enterprise, expanding population, exploitation of national resources and the individual's desire not to be bothered with civic responsibility except when he felt like it. Those forces were neither good nor bad but amoral, and they were also interlocked with one another. Nearly every element in society was making, in one way or another, its contribution of selfishness or narrowness or ignorance to the cheapening of democratic government and cultural values. No one economic or social class was wholly to blame, yet all were partly to blame. Again and again men like Lincoln Steffens tried to drive home the basic truth that it was the self-seeking and indifference of nearly every American that made corruption and injustice possible. If the public half-admired the daring and skill of men who flouted social welfare and got away with it; if it admired Theodore Roosevelt for his highhanded power politics in taking the land for the Panama Canal; if it admired Andrew Carnegie because he made millions without too much regard for the public interest, or forgave him because later he gave most of those millions away— then the public could blame only itself for the results. Americans were so busy admiring the ends that they neglected to question the means.

In fact, and in spite of their occasional complaints, most men who did not live in slums or suffer directly from business pressures and boss rule really liked their cities just as they were. Low wages, inflated land values, profits on the building or rental of firetrap apartments were often direct or indirect sources of income to a town's best citizens. It was useful to have a friend or two in the city hall who would overlook an occasional extralegal deal or do one a quiet favor. Corruption and boss rule should certainly be curbed, but there was nothing really corrupt, merely friendly and generous, about handing out cigars to the policeman on the corner in the hope that he would close his eyes to one's own minor traffic-law infractions. It was only good business to see that aldermen did not tighten up the fire laws or the building code in ways that would hurt one's own income. After all, successful business was built on enterprise and friendships. Too much regulation of a city's growth, or too rigid enforcement of its minor ordinances, might slow down progress or restrict private enterprise, or at least cause good citizens inconvenience. . . .

Since Americans did things on a grander scale than anyone else, they were not upset that their municipal graft was on as grandiose a scale as their skyscrapers—a magnificent defect of a magnificent virtue. Municipal corruption and ugliness were merely growing pains, and would somehow eliminate themselves as material progress moved toward all-round perfection. Meanwhile local scandals made interesting reading on the commuters' special or in the Metropolitan Club. Only when some episode struck directly home at him, or when conditions got bad enough to anger him, was the average middle-class citizen moved to active protest and reform. If this attitude seems an unjust analysis of the good citizen of 1913, let the good citizen of 1960 consider current juvenile delinquency or the contemporary muggings in New York's Central Park.

Nevertheless the seeds planted by the muckrakers of the first decade were germinating in the second, and the less-privileged citizens, no longer the silent and submerged minority, were beginning to assert themselves and their collective protest. The earlier planters of those seeds cannot all be mentioned, but some of them cannot be ignored.

Ida M. Tarbell's *History of the Standard Oil Company,* in two volumes, published in 1904, educated public opinion to the ramifications of big business, and the book played its part in later court actions on oil and other monopolies. Thomas W. Lawson's *Frenzied Finance* (1902) described the less-constructive activities of Wall Street, and the Federal Reserve Act of 1913 was partly derived from the public interest that book created. Ray Stannard Baker's series of articles "Railroads on Trial," which began to appear in 1905, influenced the policies and the public support of the Interstate Commerce Commission eight years later.

When Upton Sinclair published *The Jungle* (1906) and Frank Norris *The Octopus* (1901), conditions in the stockyards and the rate battles between farmers and railroads were only a little worse than in 1913, and tens of thousands who had read those books were ready to support Mr. Wilson's program of economic regulation. *The Jungle* described the preparation of meats in the midst of nauseatingly insanitary conditions; the packing of beef and pork from tubercular cattle and diseased hogs; the inadequate inspection of meats and packing plants by government officials. *The Octopus* revealed how the railroads, by adroit variations in their rates, could capitalize on the economic weaknesses of individual farmers and small towns.

John Spargo's moving story *The Bitter Cry of the Children* (1906) led to the formation of a National Child Labor Committee and brought better child-labor laws. By her book *The Spirit of Youth and the City Streets* (1910), Jane Addams made well-to-do readers in their homes on Lake Shore Drive or Fifth Avenue realize that only a few blocks away were the hovels and destitutions of the baffled immigrant, the impoverished widow, the sick workman and the undernourished child. But the book that brought the over-all problems of urban misgovernment, economic injustice, and public irresponsibility most powerfully to Americans was Lincoln Steffens' *The Shame of the Cities,* published in 1904.

There were other writers, not classified as muckrakers, who were also making Americans look more closely and honestly at their democracy and themselves. Walter Weyl, Randolph Bourne, Brand Whitlock, Herbert Croly, and soon young Walter Lippmann contributed to bring understanding and suggest remedies to the more intellectual members of society. But there was still a long way to go in 1913. The idea of planning the development of a city to make it a good place in which to live and work was still the enthusiasm of only a few men like Frederic A. Delano. One of them, George McAneny, Borough President of Manhattan, urged in March that the city create a commission to plan its future development, establish regulations to prevent overcrowding, and control the invasion of residential areas by large factories. New Yorkers heard him politely but did very litttle; to some of them the effort seemed futile. The great cities were expanding Frankenstein's monsters that had got out of human control, and they saw no hope of controlling their sprawling tentacles and concentrations.

The would-be planners received aid from some sources with personal interests at stake. Renting and building agents were expressing concern lest the "overproduction of skyscrapers" might make human concentration so intolerable that people would withdraw from the centers of cities and thus lower the values and rentals of its land and buildings. Where, asked worried real-estate operators, would all the tenants come from to fill these great new office building and residential caravanseries? Mr. McAneny said Americans would be too sensible to let such monstrosities multiply indefinitely. He predicted that the time would come when no more skyscrapers would be built in New York, and when the existing ones would be regarded as warning monuments of past unwisdom. If Mr. McAneny was a true prophet, he was certainly a long-term one.

As 1913 began, old and new voices were hammering at the need for reform in municipal affairs. In January S. S. McClure, veteran warhorse of the muckrakers days, exhorted the members of the City Club of New York to take their parts in cleaning up city politics. He compared municipal government in the United States with that in German cities, "the best governed in the world," and added that American statistics for murder, theft, and fire in its cities were higher than those in almost any European country. Professional experts on municipal government echoed his words.

In February the readers of the *Century Magazine* learned what a noted French writer thought of New York, and were not amused. Pierre Loti wrote that on reaching New York Harbor his ship entered an "infernal abyss . . . almost a nightmare, but which nevertheless attains a sort of tragic beauty by the very excesses of its horror. A thousand chimneys belch forth black smoke or white eddies of steam . . . the wharfs resemble gigantic carcasses of sombre-colored iron. . . . Enormous signs . . . in letters forty feet high . . . the shriek of whistles, the dismal moaning of sirens, the rumble of motors and the din of factories deafen the ears." In Central Park "a feeling of intolerable depression" settled on him. He saw about him "great luxury, yet something is lacking . . . perhaps . . . simply the soul of the past. . . . Even in my sleep I was oppressed by the six millions of human beings massed about me."

Mark Jefferson took a more "Hopeful View of the Urban Problem" in the September *Atlantic Monthly*, but the best he could conclude was that "no exodus from the country has occurred except as the country, exuberant and life-giving, brings forth a population in excess of its agricultural needs." This was almost as flowery as Loti's prose, though different in tone, but there were farmers and sociologists who would not have agreed with Mr. Jefferson. The farmer might have questioned the exuberance of his life, and suggested that there were more reasons than rural overpopulation for seeking work in the cities. The sociologist might have asked whether the only virtue of living in the country was to supply the city's industrial needs.

Mr. Jefferson's optimism did not solve urban problems, as Jacob A. Riis, who knew the life of the immigrant from personal experience, implied in his "Battle with the Slums" in the November *Century*. Foreign examples of municipal perfection did not move Americans to emulation, even though experts like Frederic C. Howe were busily praising German cities. Americans, with democratic perversity, seemed to prefer the corruptions of New York and Chicago to German docility under the policed regimentation of the Tiergarten.

The basic question before the American society was whether a large democracy, immersed in industrial growth and immigration, could develop a culture that would lift its people above vulgarity, scientific materialism, and economic determinism. Urban reform alone could not answer that question. Neither could the people of 1913. Few of them understood the real issue, and those who did were relatively powerless.

If democratic culture was really deteriorating in the cities, was it maintaining itself in what was left of the truly rural areas? Did the germ of cultural uplift lie in the farms and small towns? On that matter sentimentalists and realists were in disagreement. Robert and Helen Lynd's *Middletown*, sixteen years later, would supply one answer for the small city, and it would not be an encouraging one. Randolph Bourne, meanwhile, looked outside the cities for cultural growth, and found little to encourage him. He wrote in the *Atlantic Monthly* of February:

> The contest between the city and the country that has been going on for fifty years has left the country moribund and made the city chaotic. The country has been stripped of its traditions and the city has grown so fast that it has not had time to form any. The suburban town is a sort of last stronghold of Americanism [but] . . . the city swamps its neighbors. . . . These suburban annexes cease to have a life of their own, and become simply sleeping places for commuters.

In spite of Bourne's conclusion, the American city was beginning to develop a culture of its own. It was not the kind of culture Jefferson had envisaged, John Quincy Adams had represented, Emerson had recommended, or Walt Whitman had tried to see. It was not the culture of the American Affirmation, and those devoted to the earlier ideal might search in vain for it in the life and thought of Seventh Avenue or the Bronx. The new urban culture was a product of industrial progress—as yet an amorphous *mélange* of undigested habits, opinions, mores, and values, collectively as remote from the ideals of Harvard College in 1913 as from those of the Founding Fathers.

But in 1913 there was a ferment that promised better things. An increasing number of responsible citizens were realizing how much ground democracy and culture had lost while they were busy looking the other way. Sporadically and often ineptly they began to do something about it. So did the lower classes, which had their own ideas about making America more consistent with their particular democratic dream. Both groups had much to learn and far to go, for neither was a perfect embodiment of Jefferson's ideal democratic man. But in spite of their weaknesses and blindnesses, in spite of the increasing differences between them, in spite of the interruptions of world wars, strikes, and depressions, in spite of abortive popular experiments and popular fallacies, they persisted. Most of their efforts proved no more than amelioration, and most of their fruits decayed on the vine. They failed to preserve the America their fathers had loved, and they failed to create a new America they would view untroubled, but they began movements toward better government at which their successors still labor, with perhaps a little greater understanding. If one looks at the cities of 1960 only for gains, one can easily find them. The strivers of 1913 did not win their cause, but their successors have not yet wholly lost it.

XII

The Embattled Farmer

Belief in the special values and virtues of rural life antedated the Republic. Ever since Hesiod had proclaimed, "How happy is his low degree . . . who leads a quiet country life," men whose hands had never touched a plow had sung the plowman's praises. Eighteenth century poets endowed the farmer with special morality and contentment; the urban artisan Ben Franklin paid deference to agriculture as "the only honest way for a nation to acquire wealth," and even Hamilton, that famous advocate of manufactures, conceded: "The cultivation of the earth . . . has intrinsically a strong claim to pre-eminence over every other kind of industry." In the nineteenth century Whittier, Thoreau, and many other literary lights idealized country life and sentimentalized the farmer into American folklore. Rural mores so dominated American culture before the Civil War that Emerson could declare: "The vast majority of the people in this country live by the land, and carry its quality in their manners and opinions."

Until after Fort Sumter that glorification of rural life in America was almost justified. Farmers had been the chief producers of the nation's wealth; they had given stability to its politics and continuity to its culture; their interests and support had been the first consideration of the politicians. On the whole they had been the most steady and independent of Americans. More than the volatile city dwellers, they had maintained the traditions of the nation.

Myth takes over when fact departs, and long after the farmer had ceased to be the most favored and influential American everyone but himself persisted in asserting his special good fortune. Pictures of the virtuous and contented American family invariably showed it in a rural setting, and the popularity of Currier and Ives prints indicated that nostalgia as well as art associated country life with happiness. Country life bred virtue and wisdom too, and presidential candidates, to the present day, featured whatever rural origins they could claim or invent. Calvin Coolidge pretended to be more of a backwoods Yankee than he was; Franklin Roosevelt was translated by shrewd publicity from an urban millionaire to a front-porch Hudson River squire; Wendell Willkie hurried from Wall Street, in manners and vernacular, back to Elwood, Indiana; Dwight Eisenhower became the boy from Abilene. The moral and self-sufficing man with the hoe was the favorite character of political orators, and the different picture of rural life in Edgar Lee Masters' verse did not destroy the myth. Country life remained a compound of Jeffersonian tradition, literary invention, campaign oratory, urban nostalgia, and chromo-calendar sentimentality. As late as 1913, G. S. Dickerman, writing in the September *Atlantic Monthly*, could seriously aver: "The country is the national nursery . . . of . . . self-reliance, inflexibility of purpose, moral worth, religious sensibility."

All this professed admiration and literary glamorizing irritated the farmer, who was painfully conscious of the difference between the way society pictured him and the way it treated him. The more he was praised, the less he was actually deferred to, as factories and cities took away more and more of his economic and political priority. Though he was still essential to the national life and wealth, still by tradition its most valued citizen, still by myth the happiest of men, he was not even holding his own in relative numbers, influence, or income.

Hamlin Garland illustrated the change in his own experience. As a young man his literary efforts had been idyllic tributes to the charm of his rural Midwest boyhood. But when, after seven years in eastern cities reading Ibsen, Darwin, and Henry George, he returned to his old home in Dakota he found: "All the gilding of life melted away. The bread and butter realities came back on me in a flood . . . no splendor of cloud, no grace of sunset could conceal the poverty of these people . . . the gracelessness of their homes and the sordid quality of the mechanical daily routine of those lives." The average farmer of 1913 might not feel all this, but he knew that others were getting more ease, enjoyment, and elevation from life than he.

Between 1860 and 1910 the rural population had doubled while the urban population had multiplied seven times. By 1910 less than 35 per cent of Americans were in any way allied to agriculture, and less than 5,000,000 were actually classified as farmers and planters, with another 2,500,000 as wage-earning farmhands. Politicians still courted the farm vote, but they were beginning to look more amorously upon the more numerous votes of organized labor and the city masses. King Corn and King Cotton were on the defensive, and to city dwellers the sturdy yeoman had become the hick or the hayseed.

This change in the economic and social leadership of the nation was indicated by the new words coming into common use. It was not the farm but the city that created and chiefly used the automobile, turbine, telephone, phonograph, subway, wireless, airplane, dynamo, and power plant. Words like *propaganda, unionization, strike, workmen's compensation, closed shop, publicity, production line, standardization, slum, investigation, and skyscraper* bespoke an urban, not a rural society.

By 1913 the typical farmer was reaching the stage of frustration and resentment. He watched the urban dweller become the nation's chief consumer, a market to whose dictates he had to make his crops conform. He saw the city man become politically and financially better off than himself. He was increasingly dependent on urban capital to finance his machinery or next year's crop, and he had to accept whatever terms for loans the bankers cared to set. His profits were, except in unusually good years, shrinking, and city men were blaming him for the high cost of food. Something, he thought, must be wrong with the system, and he blamed big cities, big business, high freight rates, high interest rates, and the lack of some system of rural credits. And although it seldom occurred to him, he was also losing the moral strength and religious convictions of his ancestors.

The farmer was experiencing what Jefferson had feared if big cities developed, and recognizing the truth of Theodore Roosevelt's statement in 1894: "Excessive urban development does constitute a real and great danger." T. R. had gone further in a speech in Buffalo in 1901 when he urged that all aspects of urban and corporate growth should be dealt with as part of the same problem of national imbalance, and that the economy of the factory should not dominate the economy of the farm. Two years later, in his annual message to Congress, T. R. had written, "It is unhealthy and undesirable for the cities to grow at the expense of the country," and in 1908 he had appointed the first federal commission on country life. No wonder so many men from the farm belt voted for him in 1912.

That commission had reported in 1909 to President Taft, perhaps with less effect than had T. R. still been in the White House. Though the report voiced in some ways the alarms of the farmers, it tempered its picture of rural decline by asserting: "There has never been a time when the American farmer is as well off as he is today, when one considers not only his earning power but the comforts and advantages he may secure." Many a farmer thought the statement literally true but realistically specious; relative to other citizens his lot and his income were less good than his father's; though his income had gone up, so had his costs; though he had a bathtub, the comparable townsman had a Ford car and a washing machine too; and above all he could farm successfully only if he had capital, and for that he was increasingly at the mercy of bankers and other forces beyond his control. He might also have asked the commission why, if the farmer's life was so attractive, his sons and daughters were leaving it to seek their fortunes, or their pleasures, in the cities.

The small farmer had always had to face greater hazards than the townsmen or the rural myth recorded. He had never known the steady prosperity of the tradition, for nature often sent pests, droughts, and floods, and no matter how intelligently he planned, the elements could beat him. Competition from new and better farm land often beat him too. Long before 1913 the empty farmhouses, decaying barns, and overgrown fields in northern New England were eloquent evidence of the superiority of Midwest soil. The visitor in western New York

State could see miles of abandoned railway lines that once served prosperous wheat farms when Rochester was the Flour City—victims of the newer wheat belt farther west. There had always been marginal farms, but now all farm land except the best and most efficiently cultivated was becoming marginal.

What was more, the laws of supply and demand seemed to have turned against him. Each year it was more difficult to keep his costs down and sell his crops for enough to give him a reasonable profit, allowing for losses in the bad years. The small farmer who owned and worked his acres with the help of a single hired hand or a son or two found his troubles the greatest. He had no bargaining power and no margin of capital to carry him over a bad year or two. He was moving closer to subsistence farming without knowing exactly why, while he watched other men in other occupations gain in prosperity. The number of middlemen who came between him and the ultimate consumer were increasing in number, and each of them took a percentage of the revenue his crops brought in. The small farmer worked doggedly, endlessly, and sometimes not very intelligently, and his wife worked as hard. "Households of toil in the drab small towns," was what Hamlin Garland found on his return to the Midwest. It was a very different picture from the idyls James Whitcomb Riley had contributed to the agrarian legend.

The basic trouble was that the new mass-production economy was setting a pace and a standard of large-scale efficiency that the average farmer could not meet. Sometimes he was cultivating too much land without modern methods or machinery; sometimes he was depending too much on a single crop. In most areas of the country scientific practice in agriculture lagged a generation behind the model farms. There was never time or energy or capital to finish anything properly, from cultivation of the land to the new wing on the barn. The only really successful farmers were the big fellows on the best land, who could afford the newest farm equipment and had capital enough behind them to bargain with the wholesalers, the bankers, and the railroads. To be financially successful one had to stop being a farmer in the traditional sense and become an agricultural production man. Raising crops was ceasing to be a way of life, and becoming an industrial and commercial enterprise.

When a big Kansas wheat farmer shipped his crop 1,500 miles by rail and then another 3,000 miles by steamer, in accordance with prices quoted by cable, he was a very different kind of farmer from the one who still drove his grain-filled wagon five miles to town over dirt roads he and his neighbors had to keep open and repair, and sold his wheat for whatever he could get for it. The new agriculturalist had to approach his farming with the same professional skill, managerial capacity and commercial aptitude as the manufacturer and merchant. He had to become a specialist-technician in the production of goods from the soil; he had to be a clever merchandiser with a knowledge of the market and capital enough to follow its trends. He had to keep up with new hybrids, new machinery, new sprays, modern cost accounting and double-entry bookkeeping. All these things required education as well as time, and the small farmer had too little of either.

As early as 1887 a southern farm journal had seen the handwriting on the silo wall when it declared: "The time has come when the farmer must be a businessman as well as an agriculturalist," and a writer on "The Farmer as Merchant" had said in 1904: "Now the object of farming is not primarily to make a living but to make money. To this end it must be conducted on the same business basis as any other producing industry." He called the Farmers' Institute "a business meeting for businessmen." Most farmers had been very slow to take these hints, but by 1913 they were recognizing the truth, and they were not sure they liked their new role or could play it well.

The man on the farm was the victim, as much as the beneficiary, of the rising standard of living. His family wanted all the comforts and labor-saving devices they saw in the towns and in the magazines, and such things cost more money than he had. If he did not provide them, everyone was unhappy and his children might move to town; if he did provide them, he went into debt. Running water, furnaces, bathrooms, electric lights, and telephones were appearing in his neighbors' homes just when he needed to buy a horse or cultivator if he were to hold his own. If he bought the modest luxuries that had suddenly become necessities, he had to buy them on installments, or on borrowed money, or by selling some of his land, and sooner or later the day of reckoning would come. One or two years of bad weather or low wheat prices might make him a bankrupt or the victim of a foreclosed mortgage.

Farmers were not eloquent men, but one of them described his womenfolk and children as "pining for neighbors, domestic help, pretty clothes, schools, music, art, and many things they saw and wanted every time they went to town or the magazines came in." The new rural schools, autobusses, highways, and Carnegie libraries were fine things, but their maintenance had to be paid for by increased taxes on land, and it was the farmer who owned much of the land and felt he paid most of the taxes for what the folks in the town were enjoying. A man could not take much pleasure in a rising standard of living if it also meant a rising debt. "Debtors' country" was what the poet William Vaughn Moody was calling the Midwest farmlands.

The successful farmer who met all these challenges did so by becoming more of a townsman and less of a farmer than his neighbors. He had to adopt values and attitudes closer to those of the city businessman than to those of the traditional son of the soil. He no longer talked quite the same language or lived quite the same life as his less-enterprising rural neighbors, and that broke down the previous unity of the farm belt as a social, economic, and political bloc. Sometimes the businessman-agriculturalist was not comfortable at the changes he had made in himself; he stood psychologically disoriented between his inherited rural mores and his acquired semiurban ones. He had become progressive, liberal, and fluent, but at the same time retained older emotional values that frowned on those qualities. He sometimes felt a traitor to his less-prosperous neighbors. Most nineteenth century farmers had been traditionally Republican, but Republicanism seemed to have come more and more under the control of the eastern manufacturers and bankers. As the status of the small farmer became less secure, he began to care less about loyalty to the Grand Old Party and more about supporting whatever politicians offered promise of doing something that would improve his own position. Many dissatisfied wheat- and corn-belt men had supported Bryan, and others had followed T. R. into the Progressive party. Though the majority of the farmers in the northern states were still Republicans by principle, they were discontented ones.

Woodrow Wilson seemed able and honest, but he was certainly no farmer and knew nothing at firsthand of farm life and work. He showed no special interest in the agricultural problem and had talked little about it in his campaign speeches. During 1913 he did not do much to ease the farmers' lot, and made no attempt at all to cope with the long-term political and economic imbalance between city and country. There had been much talk about farm credits at the conference of governors in Richmond in January, and in the February *Atlantic Monthly* Myron Herrick had urged "adequate credit for our farmers." At long last, in his December message to Congress, President Wilson advocated rural credits as a major item in his legislative program. From the small farmer's point of view rural credits would certainly help, but they would not solve the over-all problems of the agriculturalist in an industrial and urban national economy.

The farmer was slowly beginning to alter a traditional principle in his code. He was getting ready to demand from federal government solutions to the economic problems that seemed too great for him to solve. The independent landholder of the American legend was mentally conditioning himself to be dependent. He would welcome rural credits, and then price support and subsidies and payments not to plant, and for their sakes would accept crop control and the other regimentations of the welfare state.

XIII

The Workingman

Americans before 1865 had no great interest in social and economic legislation beyond the minimum essential to safety and order. They liked personal independence better than government intercession, not wholly from a passion for self-reliance but from a dislike of interference. They wanted not only personal freedom but economic elbow room.

That laissez-faire theory had not always worked out well in practice, but on the whole America had prospered with it. Extreme individualism could flourish as long as the country was chiefly rural, almost classless, and underpopulated. Small communities with simple economic structures could breed and support men parochially self-sufficing, and proud of it. Many an American's life before 1860 was bounded by his farm, his family, his near neighbors, his church, and his four corners. The man in the smaller towns was only a little less provincial and independent, and his hired man did not think of himself as a wage slave with interests adverse to those of the employer. The rural wage earner did not feel socially inferior, and often he was not.

But as industrial civilization developed, men found it more difficult to reconcile individualism with the way economics seemed to be developing. The victory of North over South had been a victory of factories over plantations. The war had speeded up the development of industry and an industrial class, and had demonstrated that factory production and organization were the new keys to prosperity and power. Many Americans were alert enough to apply that lesson to their peacetime pursuits, and did so without regard to the ultimate effects on the individual and on society.

Railroads and manufacturers were demonstrating how effective men could be when they formed large plans and then were able to organize capital, materials, and men to implement them. But the new centralized efficiency brought new problems, and changed the hired man to the proletarian. As business expanded and corporations multiplied, it was not the men who directed the work who controlled the company, but the men who supplied the capital, and they might be remote from the actual operation and indifferent to the welfare of the workers engaged in it. This began to look to the workmen like the old tyranny in a new form; the few men controlling large industry were getting too high and mighty. It had taken all the power of President Andrew Jackson to bring Nicholas Biddle and his fellow financiers into line with what seemed to be the interests of the people, but now the railroad magnates, the bankers, and the heads of corporations were getting too powerful for the individual man, or even the individual state, to stand up against. A few men were making great fortunes, while the men who did the work for them got too little of the fruits of their own labor. The workingman began to feel the need of an organization of his own to support his interests, and of a central government that would step in to make and enforce more equitable rules of the economic game. This might mean some sacrifice of the cherished principle of individual independence, but all men can rationalize irreconcilables when they really want to. Workmen from the old American stock decided they could have more government without having less essential freedom. Workmen from the old countries were used to paternalism, and were even more ready to ask the federal government to solve their problems.

Industrialism was not only diminishing the individual status of the worker; it was also creating a new society of city dwellers, foreign-born communities, and greater discrepancies between the rich and the poor. The farmer might think he was the forgotten man, but the urban wage earner with no bargaining power was sure the farmer's lot was better than his own. The rights of private enterprise took on a less attractive meaning; they had become the right of a few men to capitalize on the skills of the rest, utilizing immigrants as cheap labor to keep all wages down, and resisting or evading the inadequate legal restrictions on monopolies, sharp practices, hours, wages, and working conditions. Corporations were even able to influence local lawmakers and law enforcers to gain their own ends. This was a form of capitalism quite different from that envisaged by Adam Smith. It was changing the relationships between city and country, producer and consumer, business and government and, above all, between employer and worker.

The new economy had developed so rapidly that Charles Francis Adams, returned from his Civil War ministerial post in London, found a different America than that he had left only a few years before. He wrote in 1871 that the five years following the war

witnessed some of the most remarkable examples of studied lawlessness, under the forms of law, which mankind had yet had opportunity to study. If individuals have, as a rule, quietly pursued peaceful vocations, the same cannot be said of certain single men at the head of vast combinations of private wealth. This has been particularly the case as regards those controlling the rapidly developed railroad interests. These modern potentates have declared war, negotiated peace, reduced law courts, legislations and sovereign states to an unqualified obedience to their will; disturbed trade, agitated the currency, imposed taxes, and, boldly setting both law and public opinion at defiance, have freely exercised many other attributes of sovereignty.

The rampant laissez faire that the muckrakers called jungle capitalism undermined national ethics as well as the economic and political systems, though workingmen did not see that fact so clearly, or were less troubled by it. They had accepted the new system because they had no alternative, and at first it had seemed to assure more prosperity and more jobs, for in spite of low wages and slums, the condition of the average workingman seemed on the whole to be improving. Naturally the factory system drew into its arms the ablest recruits from the younger generation, ambitious boys from small towns and farms as well as cities. The compelling lures of economic ambition lowered by contrast the prestige and attractions of other careers, and its values submerged any others less materialistic. Life no longer seemed rewarding unless it was economically rewarding.

Under the older system, as Thorstein Veblen had pointed out in 1904, industry existed primarily to provide men with a livelihood. Under the new system industry was operated primarily to make profits, not for the workers but for those who supplied the capital. This change in objective affected the employer's attitude toward his workmen and theirs toward him. The men at the top thought in terms of greater dividends, and those near the bottom in terms of greater wages. Since both cannot be indefinitely increased at the same time, even in an expanding economy, the conflict of interest between capital and labor was accentuated. Industrial management, led by Henry Ford, tried to end that conflict by making more and more goods at lower and lower costs per unit, and thereby also limiting purchasers to a single standardized product. The results were impressive and they raised the nation's standard of living, but they did not end the conflict. Industry became a race between constantly increased efficiency and sales on the one hand, and wages and working conditions on the other, often with diminishing regard by both parties to the interests of society at large.

As Veblen pointed out, an industrial society held together chiefly by a concern for profits leaves much, humanly speaking, to be desired. It gives a low priority to personal satisfaction in one's work, to private preference in the choice of a job, and to the consumer's choice of a finished product. Efficiency calls for the standardization of workers' talents and consumers' tastes as well as of the product made. Neither the man who makes nor the man who buys has much range of choice, and, what is even more regrettable in a democratic society, the maker and the buyer seldom if ever meet in these capacities. The system virtually eliminated personal contacts between the men who finance a factory, the men who build it, the men who work in it, and the men and women who use its product. Along the way the creative satisfactions are lost, and the choice of what to create no longer rests with the man who makes it or the man who buys it.

Long before 1900 the workingman began to protest society's disregard of his interests and welfare. He found his protest ineffective as an individual, and turned to labor organization and collective bargaining. As early as 1836 labor unions claimed a membership in five leading cities of some 300,000 men in 160 local unions. But labor unionism was not then organized on a national scale; it was neither effectively led nor aggressively demanding, and the public paid it very little attention. After the Civil War the increased imbalances and insecurities of the economy made unionism more powerful and more militant.

The first union whose activities disturbed the entire nation was the Knights of Labor, which became the chief voice of labor's protest in the 1880's. Its belligerent radicalism was replaced by the more conservative American Federation of Labor, affiliating twelve national unions. Samuel Gompers, its wise and restrained leader for almost forty years, insisted that its membership be based, not vertically on industry, but horizontally on crafts, each an almost independent association but greatly influenced by his own personality and prestige. He kept the Federation from political affiliations and activities, and was respected even by those businessmen who opposed the whole principle of labor unionism. The Federation did not challenge the capitalist system, but concentrated on securing, plant by plant, improvements in wages, hours, and working conditions. Although not so militant as the Knights of Labor, it used strikes, boycotts, and the closed shop in its fights for recognition.

The first years of the 1890's were marked by long, dramatic, and bitter strikes against the Carnegie steel and the Pullman companies. Both strikes were ultimately lost by the Federation, but it emerged from them stronger and more respected than ever before, and with the principle of labor's right to organize and bargain more firmly established. A few years of industrial peace followed, but the honeymoon did not continue far into the twentieth century. As the costs of living rose more rapidly than the wages of the workers, strikes became more numerous and effective. Although more progressive legislation was adopted between 1900 and 1910 than in the previous twenty years, the working and living conditions of most workingmen were slow to reflect it. Competition from unskilled immigrant labor held wages down in key industries like coal and steel, and the increasing use of labor-saving devices made factory workers feel insecure. Labor exploitation continued, especially in coal mines, packing houses, steel mills, and textile plants. What was more, organized labor was meeting powerful counterattacks from employers who did not fear strikes when labor was plentifully available. The courts rendered several important decisions adverse to organized labor; but though the workingman became increasingly resentful, less than 10 per cent of the total wage earners of the United States were members of labor unions.

In 1907 the ninety member unions of the American Federation claimed a membership of 1,600,000, but the unemployment that accompanied the "panic" gave large employers their chance to fight back. Corporations used the lockout, the injunction, and the company union to undermine organized labor, and even sued unions for damages under the Sherman Antitrust Law. In the Danbury hat strike, the property of workmen was attached by the court to satisfy an injunction against the union. Until about 1910 organized labor was mostly on the defensive, and had made little progress, especially in the industries concerned with metals, machinery, meat packing, shipping, and oil refining.

Economic insecurity and the defeat of moderate measures had, however, brought an upsurge of radicalism, expressed through a new labor organization, the Industrial Workers of the World. The I.W.W. was openly hostile to the capitalist system and would not sign trade agreements. It urged industrial rather than horizontal craft unions, and in addition to strikes it used the new tactic of sabotage. Its aim was avowedly to accumulate enough power and membership to call a general strike, and the preamble to its bylaws stated: "The working class and the employing class have nothing in common . . . between these two classes a struggle must go on until the workers of the world organize as a class, take possession of the earth and the machinery of production and abolish the wage system."

Though membership of the I.W.W. probably never exceeded 60,000, its strong and unscrupulous leadership by Big Bill Haywood, and its readiness for violence, made it feared and hated. So did the fact that it included such diverse but bellicose elements as tough western lumberjacks, unstable migratory farm workers of the West and Southwest, radical discontents from the factories of the East, and a few representatives of the Negro labor pool of the deep, dark South. The implications of an effective alliance between such elements of society frightened employers and public as much as the I.W.W.'s revolutionary ideology.

The I.W.W.'s greatest organization success was in winning the allegiance of the steel workers of Pennsylvania and the textile workers of New Jersey and Massachusetts. Its most spectacular strikes were in the Far West, but it won a great victory after weeks of rioting, injuries, and martial law in the textile mills of Lawrence, Massachusetts. Its success alarmed the American Federation of Labor, which feared it might have to adopt similar policies and methods or else play second fiddle to this militant rival.

But the I.W.W. proved too radical for most American workmen and for public sympathy. As economic conditions improved after 1907, its membership and effectiveness declined, and its last big strike at the Paterson, New Jersey, silk mills dragged on for five months to final union defeat. Meanwhile legislators, the public, and many industrialists were developing greater social conscience in labor matters. By 1912 thirty-eight states had passed the child-labor laws, twenty-eight had regulated (on paper) the hours of work for women, and a few states had passed minimum-wage laws.

As 1913 opened there was increasing acceptance of the principle of labor unionism, though it was by no means universal. American society was in confused disagreement about the right and propriety of workmen organizing into unions, of collective bargaining, of strikes, of labor-forced union shops and employer-forced company shops, and of interference by state and federal troops. These matters were hotly debated in public and private and tested frequently in practice and in the courts, and 1913 became a year of many strikes, the frequent invoking of courts and troops, and general confused dismay.

Every point of view was vehemently put forward. John Kirby, Jr., president of the National Association of Manufacturers, openly opposed unions in principle. Other employers accepted unionism but objected strongly to the union or closed shop. Occasionally a labor leader surprised the public, like James Bryce, president of the Trades and Workers Association, who announced he was "for the open shop because those organizations which stand for the closed shop are and have been using methods to enforce their demands that are utterly abhorrent to a man of peace."

Other men inside and outside the labor camp felt quite differently. John J. Matthews, a regular contributor to *Harper's Magazine,* presented in its June issue a liberal extreme that must have alarmed many of his readers. Under the title "Equity in a Job," he asserted: "Every man possesses the right to have work . . . [and] no effort to cure labor and poverty can be fully successful until this . . . is acknowledged."

Viewed from the relatively peaceful industrial climate of America today, 1913 appears a year of bitter and destructive economic warfare, with its riots, strikes, gunfire, martial law, and deaths. It seems surprising, now, that Americans of the time took those events so calmly and did so little to prevent them. But large strikes were a relatively new problem, and Americans had many other matters to distract their attention. Labor troubles were to most men only a temporary annoyance, and probably the majority of citizens went through the year without encountering a single striker or feeling a great personal inconvenience from a single labor controversy. Their connection with the issue was principally through street-corner and smoking-car discussions in which there was more heat than light.

They were somewhat consoled, if they needed consolation, by the reports that labor troubles in Europe were at least as bad as their own. England suffered under a railway strike that tied up all freight, with 75,000 strikers out in Birmingham and Liverpool alone. A British general strike was barely averted, and industrial war was so disturbing that employers organized a United Kingdom Employers' Defense Association, registered as a trades union "to defend their rights and freedom to bargain individually with free workers or collectively with trades unions," and raised a "war fund" said to approach $250,000,000. French labor was on the militant offensive and was even more radical than the discredited I.W.W. German socialists were doing their best to assert labor's rights in the uncongenial atmosphere of Potsdam militarism, and in April all steel workers in Belgium were on strike.

European troubles did not stop European visitors from saying harsh words about America's industrial strife. Dr. Gustav Stresemann, "a former prominent member of the Reichstag and a well-known economist" (who would be still better known in the German postwar republic) said on February 9th, after a visit to the United States, that "conditions in most American factories are simply horrible." G. K. Chesterton inveighed in the November *Century Magazine* against America's "new slavery . . . already the employer is firing his workmen; on all rational grounds of comparison he may soon be flogging his workmen. The big businesses are becoming independent states, as in the Dark Ages . . . despotic states, as in the Dark Ages. . . . Will you not fight to resist the rise of all these independent monarchies?" Americans never knew how seriously to take Mr. Chesterton, but thought that if he were trying to be funny, this time he was not succeeding.

One of the troubles was that the cost of living, and especially of food, had risen constantly for over a decade and was still mounting more than wages, yet state and federal governments did not seem to be doing anything effective to bring prices and wages into balance. The priority legislation urged by Mr. Wilson was only by the greatest indirection likely to benefit the workingman as far as prices and wages were concerned. Under President Taft Congress had adopted a law establishing the eight-hour day in all work involving government contracts, but this affected only a very small proportion of the nation's workmen, and private industry had shown no inclination to follow the government's lead.

A bill to create a federal mediation board was passed and signed by President Wilson on July 15th, under threat of an imminent rail-way strike. But mediation began only after a strike was in effect or so closely threatened that both sides had already committed them-selves. It offered little aid to the small employer or the individual workman. It was all very well, too, for Booker T. Washington, that magnificent leader of the Negro race, to write in the *Atlantic Monthly* praising labor unions because they "can and will become an important means of doing away with the prejudice that now exists . . . against the negro laborer," but solving the racial problem was not the primary objective of labor unions, and what was the use of winning economic equality for the Negro (which not all union members wanted) if the level of that equality was too low?

The comfortable American might feel personally remote from labor troubles, but if he went to New York to see the New Year in he could not avoid encountering them at firsthand. The celebrations in Times Square were dampened by industrial riots. Striking hotel and restaurant workers interrupted new-year festivities at the Hotel Astor, while twenty-five private detectives battled unsuccessfully with strik-ers trying to force their way into the hotel. The police finally drove the strikers back, but they returned with their arms full of bricks which they threw at the hotel doors and windows. Arrests were made, but the strikers continued to rush the police, disregarding the drawn revolver of Officer Bannon. Before January ended, some four-hundred strikers armed with sticks and bricks smashed the windows of the Ritz-Carlton Hotel, and there were smaller fights at the Waldorf and the Plaza. Many of the restaurants around Times Square were closed, or operated with windows boarded up for several weeks.

New York had other labor troubles as the year opened. There was a serious strike of nearly 90,000 men and women in the garment trades, and when some of them attacked nonunion workers there were many injuries before the police arrived and dispersed the mob. Elsewhere in the city police and private detectives arrested strikers who attacked workers and invaded plants, and 200,000 "white trades" workers walked out in a sympathy strike. Night sticks were freely used by police, and bricks and paving stones by strikers and their friends.

Across the nation there was even worse industrial dissension. Railway men went on strike in Maine; streetcar workers struck in Buffalo, Cincinnati, and Indianapolis. On February 2nd the American Federation of Labor called a strike of 40,000 steelworkers against the United States Steel Company "for recognition," and General Manager Jewett of American Steel and Wire told reporters that "there won't be any recognition of the Union. . . . We won't discuss wage scales and other conditions with strikers." On March 31st the motormen in New York's subways demanded an eight-hour day and recognition of their unions, and this raised questions of the right of public carriers to strike at public inconvenience and against the city government.

Violence occurred. In February and March the coal fields of West Virginia were under martial law, and the military were using "stringent measures to stamp out violence by strikers and their friends." In February, 30,000 firemen on 54 railways threatened to strike, and the New York *Times* reported that in anticipation of trouble the warehouses of the Pennsylvania Railroad "resembled an arsenal . . . rifles and revolvers and a plentiful supply of ammunition." In Buffalo 3,000 National Guardsmen fought street railway workers who attacked 700 "scabs" they said were imported to break the strike. In April contract workers on state highways in Westchester County fought with the police of Mamaroneck, and citizens of the area armed themselves with rifles, shotguns, and revolvers and formed a posse to police the highways and protect their homes. One laborer was killed and a "detective" badly wounded.

In May there were major riots and shooting by both sides in New York; strikers battled police and dynamited railroad tracks in three places in Syracuse; Cincinnati debated asking for federal troops to protect strikebreakers; riots in the I.W.W. strike in Paterson sent eighty men to jail in a single day. On several occasions mobs attacked the police with stones and fists, and Big Bill Haywood was arrested on a charge of inciting to riot. In June, nineteen national and district officers of the I.W.W. were indicted for inciting to violence in West Virginia, and the Senate planned an investigation. A woman was shot and killed, seven men were wounded by bullets, and many others, including policemen, were injured in fighting outside a hosiery plant in Ipswich, Massachusetts.

So it went during the rest of the year. Few strikes were clearly won by the unions; some were entirely lost, and most of the biggest strikes were finally settled by arbitration. A general railway strike was averted in February by arbitration, but in July it was again imminent, and both unions and railway companies were unyielding. President Wilson intervened, but three days later the unions voted to strike at the discretion of their leaders. The President finally secured an agreement to arbitrate provided the arbitration was held under what would become the Newlands Act, then before Congress as an amendment to the Erdman Arbitration Act. Under presidential and public pressure the House and Senate passed the Newlands bill the next day, but at that point the railway companies insisted that the arbitration discussions should include their grievances against the unions, and the union leaders refused to agree to this. On July 18th the railway unions announced an immediate strike. In order to prevent all transport east of the Mississippi from being completely tied up, the managements of the railroads withdrew their insistence on presenting their own grievances and the impending strike went into arbitration and was finally avoided.

All these events accomplished very little toward finding solutions for the fundamental causes of strikes, or even toward agreement upon the ground rules for industrial controversies. Once a strike began, arbitration seemed the only way to end it short of force, but arbitration did not settle the basic issues and usually left both parties dissatisfied and licking their wounds for the next round.

The thoughtful citizen of 1913 must have been troubled most of all by the failure of the government to establish clear and firm principles for adjudicating industrial conflict. What were the legal rights of labor unions, of workers who refused to join a union or join strikers, of imported strikebreakers, of company police and "private detectives," of owners of property to defend it against forced entrance, vandalism, or sit-down strikes? When and on what terms should state militia or federal groups be sent in, and how should they act when there? Not one of these questions was answered authoritatively and consistently by the courts, and it would be many years before legislators, courts, and public opinion would agree on workable formulas for any of them.

Quite apart from legal decisions, however, the public was slowly reaching its own conclusions: that labor had the right to organize; that striking workmen did not have a right to invade or destroy public or private property; that company police were an extralegal menace and "private detectives" usually no more than hired toughs; and that actions by either party that seriously impaired public safety or public convenience should not be tolerated. Public sentiment was leading the courts and Congress toward a crude canon of industrial justice and legal procedure; unions and managements were discovering that violence lost them public sympathy and that drastic methods did not, in the long run, pay. Employers were finding that the public did not like lockouts, hired strikebreakers, professional "goons" who beat up strikers, and the use of guns and night sticks by company police.

But at the end of the year industrial peace was still remote. In mid-November 5,000 streetcar workers on strike fought the police in the downtown area of Indianapolis, to the obvious personal danger of passing citizens. Governor Samuel Ralston refused requests by the city authorities to send in state troops, on the grounds that the city police were failing to do their duty. Thus inspired, the police on the following day fired a volley at the strikers to force their way into the carbarns, and a man was killed. Then the governor called out the entire state guard, and 3,000 soldiers policed the city. On December 1st the Teamsters Union of Indianapolis voted unanimously to go on a sympathy strike at midnight. They did so, and five days later "special officers" shooting at teamsters killed a Negro elevator man who happened to be in the line of fire. The public began to conclude that the only hope of industrial peace lay with stronger action by the federal government and that the federal government must make rules and enforce them.

XIV

The Upper Crust

"So with our society! As far as I can see, no one deeply cares what becomes of it!"

Henry Adams, "the long-established ghost" of Washington's cultivated inner circle, so wrote to his brother Brooks as he watched popular sovereignty overwhelm the influence and values for which that circle stood. He was nearly right—the self-appointed élite of Boston, New York, Washington, London, and Paris was politically doomed, and few men would regret its demise. Only its members would appreciate what might die with it.

Adams was more aware than most men that America was undergoing a social revolution. The rise of what Hamilton would have called Mobocracy was bringing new values to the ascendant, but it was also neglecting others that were precious to any civilized nation. For over a century a few men and women had consciously contributed qualitative leadership and aspirations to a national society that still needed both. Adams's society was not exactly Jefferson's ideal of "a natural aristoi of talents and virtues," but it had stood for standards of excellence and a sense of *noblesse oblige*. Its values were not inconsistent with the ideal democracy of Plato and Jefferson, but they were out of line with what popular tastes were defining as democratic.

Most men outside that older élite viewed the social revolution with more satisfaction than Adams did. To the majority, who did not worry about cultural excellence, democracy meant equality, and equality meant more of the good things of the world, and more of its power, for themselves and their kind of people. To a liberal journalist like Walter Weyl, the social revolution seemed necessary and promising.

It was a dynamic stage in the growth of a finer democratic society, and though its ferments and iconoclasms were sometimes excessive they were symbols of social progress. In *The New Democracy*, published in 1912, he wrote:

"America is in a period of clamor, of bewilderment, of an almost tremulous unrest. We are hastily reviewing all our social conceptions. We are profoundly disenchanted with the fruits of a century of independence."

Both men were telling the truth but not the whole truth. No single American could tell all the truth about America; it was too large, too kinetic, too fluid, too complex. What was more, Adams and Weyl were not speaking of the same thing when they used the word "society." Adams's society was the small group of educated and privileged people who had not run the country but had often guided it and, culturally at least, steered it upward. Weyl's "society" was the changing humanity he saw about him in the urban fermentation of a liberal journalist's world; his "we" were the idealists, the social reformers, the dissenters, and the urban masses seeking their place in the democratic sun. Weyl's urban society and Adams's traditional élite, taken together, did not include the majority of Americans who, distinctly ordinary citizens, were wavering between nostalgia for the stability of the old order and enthusiasm for the liberations of the new.

Adams's view had more historical perspective, Weyl's more social optimism. Adams was watching change from the isolated eminence of his home across Lafayette Square from the White House; Weyl was sharing change and experiencing at least vicariously the hopes and reactions of immigrants, wage earners, Greenwich Village dreamers, disillusioned reporters, and the young hopefuls from the high schools. Adams was looking at what the new society would lose, Weyl at what it might gain.

The private world from which Adams derived had been stable, selective, and intellectually liberal but socially conservative—an Anglo-Saxon world imbued with Puritan traditions, intent on supporting social selectivity, continuity of culture, and the superior in men and things. The world of Weyl was volatile, amorphous, eclectic, progressive and, by Adams's standards, culturally crude. Adams conceived society as an orderly vertical structure with the captain's lookout at the top. To Weyl society was a horizontal spread which should be homogeneous, and in which flexibility and equality were more important than order and cultural traditions. The two worlds were talking a different language because their basic assumptions and aims were in conflict.

Order for the sake of order is a sterile and negative goal for a democratic society, as Adams would have been quick to admit. He would have said order should exist for the sake of making democratic progress upward and enduring; that in the pursuit of democratic ideals it was dangerous to create social chaos. To destroy the old order too rapidly would create a vacuum that vulgarity and demagoguery would rush to fill. The social revolution, as it was developing, certainly provided no assurance that democracy would be led by its ablest and best, or that the pull of social change would be upward. There is a better reason for social order than order itself: human happiness and progress are uncertain without it.

One set of human affirmations is never completely and permanently replaced by another, and what emerges from a social revolution is usually something quite different from what the revolutionists planned. Neither the thinking of Adams nor that of Weyl was determinant in the America of 1913, for thought did not dominate American development. Men were impelled less by the rational process than by urges, reactions, emotions, slogans. The forces and conflicts in a changing society are not clean cut or according to anyone's specific plan. Most Americans in 1913 were less aware than Adams and Weyl that they were factors in a social struggle. They stood, in confused intermediate groups, somewhat between the two points of view.

There was, for example, the quite different society that William Allen White recalled from his youth. It was "a stable world permanently supported by cast-iron customs . . . by a ritual of living that was immemorial. . . . My mother was not behind my father on feeling that she was always right, if only because her feet were planted on the Rock of Ages, and her reply was 'We won't discuss it' if anyone questioned the laws on which our little world seemed to be built."

More Americans were still living in that world than in Adams's select society or Weyl's social ferment. Viewed from the later Age of Anxiety, the charm of prewar America lay in a sense of moral security somehow engendered by the infinite little regularities of its routine: winding the grandfather clock at the same hour each week, the unvarying menu of Sunday breakfasts and Thanksgiving dinners, the orderly parade to church, the fixed hours for bedtime, Sunday afternoon naps and calls, Saturday-night baths—for starting up the furnace in the fall, for putting on and taking off winter underclothes, for swallowing the spring tonic, for spring cleaning, for the two summer weeks at the seashore. Who could feel disoriented or agnostic in so orderly a world?

White's boyhood society was still flourishing in the small towns and villages of 1913. Frederic C. Howe, who also derived from it, remembered, or thought he remembered, other things in it at variance with its normal conservatism: ". . . a new dispensation was about to be ushered in. . . . It was good form to be a liberal. . . . Conservative lawyers, bankers and men of affairs stepped out from their offices and lent their names to radical movements. The spirit of this young American was generous, hospitable, brilliant; it was carefree and full of variety. . . . The young people believed that the truth would make us free."

Not many Americans knew such a golden age of liberalism, if it existed anywhere outside Howe's imagination. One could find or remember whatever one wanted in America, if one tried hard enough. Certainly Howe's version of small-town society was very different from that revealed by the researches of young Randolph Bourne. He too was a liberal, but he found the small towns teeming, not with liberalism, but with snobbery, class consciousness, and dissatisfactions.

Looking backward at 1913, the character of its society seems at first glance most marked by the contrast between its complacencies and its revolts. Yet that is too simple, for the backward look, like man's memory, can be misleading. Nostalgia distorts remembrance, and the written record never tells the whole story. Only the intellectuals and the discontented write things down, yet history is made and society determined by men who do not stop to record their reactions or who are not given to self-expression. Such men and women comprised the vast, solid America that habitually followed the ways of the past and yet by their work were creating a world that made that past seem irrelevant. Most of them were too busy or too unimaginative to think very much about where their kind of progress would lead America. They were the people Henry Adams thought of as "not caring," but they cared if their own toes were stepped on in the march of progress, or if the lives and opportunities of their children would be affected. They were aware of the flaws in the American system, but the flaws did not seem bad enough, most of the time, to make a fuss about. Let there be reforms by all means, if others would take the lead in them and not upset too many apple carts.

There are complacency and revolt in every society. The special character of 1913 lies in the confusions of the conflicts between them. It was in the mind of the individual American that the confusion was most significant, because least recognized and only half understood. The American was accepting with his mind the changes he resented with his feelings; he was emotionally attached to the old while intellectually attracted to the new. Because every encounter between thought and emotion is likely to be a painful collision, the man of 1913 avoided such encounters whenever he could, and thereby increased their explosive potential.

It was in urban life that the external conflict was most apparent and the victory of the new society most rapid. The change overwhelmed the physical faces of the cities, their racial composition, their cultural values, and their political control. The old, rich, and sometimes cultivated families—the "society" of Henry Adams—still had wealth, the semblance of leadership, and a lingering social preeminence, but they no longer ruled the city. They might still be the Four Hundred, but they counted less and less with the four million. They maintained their tight little islands of social exclusiveness against popular invasion, but in doing so they isolated themselves from the real life of the city. To the new urbans they seemed more and more vestigial.

But, though by 1913 the old order had been displaced in the urban centers, the new order had by no means organized its victory. Sociologically the big cities were chaos, and from chaos little can be learned. One must turn to the smaller towns and their hinterland communities to observe the subtleties of the social conflict. There the issues of class leadership still hung in the balance while community ideals and culture faltered.

Until about 1900 most small towns and cities had been quietly controlled by a peculiar group. It was not necessarily an élite of brains, culture, or ability, but it had enough of all three to hold its place for several generations. It was not exactly a plutocracy, though its members were well-to-do, and there has never been a human society in which money did not talk. It usually owned much of the land and the stocks in local banks and industries. Some of its influence came from the same source Plutarch assigned to the power of Pelops: ". . . the most powerful of the kings of the Peloponnesus, not so much by the greatness of his riches as the multitude of his children, having married many daughters to chief men, and put many sons in places of command in the towns about him."

That leading class contained almost the only sons who went away to preparatory schools, the only college graduates, the only families who went south in the winter or traveled abroad or bought "art"; the only men with business interests or social standing outside the home town. Their wives and daughters were the towns' social arbiters and set the styles; their children might mix with other boys and girls, but they were consciously and enviably "different."

The first generations of these local oligarchies had established themselves by superior energy and initiative, and had not been averse to hard work and business risks. Their descendants, inheriting comfortable mansard-roofed houses and secure incomes, had less incentive to be vigorous and more reason to be cautious in their business investments. They devoted their diminished or undeveloped talents to protecting their inherited position and property more than to enhancing them. They seldom worked full time as active managers of their banks and factories, but hired executives whom they controlled as directors, trustees, and owners of the stock.

They were not a local aristocracy in the full sense, for they lacked the aristocratic impulse to *noblesse oblige*, assuming constructive local leadership only when their personal interests were at stake. They sat almost by hereditary right on school and hospital boards, and often gave generously to charities; their wives were the routine façades for every women's organization, but they seldom put their backs into making their towns a better place for all its citizens. Though they still lived on the lands their grandfathers had cultivated, and were sometimes sentimental about keeping the old place in the family, they took no special pride in maintaining its fields. Acres once carefully tilled lay barren, and hedgerows now overwhelmed rail fences once neat and sturdy. Active farming was hard work, and it had become *déclassé* even before it proved uneconomic. More and more of the old family estates were being cut up into real-estate speculations, without much regard to town planning or community welfare. The sons of the Old Guard lost local leadership by neglecting it.

By 1913 this slightly devitalized ruling caste could no longer maintain economic barriers high enough to keep out newcomers with more initiative and enterprise than themselves. The newcomers—like the grandfathers of the Old Guard—were self-made men, climbers from backgrounds less fortunate and usually less cultivated. Little by little the older oligarchies accepted the new into their business, for it was better to have them as partners than as rivals.

In some communities the economic merger between the old élite and the upstarts was complete by 1913, but in others it was still in progress. Social distinctions nearly always remained, and the differences often dwelt in curious fields. The two groups supported different churches, frequented separate country clubs, sponsored different bridge whist circles. A man's financial standing might make him the equal of any other man in the community, but it did not give his

wife and children top social rating. Subtle nuances of social grada-
tion, understood only by the local residents, remained to show that
the social structure was not based on hard cash alone.

Beneath these still somewhat diverse upper elements of local
power lay the middle class, self-consciously distinct from the "rich
folks" above it and the "working class" below it. In the *Atlantic
Monthly* for September, 1913, Randolph Bourne described the distinction after small towns became suburbs to larger ones.

The middle class . . . have their own society and their own exclusions.
. . . In business matters the line between the two classes is equally sharp.
The members of the ruling caste hold, as a rule, business positions of considerable importance in the neighboring city, while the middle class is engaged largely in local trade, or in smaller functions in the city . . . the city
is . . . the goal of all the socially ambitious. There is a distinct prejudice,
also, on the part of the ruling class, against anything that savors of mechanical labor. . . . The class membership of the [fraternal] organizations is very evident. . . . The dramatic political contests are . . . between the old residents and the new, between the natives and the
commuters . . . no lover of his town wishes to see things turned over to a
loose herd of temporary residents. . . . [Nevertheless] political control
has long since passed out of the hands of the old leaders into those of the
commuters.

Bourne had found that he could not study the small towns without
encountering a new American development—suburbia. By 1913 many
towns had become satellite dormitories to nearby big cities, and villages had become residential annexes to the towns. This introduced
new complications to local society and politics, and split the community into peripatetic and hereditary residents. The suburbanites
tended to be indifferent to local mores and carefully adjusted local
social gradations. They might make sporadic incursions into local
affairs, but they lacked knowledge, and the desire to accept con-
tinuous civic responsibility.

Since neither the Old Guard nor the new plutocrats nor the
suburbanites were exerting local leadership, it developed upon a little
band of middle-class conscientious do-gooders—mostly women—to

carry the load for the improvement of local government, schools, hospitals, and general culture. It was they who arranged and sponsored local lectures, political reforms, community houses, concerts, Boy Scouts, drama clubs, and reading circles. The rest of the middle class were at best only occasional workers for civic causes. To them the pursuit of culture seemed a proper avocation for schoolteachers, rich men, and their own wives, provided it did not interfere with their domestic efficiency or their husbands' business interests. As for intellectual attainment, it should of course be encouraged, but only up to a certain point. The highbrow and the college professor were viewed with mild suspicion as carrying theory beyond practical common sense. Except for a few of its members, the middle class of the small cities and towns was not overwhelmed with a sense of civic and cultural responsibility.

Nor did its members foresee the split within their own ranks. The real issue of their generation was the increasing demand by the less privileged for greater opportunity and power, and one of its results would be to divide the middle class horizontally between those who supported and those who opposed that demand. The more prosperous or socially ambitious of the middle class would identify their interests with the more privileged above them. But the small businessman with only a little less income, the bank clerk whose home mortgage was still large, the farmer with no reserve of capital, and the schoolteacher resentful of his low pay and low prestige would join the rising workingman in a claim for a greater share of the nation's wealth and power. Too often he would also accept the lower-class cultural levels that were overwhelming those of Henry Adams's élite.

In the smaller communities that division of the hitherto solid middle class was not yet evident. The underprivileged and underpaid had hardly begun to assert themselves; there was no voting solidarity in the working class; labor unions had not yet established themselves in most smaller cities and towns, and the lower-middle-class sympathizer had not yet declared his affiliation with the popular surge. On the surface of small-town society there was little to suggest how much ferment was developing underneath, or how rapidly it would coalesce into class solidarity and protest.

There were some straws in the wind, and one of them was the new servant problem. The wives of the rich and the moderately prosperous were complaining more than ever before that it was hard to get good domestic help, and harder still to keep it; that the girls of the lower class were untrained or unwilling to work or dissatisfied with the wages and hours of domestic service. The new cook or maid seemed to take no pride in doing her work well, and the number of days off she demanded were outrageous. Frequently she was actually "sassy" to her mistress. These young women seemed to prefer jobs in offices or shops or even factories, where they got bigger wages or shorter hours or more independence or met more young men, and did not have to get the permission of the lady of the house to have "followers."

The young women in question were simply expressing in natural ways the resentment of their class against the long domination of those who had thought themselves better. They did not like to take orders from a housewife; the orders they had to take in offices or factories were more impersonal and less belittling to their newly insistent self-respect. They did not like to call an employer "madame" or even "madam," to make other people's beds and cook other people's meals. Domestic service was suddenly down-graded by girls whose mothers had regarded it as the most natural and desirable of jobs before marriage. Such girls were expressing emotional resentments, long cherished but only half conscious for generations, of what had been called the "lower class."

Resentments were especially natural in children of immigrant parents, who had been treated as no more than second-class citizens and often segregated geographically as well as socially. Even towns of ten thousand had their Polish quarters, their Italian quarters, and their Irish sections and Negro streets. "It can hardly be possible," wrote Bourne in 1913, "that these people have left anything worse in the old country than this collection of indescribable hovels . . . but their fearful squalor . . . has not seemed to distress their American neighbors in the least. . . . It would be difficult to find any way in which they really count in the life of the town. . . . The town seems to have a whole class living in it, but not of it, quite apart and detached from the currents of its life."

Not all settlements of the foreign-born were squalid. A few had a community life of their own, sometimes gayer, more colorful, and more artistic than that in the drab respectability about them. Those foreign communities were largely self-governing, though extralegally so, with unofficial mayors whom the constituted authorities gratefully let alone to handle settlement problems in their own ways—ways sometimes inconsistent with American law or mores. From the point of view of the ardently 100 per cent American these people were restricting Americanization, yet it had been the 100 per cent Americans who had crowded the immigrants into isolation. The only time the "good citizens" courted the "wops," the "Poles," and the "shines" was when their votes were wanted. "The sense of inequality," wrote William Jewett Tucker in the *Atlantic Monthly* for October, "is becoming a matter of class resentment." The class resentments thus developed would take a further toll on American thought and progress for decades to come.

There were deeper causes for the frictions and confusions of American society than any derived from immigrants or labor unions or upper-class indifference alone. Americans had not faced up to the social changes they were bringing upon themselves through industrialization, materialism, and new definitions of democracy. All they knew in 1913 was that the foundations seemed unsteady and the changes sometimes unpleasant. The inheritors of the affirmations had lost their way, and even the most confident liberals were often merely whistling through the woods. As a result, society's progress was not straightforward, or even always tangentially upward, but, like that of a wandering child, guided only by the distractions of the moment, the vacillations of experience, and the fluctuations of emotion. For this the men and women of the middle and working class were less to blame than those who had the power and leadership in their hands, and neglected it.

Flaubert once wrote of "the unique moment, between Cicero and

Marcus Aurelius, when the Gods were no more, and Christ had not risen to take their place. Man was alone."

Americans, for somewhat comparable reasons, were in 1913 victims of their own spiritual vacuum. They would soon find themselves more culturally penniless and spiritually lonely than they knew.

XV

The Man in the Middle

For over a century the ordinary citizen had been called the common man. As the twentieth century opened, that phrase was no longer acceptable in America. It no longer seemed democratic. The common man became the average man, and the change was significant.

Eighteenth century liberal thinkers had exalted the common man as society's most promising unit of character and virtue. The nineteenth century accepted that tradition; but as its decades wore on, the common man lost his special halo and found the chances for his personal advancement less infinite than the theory had promised. The phrase acquired an overtone of patronage and an undertone of class distinction. The common man was becoming too much the proletarian to suit him.

To call most men common was to imply that some were uncommon—superior because of birth, education, ability, or wealth. Early democratic society had recognized superiority in men like Washington, and had accepted Jefferson's principle that democratic society needed an aristocracy of talents and virtues. The Founding Fathers had said all men were created equal, but they did not mean it literally. They meant that talent and virtue could be found and recognized among ordinary men as well as among the better born, so the occasional common man would become an uncommon one. Democracy had not yet become confused with egalitarianism; even Andrew Jackson, who professed to represent the common man, did not regard himself as one.

The theory that democracy would bring leadership by the ablest and most unselfish had not worked out too well in practice. Before

1840 some Americans were thinking that too much power had fallen
into the hands of a few rich men—that democracy was becoming
plutocracy. They began to work toward popular democracy, and to
insist that democracy meant equality and that any man was, in matters of political judgment at least, as wise as any other. The common
man still accepted leaders, but he declined to regard them as inher-
ently any better than himself—or if they were they had no right to be.

Another force was also changing the common man to the average
man. Standardization had become the accepted method of industrial
production, and the concept of standardization subtly crept into
men's social thinking. If the standard methods and products made
manufacture more efficient, then standard tastes and values should
make democratic society more efficient too. Those who reached this
casual conclusion did not consider that standardization was achieved
at a sacrifice of superior quality.

The more Americans could be induced to want the same thing,
the more cheaply or profitably manufacturers could supply it, and
they developed ways to find out what the majority of the people
wanted. They introduced the "science" of market research, and market analysis meant statistics and statistics meant averages. The man
who fitted into the statistical majority, the nation's greatest consumer,
became the average American. The change added to the *amour propre*
of middle-class Americans, for it was nicer to be average than to be
common. But the common man had been esteemed for his virtue and
promise, while the average man was esteemed only as a standardized
purchasing unit. The common man, under a new name, was in the
saddle, but it was a very common saddle.

The next step of the manufacturer was to get the public to want
what his factory could most profitably make. Advertising and sales
promotion suddenly became major industries, and the power and
uses of propaganda multiplied. Average men were not only being
induced to want the same thing, but to think they wanted what the
manufacturer had to sell them.

If the factory system and the new self-assertion by the lower
classes had not created the average man, the politicians would have

done so. The new democracy was by definition run by the average. Since popular sovereignty meant the rule of the norm, the politicians who acted for the people must first find out what the people wanted. By 1913 the politicians, as well as the press and the advertising men, were engaged in an all-out effort to make average tastes the national ideal. Having established the average man on the throne, the next step was to influence him; by catering to him they could rule him, politically as well as economically.

The change went to the roots of American political and social philosophy, and helped turn the older individualist affirmation into myth. A people whose traditions were nonconformist began to embrace conformity by welcoming the impersonal anonymity of the average. A society erected on the leadership of the exceptional was deferring to the ordinary. In its effort to maintain a classless society, American democracy was creating a new and faceless ruling class in culture as well as politics—the statistical majority.

The forces that brought about this change were not pursuing a political or social idea but their private ends. The politician praised the average man in order to win his vote; the advertising man in order to sell him goods; the manufacturer in order to simplify his production line; the labor leader because class solidarity was the source of his power; the sociologist because generalizations and statistics were the breath of life. The procedure was not a new one; demagogues had always sought the lowest common denominator and flattered the plebs to gain power. But never before had such universal deference to the average so characterized a national society, or led to such enthusiastic acceptance of statistical collectivism and the cultural mean level.

In spite of market statistics, preference polls, and outward conformity, the average man was still only a figment of print and oratory. America still consisted of individuals, and the so-called average man was simply one who, by purely arbitrary mathematical measurements, happened at the moment to stand in the middle of society. Though his feet were mired in the sticky soil of the common ground, he was still, when sufficiently pressed by his own concerns, capable of asserting his individuality. In 1913 things were happening to him and around him that stimulated him to do so. On the surface he was reasonably content; was he not the Ideal Consumer of the market analyst, the democratic ideal of the politician, the predictable citizen of the polls? He was living in a better house than his parents had lived in; eating better food, moving more widely through society, and providing greater opportunities for his wife and children. He had many reasons to be satisfied, and was by conditioning optimistic.

But there were times when he wondered if he was really as well off as the hucksters and politicians told him he was. His income was going up, but so were the prices of the things he had to buy, or his wife and children urged him to buy. The world seemed to be becoming more and more complicated, even in the little daily things . . . and the area of his life within his own control seemed to be getting smaller and smaller. The advantages of the new system were partly offset by the added problems and demands that came with them. Every new implement of progress brought its cost or regimentation or responsibility: the income tax that came when his income reached $4,000, the driver's license that he had to get to use his Ford, the union he had to join to be sure of his job. If he was a small businessman he had to meet the competition of the new big companies, and more and more men of his kind were selling out as independent operators and working on salary for someone else.

The man in the middle was beginning to feel crowded from all sides, and not so important or free as he used to be. It was not the principle of big business he objected to, but the power of big business in local communities and sometimes in the state legislature, and its impersonal indifference to what happened to him and the community he lived in. Much the same thing could be said of the labor unions, and when either the corporation or the union started to push him around he could find no way to get at the key man to push back.

There had always been low-wage workmen in the country, the men who did the rough work in fields and mills and mines. The man in the middle had gone to school with some of them, had called them by their first names, and had occasionally hired one of them to help him turn over his garden or move his rock pile or cut his wood. He and his hired man had worked together at such jobs, and had felt themselves to be the same kind of people, with the same background and much the same opinions. But now the workman had become a member of a labor class, and seemed to think his interests were different from those of the man in the middle. The old mutual respect between employer and employee was lost in the factory or steel plant. What was more, many local laborers were no longer men with familiar names and backgrounds, but immigrants with foreign names and ways. Many of them were respectable and hard-working men, but it wasn't the same as in the old days. . . .

It was clear to the man in the middle that workingmen ought to get better pay and that the conditions under which many of them worked and lived were very bad. But to refuse to work and to force other men to stop work, to smash windows in factories and fight policemen was intolerable and, what was worse, un-American. On the other hand, some of the things that company police and imported strikebreakers were doing were just as bad. The big unions and the big corporations were carrying on their private wars without much regard for what was legal and what was reasonable, or what the effects were on those in the no-man's land between them. "A plague on both your houses!" he sometimes felt like saying.

Thoughts like these flitted only occasionally through the mind of the man in the middle, for he was busy, good-natured, and not one to borrow trouble or think very hard unless he had to. The topic most constantly on his mind was the increase in the cost of living. All this complicated structure of subsidiaries, interlocking directorates, middlemen, lawyers, unions, and advertising men seemed to come between him and even the smallest thing he wanted to buy, and to mess up the natural law of supply and demand. As the cost of living went on mounting each year, it seemed more and more clear that no one except the government could stop it.

Professor Irving Fisher, of Yale, said to be one of the wisest economists, began the year with the statement that the average price of all commodities had risen 60 per cent since 1896, and that wages and salaries had not gone up in proportion. This was not news to the man in the middle, though he had not known the exact figures, but he was not happy when the professor added that prices during 1913 would go still higher. Labor was winning better wages by fighting for them; millionaires were getting still richer; but the man in the middle was hardly holding his own. He had no organization to fight for him, and he was beginning to think it was time the government paid some attention to his problems.

From the mountain peaks of 1960 prices, those of 1913 do not seem high, but fantastically low, until one looks at the salaries and wages of the time. Here are examples of both, taken from contemporary records and advertisements in the New York *Times:*

New York department stores were offering men's woolen suits for less than $30, and the Glen Rock Woolen Company of Somerville, New Jersey, was ready to provide any man with an all-wool suit "cut to your measure according to the latest New York style and guaranteed fit, material and workmanship or your money back . . . for $10 . . . the kind for which you'd pay $18 to $30 anywhere." Style as well as price counted. The American Woolen Company offered a "nobby suit" with "classy linings and millionaire trimmings and a swell cut" for which the purchasers might have to pay as much as $30. Saks offered women's corsets "in a liberal range of the smartest models . . . to suit all types of figure" for as little as $1.95, though the price of the finest in the store was $8.00. Style counted still more with women, even in things unseen, and Lord and Taylor offered a big sale of women's finest muslin underwear, nearly all "lace or embroidery trimmed," for as little as $0.80 a garment.

Rents in New York city will also arouse envy in urban dwellers of the 1960's. "High class elevator apartments" of five, six, and seven rooms could be rented at the Berkeley Arms on West Ninety-fifth Street for $50 a month, and larger and better ones at fashionable 55 East Seventy-sixth Street for $1,000 a year. A large furnished room with private bath, steam heat, and elevator service included, was available at 24 East Sixty-second Street for $20 a week.

Those able to enjoy the finer things of life could take the Bay State Line overnight from New York to Boston for $2.40 first class, and have an outside private cabin for a dollar more. One might go round the world in one of the Canadian Pacific's "magnificent new ships," the *Empress of Russia* or the *Empress of Asia*, for $639, including some shore excursions. Table d'hôte steak dinners at good New York restaurants seemed very expensive to out-of-towners at $1.25, but one could tip a dime and be thanked for it. Good bourbon whisky was $3.50 a gallon and Sandy River 100 proof was $0.60 a quart.

Those prices did not seem low to the cashier of a small bank on Long Island who owned his house and four acres and supported a wife and two children on a salary that came to less than $40 a week. Steak dinners at $1.25 were out of the question to girls earning $4 a week in the lower Broadway garment trades. On January 9th the *Times* reported the following average current wages in New York City per week: clerk, $15; accountant, $30; stenographer-bookkeeper, $15; mechanical engineer, $25; senior C.P.A., $36. The average family income in the United States was below $900, and not more than $750 in the South Central states. In 1910 the Massachusetts Labor Bureau reported that 30 per cent of the state's population saved nothing. The average banker's salary was $7,726; the average lawyer made $4,169 a year; the average physician, $3,907; and the average college professor, $2,878.

In June it was reported that the cost of food had mounted even more than other costs. Every article of food except sugar had gone up steadily since 1900; corn had doubled and beef and milk were up about 50 per cent. Yet the farmers were complaining that the prices they received were barely enough to keep them solvent. Like the farmer, the man in the middle was baffled; there was something wrong here. Someone between producer and consumer must be taking an excessive profit, or else there were too many middlemen. In August the news was still worse. The new Federal Bureau of Labor's statistics predicted that food prices, up 8 per cent in the past year and 15 per cent in the past two years, would go higher. By winter beef might be as much as $1.00 a pound in the cities and eggs $0.75 a dozen. Other prices were rising too, and the motorist was paying nearly twice as much for gasoline as he had paid a few years before.

Concern about food costs filled many columns of the newspapers and magazines, though federal price and wage control was not even suggested. Most of the discussion centered upon farm production. The experts praised the European farmers' cooperatives, but since most of them were operated or controlled by government most Americans were dubious about importing them. In *Harper's Magazine* for September, John J. Matthews suggested that American farmers provide their own capital to establish cooperatives free from government control, but the farmers said they had no capital to provide. The *Independent* magazine blasted the hope that the new lowered tariffs would appreciably reduce food costs, and said the basic cause of high prices was the tripling of the gold output since 1890. The man in the middle could not understand why, if cheaper gold made higher prices, it did not also bring higher wages and profits to him.

The loudest complaints about food prices came from organized labor, but it was the white-collar workers and the lower-level professional men who were in the most difficult long-term position. Union workers might get their wages raised, but the unorganized man in the middle had no weapons like strikes and collective bargaining to get his salary or income increased. Where, he wondered, would he end in this race between wages for labor and profits for corporations? What could he do to help himself against the special interests of corporate capital above him and corporate labor beneath him? Ray Stannard Baker had raised this question in *McClure's Magazine,* but no one seemed any nearer to the answer.

When urban workers complained or farmers fulminated, the politicians listened, but they did not seem so interested in the troubles of the men in between. The farm and labor problems were political issues, because farmers and laborers presented solid voting blocs, but no one worried about the problems of the unaffiliated shopkeeper or bookkeeper—except himself. He applauded President Wilson's gesture of eliminating the costs of the inaugural ball, but he wanted to see some more effective action toward economy by the government. In August the President began an official inquiry into the high cost of living, but prices kept on going up.

All sorts of explanations were offered. Professor Fisher said Americans should "give less attention to earning money and more to producing goods." That made sense so far as the other fellow was concerned, but the man in the middle wondered how he could make both ends meet if he paid less attention to earning money, and he was not himself a producer of material goods. He could not even understand Professor Fisher's proposal "to create a standard monetary yardstick, an unshrinkable dollar—a scientifically standardized dollar," but he was dubious about anybody fiddling with the currency. On the other hand, Charles Whiting Baker, editor of the *Engineering News,* seemed sensible when he blamed rising prices on the growing public debt, which, he said, was a menace to national prosperity and would burden future generations to pay for "what profits outselves." The man in the middle knew what debt was, and that in the long run he would have to help pay it.

Just as government was mortgaging the nation's future, Mr. Baker continued, individuals were mortgaging their own. "These are times when everything is bought on the installment plan, when people mortgage homes to buy automobiles, when men prefer running risks on borrowed capital to carrying on a safe business of their own." The man in the middle was financially conservative, but if his wife thought she had to have one of those new electric vacuum cleaners, or he had to have a new bicycle, he saw no option to buying it on time. . . . History repeats itself, and so do wives and installments.

The man in the middle, that "average man" of 1913, was still devoted to free enterprise; along with the farmer, he was its chief exponent in practice. He was the last man in America to like the idea of government interference with his private affairs, but as he surveyed the conflicting forces around him they seemed too complicated and too powerful for private citizens or even state governments to control. Corporate monopolies, militant labor unions, the cost of living, the farm problem, the currency problem, the tax problem, the growth of cities and their slums and crime and corruption—these must all be interlocking problems derived from forces that only the federal government was powerful enough to control.

So, in spite of his convictions about independence and self-sufficiency, the man in the middle was ready to demand more federal intervention in economic affairs. He was prepared to accept more domination by big government if it would bring less domination by big business and big unions. He did not analyze the causes of these troubles in any deep and comprehensive way; he simply wanted quick remedies for specific defects. They made him feel insecure about the future, so he turned to the society around him to provide the sense of stability and importance, collectively, that he could no longer feel alone. He was approaching, slowly, the faceless nepenthe of "togetherness."

The man in the middle could not possibly have seen how far government would go when it began to untwist the tangled skeins of the new economic forces, and how little might be left of private enterprise after the government had finished saving it. He would not have believed that he was heading down the road to state socialism and social conformity. He thought all he was proposing was that the government force trusts and bosses and unions to "give the government back to the people."

There were of course some men, not quite average, who did not think the solution so simple. They knew that these national problems had roots too deep to be reached by government cures alone and that the medicine might prove as bad as the disease. To them the evils of the American system were symptoms of a slow corruption in American standards and character. A man could succeed in the new America, and even sometimes succeed more quickly, if he cut legal corners and was not too considerate of the welfare of the public. Popular sentiment not only tolerated such men but sometimes applauded them, and the air was full of compromises, rationalizations, and evasions. The national way of life seemed to be degenerating into a cynical struggle for power by contending interests and classes, with the most numerous class, the lowest, certain to set the standards in the end. The issue was really one of national moralities, national values, and national standards of excellence.

Some men were openly protesting that Americans were losing their

souls in a scramble for material wealth and comforts. Winston
Churchill, the American novelist, had just published *The Inside of
the Cup*. On the very first page Mr. Churchill had described an
American city:

"A city overtaken, in recent years, by the plague which has swept
our country from the Atlantic to the Pacific—Prosperity."

But most men did not think of the new prosperity as materialism.
They called it a socially beneficial drive to raise the standard of
living. They said it was a step on the road to the old ideal of the
pursuit of happiness. They insisted that once all Americans had
gained high levels of security, health, wealth, and comfort, they would
turn to cultural and spiritual values, and attain them by an equally
ardent and mass-organized effort. They predicted that on the material
foundations Americans were now building they would in time erect
towers of character, wisdom, and beauty. But as one watched most
of these men in action, they seemed to be concentrated not on raising
the standard of living for all Americans, but only for themselves and
others like them. There were still slums and wage slaves, while national expenditures for entertainment, cosmetics, luxuries, and gadgets continued to mount. The gap between the rich and the poor was
widening, not narrowing, as the result of their efforts. Might not
the only towers they ever built prove to be taller skyscrapers of mammon, monuments to unrelieved materialism? A few men had such
thoughts in 1913, but their voices were drowned out by the strident
enthusiasms of the urgently acquisitive average.

XVI

Ferment in the Arts

"Americans never did and never will look in the right quarters for vital art. They are imitative, with no real opinions of their own."

This indictment by the British novelist Arnold Bennett, vouchsafed in 1913, perhaps revealed his own limitations more than America's. But, like the opinions of most British critics of a nation they hardly knew, his words had a grain of truth. Only American popular arts had vitality and independence, and no one could call them great art. In the more formal arts most Americans followed the judgments of Europe.

Though Americans might be adolescent in the fine arts, as purchasing patrons they were both important and precocious. They might start as mere newly-rich Philistines, but most of them soon became too discriminating to be patronized or gulled by the dealers of Bond Street or the cognoscenti of the Rue Royale and the Piazza Spagna. American public and private collections were beginning to rival the best in Europe. Operas and symphonies were performed and appreciated as well in New York as in London, Berlin, and Milan. Broadway's theater was, in quality as well as quantity, unexcelled in foreign capitals. American writers were producing books with a vigor, scope, and originality unknown in England since the Elizabethans.

Manhattan was the Mecca of American culture, but much of Manhattan's culture was not American. In those two facts lay the weakness of the fine arts in the new democratic society. With a few exceptions its vast hinterland offered little encouragement or appreciation to creative culture in its higher qualitative expressions. And though New York patronized the arts, much of what it produced and admired was not authentically American. Its best music was written and played or sung by Europeans; its best paintings were imported; most of its finest theatrical productions leaned heavily on European dramatists or actors. Though New York's bookshops sold novels by Americans in the greatest quantity, only a few critics dared pronounce American work to be equal in literary excellency to the best imports from England and the Continent.

As far as more or less cultural entertainment was concerned, Broadway was unquestionably the national center, and as the year 1913 opened, holiday visitors flooded the city and paid exorbitant prices to see its sights and enjoy its shows. Broadway's bill of fare was varied enough to suit all tastes—from Sarah Bernhardt and symphony concerts to Keith's vaudeville house and the "burlecue" shows on west Forty-second Street. The holiday crowds were after entertainment, not culture, and with indiscriminate enthusiasm sopped it up in all its native and imported varieties. There was nothing self-conscious in the people's pursuit of the popular arts; they did not go to the theater to elevate their minds or even to put their familiar world behind them. To them the theater was not an escape from reality but a distillation of familiar life, a month's worth of normal laughter or tears packed into two exhilarating hours.

The comic spirit of the time was more natural and relaxed than it became under the tensions and disillusions of later decades. It did not pretend to be sophisticated or imbued with inner psychological meanings, and the Broadway crowds of 1913 would have been honest enough to find Sartre silly and Noel Coward a little precious and effeminate. Cyril Maude and Forbes-Robertson were offering light and heavy comedy in the best British tradition, in which emotions were controlled and wit was seldom tortured, and George M. Cohan was contributing his talents to a less cerebral American music-hall humor. Compared to the affable apings of Fred Stone, the frenetic antics of Jimmy Durante and the cynicisms of Groucho Marx would have seemed to the theatergoer of 1913 nervously effortful, as if the actors were saying to themselves: "I will be amusing in spite of everything; I will make these people forget the strains of life no matter how much

I may have to distort life to do it; I will fiddle my fun even if our Rome is burning." Even the highbrows of 1913 were not too sophisticated to enjoy slapstick or yield to belly laughs.

The more serious drama was seldom esoteric or fraught with symbolism, and if it were cerebral or even deeply meaningful, that was incidental to the fact that it was a good play. But the Broadway of the new year was nevertheless offering plays and actors equal to the best in 1960. In addition to the Divine Sarah in *Camille* and *Phèdre*, there were Jane Cowl in *Within the Law,* Mrs. Fiske in *The High Road,* Grace George in *Divorcée,* and Nazimova in *Bella Donna.* None of these indulged in the wallowings of disillusion for the sake of disillusion, or introspection for introspection's self-torture. *Camille* and *Phèdre* looked backward to the French classical tradition of the drama, and though plays like *Within the Law* gave modern society a serious treatment, they were closer to the clinical approach of Eugène Brieux's *Damaged Goods* or the witty animadversions of Oscar Wilde than to the deeper psychological probings and emotional appendectomies of Eugene O'Neill or T. S. Eliot. The theater of 1913 was adapted to the society that was culturally extrovert and healthy-minded, if psychologically naïve. There were no beatniks in 1913.

Those who sought their culture more conscientiously could find it at the Metropolitan Museum and the Metropolitan Opera. On a different level they could improve their minds at Burton Holmes's five travelogue lectures, with colored slides, at Carnegie Hall at $3 for the course. Theatergoers with children or sentimental tastes made a happy choice if they went to *Peter Pan,* where Maude Adams's impish charm captivated every male from seven to seventy. As for straight comedy of the bourgeois type, none since World War I has had a more genial appeal than *Potash and Perlmutter,* which rollicked through the business escapades and family squabbles of two Jewish merchants with an atmosphere so free of any sense of strain over racial relations that it could meet the problem with warmhearted frankness and submerge it in *gemütlich* sentiment during one of the longest runs in stage history.

Musical shows were at a high level of song, setting, and undieted pulchritude—almost as high as the holiday prices the scalpers exacted for their tickets. That unparalleled girlie show known as the Ziegfeld's Follies was at its peak, and the 1950's offered no group of musical shows on the stage at one time superior to Laurette Taylor in *Peg o' My Heart*, Billie Burke in Pinero's *The Mind-the-Paint Girl*, George M. Cohan in *Broadway Jones* and Montgomery and Stone in *The Lady and the Slipper*. They were all, by modern standards, florid and naïve, but they had a spontaneous quality that makes the later sophisticated romps of the Noel Cowards, the war sentimentalities of the *South Pacifics*, and the physiopsychology of Tennessee Williams seem a touch neurotic. And one can find on the 1913 stage no evidence of whatever psychoses in current society account for the orgiastic adulations of plastic idols like Sinatra, Liberace, and Presley. The theater of 1913 was not air-conditioned, but its psychic atmosphere was fresher than in 1960.

In April, 1913, thousands of Americans asserted their opinions in the field of modern painting with an independence that refuted Arnold Bennett's charge. In numbers and with an interest never before equaled, ordinary Americans were flocking to the International Exhibition of Modern Art in the New York Armory. They might or might not be looking in the right quarter for vital art, but they were looking very closely and formulating their own opinions about cubist, futurist, and post-impressionist paintings they saw there. Whatever the merits of the modernists, the interest they caused was a stimulus to all art and culture in America.

That first extensive view of the creations of Picasso, Matisse, and their disciples had devastating results in the American art world. They challenged the traditional canons as they had not been challenged since the Renaissance. During the first weeks after the exhibition opened, both critics and the public were in a state of post-impressionist shock. The cubist paintings aroused "awe, scorn, disgust, amazement, pleasure, amusement, puzzlement and adoration. The art critics are cowed, and a considerable proportion of the public has been brought into a condition where it is ready to swallow anything," according to the *Independent* magazine.

The critics may have been cowed, but they were by no means reduced to silence. Frank Jewett Mather, of Princeton, one of the nation's art pundits, analyzed the new art:

In such a view lies either lamentable self-deception or utter charlatanry.
. . . So far as post-impressionism rests on a desperate struggle for originality and a false theory of the emotions it is a negligible eccentricity and
will run its course. . . . It is conceivable that an occasional cubist like
Picasso their leader may believe in this geometrical mode of expression, but
in the main this perversely ingenious work seems a mere hoax of mechanical
draftsmen. . . . The unwholesomeness of the new pictures is their most
striking and immediate condemnation.

Royal Cortissoz let himself go in less academic language. He
called the post-impressionists responsible for "a gospel of stupid li-
cense and self-assertion which would have been swept into the rub-
bish heap were it not for the timidity of our mental habit." Kenyon
Cox, who with Mather and Cortissoz could be called the big three of
American art criticism, denied that the new paintings represented an
advance in art. "Being no longer intimidated by the fetish of progress,
when a thing calling itself a work of art seems to us hideous and de-
graded, indecent and insane, we shall have the courage to say so. . . .
Detestable things are being produced now. . . . Even should such
things prove to be not mere freaks of a diseased intellect that they
seem, but a necessary outgrowth of the conditions of the age and a
true prophecy of the art of the future, they are not necessarily the
better for that. It is only that the future is very unlucky in its art."
Byron Cox, member of the National Academy, said much the same
thing more tersely with "Cubists and futurists are making insanity
pay." Even Theodore Roosevelt donned the toga of an art critic and
commented that at the armory exhibition "The lunatic fringe was
freely in evidence, especially in the rooms devoted to the Cubists and
Futurists."

Modernist painting gave some writers an excuse for relieving
their feelings on other matters. They repeated William Dean Howells's
dictum that "Art must serve morality," and saw in the new art a bar-

barism that flouted disciplines, ignored beauty, and laughed at morals. Some thought cubism and futurism were examples of the rush from civilized values to decadence, and a writer on Futurist Manners in the *Atlantic Monthly* found similarities between the crude self-expression of the cubists and the manners of callow and undisciplined modern youth. "In art as in life this need of immediate self-expression is too often gratified at the expense of beauty and order. The new pictures render directly the vibrations and rhythms of life? So does a herd of stampeding cattle; so do our sons and daughters on the city streets."

No one could be certain where his closest friend would stand in this battle of inkpots and paintpots. Dinner parties on Park Avenue or faculty tea parties in Ohio might suddenly erupt with vociferous disagreements over the merits of "The Nude Descending the Staircase," one of the most striking of the armory exhibits, and one that its creator, Marcel Duchamp-Villon, said, in the late 1950's, he had painted with no intention other than that of amusing himself. The *Independent* magazine, normally self-consciously open-minded, this time lined up with the conservatives: "We are willing to admit that the world is now so old that the period of its second childhood in art has arrived. . . . The public has been fooled by a common fallacy that all propositions are reversible; that because all great art is upon its first appearance called unnatural and absurd, therefore all art that is now called unnatural and absurd must be great."

But the more the highbrows protested, the more the public was intrigued. Some professed to admire the bizarre creations in order to seem liberal or in the sophisticated swim, and, as Kenyon Cox wrote ruefully: "Even the gasping critics, pounding manfully in the rear, have thrown away all the impedimenta of traditional standards in an effort to keep up with what seems less a march than a stampede." The British public, whether more balanced or more inert, viewed the new art creations more calmly, and the French dealt with them more arbitrarily. In Paris the Autumn Art Salon declined to admit cubist paintings with the simple statement that they were not art. By taking modernist painting so seriously the American public made most of it more important than it later turned out to be. The mellower judgment of forty years indicates that those who saw no merit in the work of Picasso and Matisse were very wrong, but in condemning most of the other extremist creations of 1913, now forgotten, they were wholly right. Public acceptance of modernist art must have made conservative critics feel like Anacharsis when he first saw democracy in action in Athens, and commented that the wise men spoke but the fools decided.

In spite of this furor over the Ideas of March, normal American preferences in art soon reasserted themselves. George Bellows's prize fighters pleased the average man far more permanently than cubism. But what pleased him most of all in 1913, for reasons that transcended the purely aesthetic, was the strictly representational painting of a shy young girl caught bathing in adolescent nudity called "September Morn." There were few American males over sixteen who did not openly or covertly admire one of its innumerable calendar or post-card reproductions. It was far less risqué than thousands of girl-art pictures that now decorate advertising posters and the pages of *Esquire,* and on one point even Cortissoz and Picasso would have agreed: "September Morn" was certainly not great art. But it was popular art, and perhaps all the more popular as a relief from post-impressionism. When in May a shrewd New York shopkeeper on Forty-sixth Street displayed the original in his plate-glass window, the crowds stopped the traffic and his trade increased. So did the head-lines when Anthony Comstock, New York's self-appointed guardian of public morals, thundered against it. But that excitement yielded in turn to the World Series and the slit skirt, which drew male interest in beauty back to reality.

In music New York's offerings as 1913 opened were extensive, and some of them were first-rate. Walter Damrosch was conducting the Symphony Society with Mischa Elman as violin soloist at the new Aeolian Hall, and the Metropolitan was offering Italian and German operas with such stars as Enrico Caruso, Nellie Melba, and Antonio Scotti. There were scores of concerts and recitals, and New York's Tin Pan Alley, led by Irving Berlin, was determining the nation's tastes in popular music. The battle between classical and modern in music had not yet fired off its biggest guns, but there were preliminary skirmishes. Stravinsky's *Le Sacre du Printemps,* with Nijinsky and the Russian ballet, was hissed off the stage in Paris, but the premier of Moussorgsky's *Boris Godounov* made "a deep and favorable impression" on the Metropolitan audiences, and the critics called its music "original and strong." Moussorgsky's tones did not offend the unaccustomed ear as did Stravinsky's dissonances, but there were indications that New York musical audiences were at least as sophisticated and tolerant as those of Paris and London, and more ready to welcome the new. Perhaps that was because Americans were already accustomed to the pace, syncopations, and stridencies of American jazz, from which would soon develop uniquely American music of high quality. George Gershwin was on his way.

All the arts in America were highly commercialized. More than in the 1950's, New York's monopoly of the arts rested in the hands of the professionals. Its critics guided national tastes in literature, music, and painting. Most of the nation's books were published in the New York area, and half the copies sold in America were sold there. New York newspapers set the standard for the country in editorial opinion as well as in news coverage. What appeared on stage and screen depended greatly on New York producers and financial backers. The artist and his inspiration might originate elsewhere; jazz and blues in New Orleans and Memphis and the realistic novel in the Midwest; but the artist and his work were soon drawn into the orbit of New York and the maw of its commercial entrepreneurs.

In the new democracy, where popular culture was becoming more and more sovereign, good art became, commercially, what the masses and not the élite said was good art. If the cognoscenti did not agree, there was little they could do except to fulminate and wait for time to prove them right. But the popular taste in music, art, and letters was not wholly spontaneous and unguided; it could be implemented only through dealers and publishers, who therefore assumed increasing importance. The newly rich American with a sudden interest in the arts could see and choose, but only from what the dealers put before him, and he welcomed their advice as to what was worth buying. The unestablished creative artist could sell only what the dealers were willing to sponsor and display.

Art has always had its commercial aspects. Even the Bachs and Cellinis had to eat to live, and could not treat too independently the tastes of their patrons. But Florentine and even German princes had usually been bred to good taste or were ready to be guided by men who had it, and some of them even gave the artist a free hand. The earlier artist usually had to please only one patron at a time, and he was predictable. The artist or musician of the twentieth century is not the pet of a single patron, and at first glance seems more independent. Actually, he has only multiplied his masters, who no longer have individual personalities familiar to him, but blank faces and volatile tastes. Yet if he ignores their judgments he is likely to go hungry; if he yields too much to them his work loses integrity and moves toward the second-rate.

Both the commercially successful artist and the aspiring but unknown one were drawn to New York, but their New York worlds were separate. Those who had gained recognition usually established themselves in the uptown area where dealers, publishers, and lion hunters might make much of them. Those not yet accepted, or stubbornly Bohemian even after success, made Greenwich Village their spiritual and usually their temporal home. In 1913 the Village was as unique a hotbed of artistic aspiration and rebellion as the Left Bank in the nineties. There ambitious youth and still hopeful middle age argued, experimented, and flouted the conventions. There the Bohemians scored as Philistines the successful artists and dealers of Fifth Avenue and Fifty-seventh Street, even as they envied them and sought their patronage. For it was the uptown shoppers for culture who were the consumers of art, and the Greenwich Village aspirant had to renounce commercial success or else produce what the dealer, the publisher, or the musical director said the buying public wanted. Max Eastman, leftist intellectual of the Village, branded the system as "business art," and tried to find ways to offer directly to the public "what is too naked or too true for the money-making press." He did not really succeed.

Greenwich Village was as fluid as the opinions and careers of its residents. Every man who has described it has seen in it the light of his own interests and experiences there. Robert Herrick, whose novels were popular in boudoirs, said the dominant atmosphere of the Village was derived from "the restlessness of women." Floyd Dell, later to publish *Intellectual Vagabondage* and *Love in Greenwich Village*, saw it as the home of youth, fleeing from the Babbitry of small-town origins, groping for orientation, repudiating "the hypocrisies of traditional thought" and revolting against "tribal customs." To Max Eastman, teaching philosophy and burning for Utopia, the Village was a coterie of social reformers with passionate liberal convictions, influenced by the muckrakers and the examples of Lillian Wald, Jane Addams, and Jacob A. Riis. Phrases like "social conscience" and "young intellectuals" had the uplifting excitement of newness, and there was "a feeling of regeneration in the air," as of "just before the dawn of a new day." Actually, there was no typical Greenwich Villager; some were genuinely creative, some imitative, some sincere, and some charlatans; some were mature and many only half baked.

Young men and women then fermenting in the Village became leaders in the kind of thinking that led both to parlor pinks and to the New Deal; others, twenty years later, were established citizens who voted Republican and laughed a little apologetically at their earlier dissents and enthusiasms. A few ultimately wrote best sellers; more went home again and "adjusted." Robbed of its élan and swamped by the pseudo-art and pseudo-radicalism of its camp followers, the creative spirit of the Village declined after World War I and was engulfed in Bohemian mediocrity. Later crops of Village artists and social rebels would imitate the unconventionalities and defiances of their predecessors more successfully than their sincerity and talent. But the Greenwich Village of the prewar years played its part in stimulating America in the creative fine arts and in political reform, and in changing, for better or worse, the values of American culture and the concepts of democratic government.

XVII

Truth and Fiction

There had been plenty of realism in nineteenth century American life, and perhaps that was why there was so little in its literature. Its writers had romanticized American history and sentimentalized American life, perhaps because its practical pursuits had discouraged romance and sentiment in daily living.

Yet Americans have always been more influenced by books— sometimes by books they had never read—than most of them have realized. Tom Paine's *Common Sense* helped to make the Revolution, and *Uncle Tom's Cabin* the Civil War. Writers like Irving, Cooper and Mark Twain built up a national tradition of Americanism that the nation accepted and that still influences its emotional reactions.

"History," said Voltaire, "is a fable agreed upon." Led by its literary lights, the American people made a fable of their history, and cherished that fable even after it had little relation to reality. As society discarded in fact its pioneer and rural folkways, it embraced them more warmly in fiction. The more remote the revolutionary forefathers, the more heroic they became; the more unfamiliar the crudenesses of log-cabin life, the more they were glorified. The fable satisfied an emotional need of Americans immersed in urban complexities who feared they were neither very strong nor very valiant; they could imagine themselves endowed with heroic qualities by their idealized forefathers. Even in 1900 they saw themselves, not as they were, but in the warming light of a romanticized history that fortified their self esteem. McDougall the psychologist would soon point out that Americans were uniquely ready "to believe and assert that the state of affairs which they desired to see, already obtained."

The true story of the nation's growth was epic, and merited preser-
vation, as an epic, of times forever past. But epics get reshaped into
romances, and when they do they lose vigor and reality. The American epic was watered down by the distortions of its romantic exalta-
tion. Every forefather became a strong and silent hero, every asser-
tion of self-interest became enterprise, every resistance to European
culture another Declaration of Independence. The real significance
of actual heroes was lost in exaggeration. Davy Crockett would not
recognize himself in his twentieth century reincarnation.

It was a good fable as fables go, an appealing romance when recognized as fiction, but taken as history its falsifications perpetuated
the adolescence and supported the illusions of a nation called upon
to be clear-sighted and mature. Sentimental romances and boys' ad-
venture stories have their values, but those who cling to them too long
fail to grow up and face the facts of life. By 1900 the fable of American
devotion to the simple virtues, to rural life, social equality, religious
faith, self-sufficiency, and social independence was no longer reality.

The reading public preferred historical romances about America
to any other literature, but stories had to have happy endings, and
writers and publishers gave the public what it wanted. No less a
literary pundit than William Dean Howells wrote in his *Criticism and
Fiction* that American realism should concern itself with "the large
cheerful average of health and success and a happy life, [since] the
more smiling aspects of life [are] the more American." This insistence
on the smiling aspects of life did not encourage aspiring young writers
to picture real persons and real contemporary problems, and the variety and quality of American literature suffered as a result. In 1913
the editor of *Harper's Magazine* wrote rather regretfully of "the overwhelming prevalence of fiction" in the American market, and George
P. Brett, the distinguished head of The Macmillan Company, said in
the *Atlantic Monthly* that it was seldom that a novel "of merit and
value, representing honest work and real convictions . . . finds its
way into the ranks of the 'six best sellers.' Their appeal is to that part
of the public which still discriminates in its reading, a smaller per-

centage of the whole, I fear, at present than at any recent period in our history."

The romantic legend took many forms. Horatio Alger's success stories for boys sold in numbers second only to the Bible. Since 1867 he had been turning out his infinite versions of the poor boy's rise to power and riches. His heroes invariably reached success by courage, honesty, hard work, and an eye to the main chance. Their piety and morality—especially their practical morality—always triumphed; the goal and the reward were material success. It was significant that Alger adapted the log-cabin fable to the new urbanized America. His country boys were drawn to the dangers and opportunities of the big city and made their fortunes there, an inverted version of the challenge of the frontier.

Samuel Merwin and H. K. Webster began to supply in about 1900 the equivalent of Alger's boys' stories for older readers assumed to be adult. In *The Short Line War* and *Calumet K* they had recounted admiringly, in a style as brisk and unconventional as their heroes, the bustle and trickery of ambitious men in a dog-eat-dog version of American enterprise. Their heroes were Alger's heroes grown up and morally somewhat shopworn in the process. They had brass, energy, fertile brains, thick skins, few ethics, and no values higher than power and profits. Though dressed in a kind of natty realism, these two novels were merely a modernized commercial version of the pioneer romance, and a cheapened one, with rules of conduct as adolescent as those of a boyhood gang. The books went through many editions between 1900 and 1913.

The success myth had nonfiction versions just as popular. The inspirational books of Orison Swett Marden, with their blend of cheapened Christianity and material success, were said to be on every fourth living-room table in America, and his *Success* magazine was widely read until, paradoxically, it failed. Many another uplift author imitated Marden in telling Americans how to make the best of both worlds by "practical Christianity"—America's new-found tool to build spiritual satisfaction through material success.

There were other variations of the fable, each emphasizing some virtue believed to be uniquely American. Virility was glorified by Jack London, who romanticized in swinging verse and fiction the crudities of Yukon life, and created a youthful cult of admirers of the hard-drinking Alaskan with a heart as well as a pouch of unrefined gold. Robert W. Service rang changes on this theme, and there was probably not a college sophomore in America who could not quote lines from both. Joseph Vance tempered robustness with sentiment, rather less flamboyantly. Meredith Nicholson offered somewhat tamer versions of American manhood in his Indiana heroes in books like *A Hoosier Chronicle* (1912) and *The Provincial American* (1913); they emphasized the virtues and sweet flavors of Midwest life more truthfully than its narrownesses and hypocrisies.

Booth Tarkington depicted with more uncritical affection the adolescent lives of boys and adults in a special Edenized Indiana of his own, where local realities were sweetened by sentiment and happy endings, and where old and young Tom Sawyers were more successfully civilized than their original by public schools and Aunt Pollys of both sexes. Whatever protests Tarkington implied against American values were little more than expressions of the nostalgia for the older, simpler ways. But though he disliked large cities and recoiled from the current admiration for everything big, he shared some of the tastes that led to megalomania. Occasionally one of his characters would punch through the sentimental gloss, and *The Gentleman from Indiana* pictures political skulduggery so convincingly that his friend Theodore Roosevelt reproved him for it. Such social criticism was, however, only an incidental to Tarkington's best-of-all-possible Indiana worlds.

More than their readers realized, these fictional soporifics were escapist literature. Each reflected American life in its pleasantly distorting mirror. Every society has its dream world, but the nation-wide popularity of Eleanor H. Porter's *Pollyanna* indulged the nation in its greatest orgy of sentimental optimism. It was the American myth's most blatantly saccharine tribute to its faith in simple goodness and to the proposition that all was really for the best in a disturbingly mechanized world. Its readers, perhaps with an unconscious sense of guilt for their own infidelities to their nursery-taught virtues, cherished Pollyanna somewhat as a prosperous madame cherishes her memories of vanished innocence. A victim of crippling injuries in early childhood, Pollyanna discovered that there were some eight-hundred texts in the Bible telling people to be glad, and so impressive a quantitative sum of exhortation convinced her that He must have meant it. So she made happiness her religion and spread it about with a very thick trowel and a rather irritating cheerfulness. All her enemies and obstacles, including her own crippling injuries, were overcome by it before the last chapter. "The glad girl" was the era's most synthetic darling and sentiment's best anwer to the social problems of the new century. If Pollyanna, so unfortunate, could be glad and good, then so could the unfortunates in slums and sweatshops, if they only would.

Pollyanna was not the only child idol in contemporary literature. Adolescence was admired and perpetuated for decades in a flood of fiction and quasi-autobiography. From Washington Irving and James Fenimore Cooper to William Dean Howells and Stephen Crane, almost every leading American storyteller wrote at least one book glorifying childhood. In addition to Huck Finn, Tom Sawyer, Pollyanna, the Little Women, and Alger's virtuous bootblacks, there had been Lucy Larcom's *A New England Girlhood*, Edward Everett Hale's *A New England Boyhood*, Thomas Bailey Aldrich's *The Story of a Bad Boy*, Noah Brooks's *Boy Emigrants*, Charles Dudley Warner's *Being a Boy*, William Dean Howells's *A Boy's Town*, Hamlin Garland's *Boy Life on the Prairie*, Booth Tarkington's *Penrod*, Augustus Hoppin's *Two Compton Boys*, William Allen White's *The Court of Boyville*, and all the cheap series of Minute Boys, Motor Boys, Submarine Boys, and the rest.

All of these writers perpetuated some aspect of the old affirmations or adapted them to factories and slums. The kind of literature that soothed the minds of its readers sold best in 1913. A quite different kind of writing was required to stimulate thought and action to meet the new world on its own terms, and the important books of the new century were those that sought reality or expressed dissent. By 1913 a very different set of literary men was pointing out the discrepancies between legend and the actuality. Those writers did not constitute a unified literary coterie; they wrote as individuals, and would have objected strongly to being classified together. Nevertheless their influence was collective. Not one of them was able to present the entire American scene, but their piecemeal contributions made up a disillusioning mosaic Americans could no longer ignore.

When democracy finally accepts a disillusioning truth, it is likely to move from excessive confidence to excessive uncertainty, as in the case of Russian satellites. In 1913 fiction was on its way from overromantic myth to overstark reality, from excessive self-adulation to excessive self-debunking. The new realists, overwhelmed by the actualities of their society, sought scapegoats, and concentrated their fire on the more obvious targets of American sin. The change was not so sudden or complete as it appeared at the time. Americans have never been without a sense of reality, and in the nineteenth century a few native voices had joined some from Europe in criticism of American ways. Though almost all were drowned out in the universal paean to America, they left their mark on the national consciousness. James Fenimore Cooper's caustic criticisms condemned him to social outer darkness, but by the last quarter of the nineteenth century other critics of American complacency were being given a hearing, at least by the intellectuals.

One of these was William Dean Howells, the writer who in 1894 had recommended that American realism should limit itself to "the more smiling aspects of American life." The change in Howells's reactions to America, which led him to disregard his own advice, mirrored the change in the spirit of the times. By 1900 Howells was writing that "the struggle for life has changed from a fight to an encounter of disciplined forces, and the few fighters that are left get ground to pieces between organized labor and organized capital." In 1913 Americans were reading in his *A Traveler from Altruria* of the mean and selfish aspects of contemporary capitalism. He predicted that the Age of Accumulation, with its gigantic monopolies gathered into ever fewer hands, would lead inevitably to state control over all industry. Big industry would fall like a ripe plum into the maw of the state, whose engulfment of private enterprise would be peacefully ratified by the voters. Howells was preaching the socialism he had come to accept, but he sugared the pill so tactfully, and had such a following among the well born and well heeled, that few readers denounced dear Mr. Howells as subversive.

A less popular but equally significant book had appeared in 1891. H. H. Boyekin, a professor at Columbia, saw the economic morals of the times as little better than the law of the jungle, and American culture as the acceptance of plutocratic crudities. In his *Mammon of Unrighteousness*, the character of Horace Larkin was the first serious presentation of the new American man of business. He is attractive because of his aura of success, his supreme self-confidence, his high intelligence, and his almost feline directness of action. His ethics are a conscious justification of the right to turn democracy to his personal advantage:

"The majority of our politicians," said Larkin genially, "are a low-lived lot, and many of them are corrupt. But they have the courage to be American—crudely and uncompromisingly American—and that is, in my eyes, a virtue which is not to be lightly rated."

"And may I ask, Mr. Larkin, what do you mean by being American?"

"Being frankly, ably and enterprisingly plebeian. It is the plebeian who after all shall inherit the earth."

"I beg your pardon. According to the Bible it is the meek."

"I must differ from the Bible then, for the meek, in my opinion, if they inherit anything, never manage to keep it. It passes, sooner or later, into the hands of the strong, the self-assertive, the grasping. But these, as you will admit, are plebeian characteristics. A universally prosperous, comfortable, independent and enterprising mob—that is the real goal toward which we are steering; and in my opinion it is a good and desirable one."

Those earlier novels had no wide influence on most Americans of their time. But when a dozen books of revelation and protest appeared within a few years, the public began to pay attention. There has been no decade in which, as Bruce Catton recently put it, "a few ink slingers did more to change the climate of opinion." The muckrakers wrote to be heard, and for the first time in several decades

America listened to writers who were critically evaluating its ways. They opened the door to the realists in fiction, who were already beginning to set a new tone in American letters.

One of the most powerful of the realistic novelists was Theodore Dreiser, busily piling up the pedestrian details that made his books massive attacks on the business barons of the Age of Accumulation. In *The Financier* and *The Titan*, Dreiser threw harsh light on the social effects of plutocracy, though he could not conceal a sneaking respect for the strength and ability of his hero-villains. His readers found his portraits too convincing to deny, too just to ignore, and too devastating to accept. How could admirers of the American Way of Life approve a man who said he could no longer abide American complacency after seeing Pittsburgh? How could professed Christians accept a concept of their society implicit in his "stony universe whose hard, brilliant forces rage fiercely . . . forces of which the lesser is nothing to the greater. . . . We suffer for our temperaments, which we did not make, and for our weaknesses and lacks, which were no part of our willing and doing." Such determinism left no place for Sunday-morning smugness.

Dreiser's heavy indictment made other realists who wrote more readably seem mere triflers of dissent, but some of them were more persuasive than he because they were less Promethean. Jane Addams, daughter of a Quaker millowner, preached through the good works she began at Hull-House in 1889, and helped to open eyes to the plight of the underprivileged. Rejecting Dreiser's determinism, she saw hope of improvement through legislation and social work. Many who never read a word she wrote knew what Jane Addams stood for, and her example set new goals for an awakening sense of social responsibility.

Novelists remote from Dreiser's philosophy were also nibbling in their various ways at the edges of social injustice and complacency. Hutchins Hapgood pictured the moral disintegration of an honest and well-meaning man caught in the pressures of the industrial system. David Graham Phillips genially assaulted the "light-fingered gentry" in their worship of "the Great God Success." Jack London, abandoning his muscle-men of the Yukon, wrote crudely revealing

stories of America's unacknowledged class warfare. In *V. V.'s Eyes*
and *Queed,* Henry Sydnor Harrison recounted the adventures of naïve
young men stirred to action by the social injustices they stumbled on.
The miseries of the poor, the indifference of the rich, and the pressures
toward conformity kept creeping into Robert Herrick's romances.
The American Winston Churchill underwent, like Howells, a change
in the subject matters of his novels. At the turn of the century *Richard
Carvel* and *The Crisis* had established him as a popular and skilled
writer of historical romances. But like Theodore Roosevelt, whom he
admired, he developed an increasing concern about social and economic inequities. *The Inside of the Cup* in 1913 treated upper-class
indifference with an artistry and depth seldom equaled by the more
strident protesters. His ardent clergyman's soul searchings over the
hypocrisies of the well-to-do pillars of his church is one of the most
significant novels of the time. William Allen White stretched a point
when he pronounced Churchill "the first of the literary reformers,"
but Carl Van Doren did him less than justice when he called him
"morally eager, intellectually belated."

Protests came from unexpected places. No established writer lived
in circles less inclined toward social revolt than Edith Wharton, ir-
reproachably well born into a conventional New York family that
viewed her literary efforts as inappropriate and her literary success
as a matter best overlooked. Her novels described her own upper-class
society "in all its flatness and futility," and showed how it could half
destroy those who even only mildly defied it. She could even make the
heart of her hero ache at "the bitter throes with which the human machine moves on." As a critic of all but her own social set, she lacked
firsthand knowledge, and Edmund Wilson called her "a brilliant example of a writer who relieves emotional strain by denouncing her
own generation," but whatever her motivations, her books helped to
stir the upper-class conscience.

Two other women writers, just making their reputations, contributed to the new realism. Kathleen Norris in *The Rich Mrs. Burgoyne*
(1912) deplored the manners as well as the morals of plutocratic society. Edna Ferber in *Roast Beef Medium* (1913) developed her

talent for realism. On the other hand an immigrant woman, in *The Promised Land* (1912), though utterly truthful in fact, supported the legend of America as the best of all possible worlds. Mary Antin found her new country a wonderful place of friendliness and opportunity, but her character was exceptional and so was her experience. Hers was a rosier picture than most immigrants of the time could honestly have painted.

Not all the criticism of American life and myth was in fictional or biographical form. Professor Charles A. Beard's *Economic Interpretation of the Constitution* created a new school of historical writing that deflated some of the rosier versions of the motivations of the Founding Fathers, Walter Lippmann, only a few years out of Harvard, stimulated in his *A Preface to Politics* the search for a sounder pattern for political progress in a democracy. Young Randolph Bourne, whose early death was a great loss to American liberalism, analyzed the values and mores of small town society with perceptive and disillusioning vision.

Some of the new poets were also declining to look at American life through the rosy spectacles of the conventional tradition. Edgar Lee Masters stripped the petals from the artificial flowers of Midwest contentment in his *Spoon River Anthology*. His Miniver Cheeveys were as different from Tarkington's contented Hoosiers as the Chicago stockyards of Frank Norris differed from the smiling estates of their North Shore owners, and more than any other poet of his time he set the stage for the literary disillusionists. He stressed the blindnesses, hypocrisies, and barren respectabilities that dominated much of small-town life and thought, and prepared the way for Sinclair Lewis, Eugene O'Neill, and T. S. Eliot.

A society that could at the same time embrace Pollyanna and plunge into the chill waters of Spoon River was in need of spiritual reorientation. In *Winesburg, Ohio* and elsewhere Sherwood Anderson protested against a mechanized society that left its victims frustrated and robbed of creative ability. He saw Americans as "confused and disconcerted by the facts of life." The only escape for the creative man lay in reaching down "through all the broken surface distractions of modern life to that old draft out of which culture springs."

But though verse was regaining literary recognition, most of it was trivial. For every man who read Masters or Anderson a hundred swallowed the daily syndicated sugarplum rhymes of Edgar A. Guest. Intellectuals like Amy Lowell of Boston might encourage the ardent poets of the new revolt, and Harriet Monroe might launch *Poetry* magazine (with an annual subsidy) to publish new serious poetry, but Kipling's "If" was probably the most popular poem in America, with Joyce Kilmer's "Trees" a close second. The new verse had a long way to go when critics could find John Masefield and Wilfrid Gibson iconoclastic, and Robert Shafer could write in the *Atlantic Monthly:* "Of course both men have cut loose from the trammels of convention and have antagonized those pious souls who can see only technical experimentation in their work. But . . . here we have . . . the first poetic expression of a movement which bids fair to sweep the whole Western world. . . . I mean of course the whole socialist conception of life and government."

To broaden an American culture that thought Masefield iconoclastic, a number of new periodicals, all protesting something or other and all visualizing a better world of some kind, sprang up during or about 1913. Among these were the *Masses,* the *Little Review,* the *Dial,* the *New Republic,* the *World's Work* and the *Independent.* Most stimulating of all to the creative urge was the *Seven Arts Magazine,* started by Van Wyck Brooks, Waldo Frank, Louis Untermeyer, and James Oppenheim. It looked toward "a new international life, an interweaving of groups in all countries, the unspoiled forces everywhere who share the same culture and somewhat the same vision of the new world . . . a mixture of art and revolution." So noble an ambition was too good for this world, and the *Seven Arts* died young. But all this fresh vigor led Alfred Noyes, the English poet, to predict, quite mistakenly, in March, 1913, that "poetry is going to dominate the next age."

Highbrows and would-be highbrows still held American writers in less esteem than imported ones. Inability to read foreign languages limited most seekers for European culture to those who wrote in English, for the Knopfs had not yet embarked on their mission of printing foreign books in translation. Romain Rolland's *Jean Christophe* was, however, displayed on many a living-room table. So were the Irish leprechaun fantasies of James Stephens's *The Crock of Gold*, so were John Galsworthy's *The Dark Flower* and *The Inn of Tranquility*, and Hall Caine's *The Woman Thou Gavest Me*. Galsworthy was not without his criticisms of the mores of English society, but few would have called him an ardent dissenter, and Caine's novels were not profound or charged with social concern, though his formula challenged conventions just enough to lead some careful American mothers to try to keep them from their daughters. Arnold Bennett's *Those United States* seemed to many an American reader more fiction than fact, though they also waded respectfully through his faithfully dull reproductions of the dullness of lower-middle-class life in the Midland industrial cities. If Bennett had strong opinions about social problems, they did not inspire him to constructive protest, and he contributed little to the widening of American cultural horizons.

That was not true of Bernard Shaw, the new enthusiasm of eager intellectuals—more popular in America than in England in 1913. As an intellectual cocktail he was stimulating, but as a purveyor of social wisdom his value was dubious. His epigrams and iconoclasms were often taken more seriously than they were worth, and his parlor socialism did more to arouse than to deepen the American mind. His effect on his younger admirers in America was to make them think, but also to make deference to traditions, conventions, or one's elders unfashionable. Those who assumed the role of advanced intellectuals hailed him as a seer and philosopher and classed him with Ibsen and Nietzsche, a concatenation of literary sputniks that showed how confused they were.

Next to Shaw, H. G. Wells was the most widely read Englishman in America. His refreshing ideas about science, history, government, and any other matter called to his attention, as well as his highly readable style and his intellectual ebullience, made him irresistible to those who liked their intellectual stimulants to be heady without headaches, and who were chronically in quest of the simple solution. He was a strong force toward discarding the old and embracing the new; as he once said of himself, he "had a flair for what was coming." His *Marriage*, published here in 1913, was not one of his most popular books, but it deflated conventionality in that field as he had deflated it in others. As a stimulus to American thought he was healthy and helpful.

To Americans of 1960, who have lived with the realities of wars and nuclear threats, the 1913 brand of horrid truth seems mild. They wonder that Shaw could have seemed so shocking and the muckrakers so disillusioning. But to the mores of 1890 the realism of 1913 was iconoclastic. *Spoon River* shook prewar America because it was so different from Whittier's Barefoot Boy; there was a wider gap between them than that between Masters and T. S. Eliot or Shaw and Sagan. Then, too, the realist of today is talking a universal language; the realist of 1913 was addressing his fellow citizens in a way polite society had thought taboo. In *America's Coming-of-Age* Van Wyck Brooks described the psychic background of the 1913 literary world. The American of the time, said Brooks, had been reared in "a sort of orgy of lofty examples, moralized poems, national anthems, and baccalaureate sermons; until he is charged with all manner of ideal purities, ideal honorabilities, ideal femininities."

Americans in 1913 had not yet taken the full plunge into disillusion; a new young writer would soon hold up to them a mirror with reflective harshness and power equal to anything provided by the angry young men of the fifties. Words like these were already forming under the bludgeoning pen of Sinclair Lewis:

The United States of America are peopled by a mighty herd which . . . drives foolishly in whatever direction their noses point—a herd endowed with a tremendous blind power, with big bulldozers, but with minds rarely above their bellies and their dams . . . with a herd power that sweeps majestically onward in a cloud of dust of its own raising, seeming to be lords and masters of a continent. But in fact they are somewhat stupid, feeble in brain and will, stuffed with conceit of their own excellence, esteeming themselves the great end for which creation has been in travail; with a vast respect for totems and fetishes; purveyors and victims of Bunk— a vast middleman herd that dominates the continent but cannot reduce it to order or decency.

XVIII
Progress

"Progress! Did you ever reflect that the world is almost a new one? The modern idea is to leave the past and pass on to something new."

Woodrow Wilson wrote those words as an authority on progress, who had promised that his administration would lead the American people onward and upward. Whatever, as a former historian, he may have thought of turning his back on the past, the reforming statesman had his eyes chiefly on the future.

The President seemed to be making good his promise, and the nation was moving forward with him. To most of its citizens, all expansion was progress, whether in population, production, or wealth. Immigrants were still flooding the country at the rate of nearly a million a year, and the total population was nearing the 100,000,000 mark. Per capita wealth had passed $1,300, the equivalent of more than twice that much today. Industrial production was greater than ever before.

The America of 1913 was excited about its new mechanical civilization. Telephones and typewriters were increasing office efficiency and home convenience. Motorcars were beginning to become universal carriers, and Henry Ford alone was producing them in numbers unthinkable only a decade earlier. Ships of unprecedented size, speed, and luxury were crossing the Atlantic every week: the *Olympic, Aquitania,* and *Imperator,* all of fifty thousand tons. The Panama Canal would soon be opened, with its promise of increasing American trade, naval power, and world influence. America had defeated Spain, taken over its colonies, and made a beneficent world empire its "manifest destiny." The new Roosevelt Dam offered expansive vistas of what harnessing natural resources might add to America's food and power, and New York's skyscrapers were a symbol of the nation's towering ambition and confidence in the future.

Such achievements seemed to be only the beginning when one considered the progress of science. The death rate was falling and the life span increasing. Americans had become germ conscious, and were setting higher standards of sanitation than any nation in history. Medical science had conquered yellow fever in the American tropics, and malaria and hookworm might soon vanish north of the Rio Grande. In January, Surgeon-General Charles G. Stokes announced that since the introduction of inoculations against typhoid eleven months earlier, not a single case had appeared among 64,000 enlisted men. When, in May, research in cancer was begun at the Harvard Medical School, most laymen thought that within a few years that menace too would be overcome.

The physical sciences were promising an even more startling new world. In March the first transatlantic radio signal was heard between the Eiffel Tower and Arlington, Virginia, and only four months later clear messages were being exchanged between Berlin and the new wireless towers at Sayville, Long Island. This was the greatest miracle of all; it seemed almost godlike that human beings could send their voices across the ocean through the air. It had endless possibilities, and one of them was demonstrated in October when the liner *Volturno* caught fire in mid-Atlantic. Ten ships notified by wireless came to the rescue and saved 521 lives otherwise almost certainly doomed. . . . And very soon, someone would fly clear over the Atlantic Ocean.

Even such miracles, according to the scientists, might be nothing compared to what was coming. Henry Smith wrote in *Harper's Magazine* about Ernest Rutherford's exploration of the atom, and of the discovery of the electron, and added that "this infinitely minute particle . . . is . . . far and away the most important thing in the universe." In August, Sir William Ramsay wrote even more impressively about the possibilities of the atom if its power could be unleashed and controlled, and concluded that "a new chapter in the history of science . . . has been opened."

To most Americans such scientific research was important because it promised progress as they defined progress: the creation of more and bigger things to buy, sell, use, and admire. Everyone knew that scientific progress and education should go hand in hand. Since education was the germ of progress, the more of it, the better, in numbers of bricks and students, in areas of knowledge and instruction, in the size of libraries, laboratories, lecture halls, and gymnasiums. To make education available to all, on equal terms, it must be standardized and made as efficient as Henry Ford's assembly line. So education, too, was expanded. Classes were enlarged as well as institutions, so that each teacher could achieve maximum numerical efficiency; and instruction, as well as new buildings, moved toward uniformity and prefabrication. By 1913 educational progress had been so great that the public schools had an enrollment of nearly 19,000,000 pupils, a number so impressive that few considered the significance of the facts that some 6,000,000 of those registered did not attend school regularly; that the number of trained teachers had not increased in proportion; and that by qualitative standards it was doubtful that education had progressed at all.

The colleges were expanding too, and that was bringing changes in their atmosphere and values. In the nineteenth century they had been almost exclusively the privilege of the well-to-do, an easygoing clientele that accepted the traditional collegiate emphasis on liberal and humane learning. The new expansion brought to higher education tens of thousands of students from less prosperous homes, who demanded that the classroom prepare them for earning careers, especially in the promising fields of science, engineering, and business. Though some educators deplored the trend, the colleges turned more and more to the dissemination of the usefully factual and the profitably technical. The atmosphere of the campus became less concerned with the pursuit of the good mind and the good life than with the pursuit of a good job.

In school education the disciplines of learning were losing caste.

Parents as well as teachers, influenced by the new child psychology, began to abandon the former theory that to spare the rod was to spoil the child. Madame Montessori's doctrine of "free self-development" led teachers at all levels to demand less of their pupils in hard work, discipline, and foundation knowledge. Progressive educators of 1913 were beginning to condemn "the concentrated authority and blind obedience" of the traditional school educational system, and to encourage boys and girls to substitute for the authority of traditional knowledge and experience their own half-baked conclusions. The results bequeathed to the current generation the virtues of flexibility and self-expression and the vices of indiscipline and sloppy thinking.

Not everyone approved the change. The *Independent* suggested: "The principle business of our elaborate machinery of education . . . just now seems to be to convert ignorance of the plain or elemental kind into the complicated variety . . . our educational institutions are not doing their job." A writer in *Scribner's Magazine* said: "The spirit of self-assertion has so permeated all classes of our population that even the babes and sucklings brought up under the Montessori methods are showing the influence." The editors of the *Century Magazine* deplored the fact that "not only in Congress but elsewhere . . . there is a veritable contempt for learning."

Because the democratic government did not seem to be working out quite so happily as expected, there was much talk of the duty of the colleges to be "training schools for democracy." To the public this seemed to mean making the colleges and their requirements easier and their undergraduate bodies self-governing, their studies more ephemeral and their extra-classroom activities more ardent. As a result the colleges became more and more like vocational country clubs with thousands of young people who had few intellectual qualifications and still fewer intellectual interests doing very much what they pleased. Some educated "traditionalists" protested that this was lowering the intellectual tone and qualitative standards of education, and would lead to cultural mediocrity. But the wave of egalitarianism in the name of democracy engulfed nearly everything in education, though democracy broke in futility against the social Gibralters of the collegiate fraternities. Even Woodrow Wilson had failed to abolish the clubs at Princeton, and in nearly every college the fraternities and sororities continued to perpetuate the American brand of social snobbery and ward politics.

Educators and students were not, of course, the only groups that did not always practice the virtues they preached. In spite of all the talk of social justice there were forty-five cases of recognized lynchings during the year, and a much larger number of interracial brutalities. Racial discrimination was even more prevalent and more widely accepted in 1913 than in 1961, and it appeared not only in southern schools. In Jamaica, Long Island, upper-middle-class white women stormed local municipal and real-estate offices to protest against the sale of land near their homes to Negro families. In the "free state" of West Virginia there were clear cases of discrimination against Negroes in the public schools. In Washington, the National Association for the Advancement of Colored People complained to President Wilson of the segregation of Negro employees in certain buildings of the federal government, and of discrimination against Negro civil service employees in appointments and promotions, in direct violation of the federal laws. The new freedom in which society was indulging did not include freedom from prejudice. In view of such events, only a very sentimental person would feel that the issues of the Civil War were really settled, even though on July 4, 1913, some 57,000 Union and Confederate Army veterans camped garrulously together on the battlefield of Gettysburg.

Progress also meant increasing independence of social and of moral conventions. Men and women were making the most of their legal freedoms to escape from marriage bonds, and one marriage out of every four was ending in divorce. The divorce rate was rising annually, and in 1913 was higher than in any other country except Japan. Switzerland was a poor third, with only half as many divorces per capita as the United States, and Great Britain was fourth with $\frac{1}{36}$ of the American rate. This easing of the marital contract did not necessarily indicate lowered sexual morality, but it did open the door to legalized promiscuity.

In the relation between the sexes mechanical progress played its part for greater freedom. The motorcar enabled young people to escape the supervisions and limitations of the front parlor; the "movies" gave their audiences expert examples of the amatory art for their stimulus and emulation; the telephone made "dates" and assignations easier to arrange, and the new knowledge of birth control made copulation less indiscreet. In conservative circles chaperons were still in the tradition but not much in the picture, and most young people regarded them as amusingly vestigial. The fires of sexual indulgence may have burned no higher than in Victorian times, but they gave off much more smoke. Some regarded these changes as the healthy elimination of hypocrisies and inhibitions, but others deplored what the editors of the *Century Magazine* called "The Tidal Wave of Indecency."

Another of the causes of the revolution in social conventions was the new psychology. Though the theories of Dr. Freud had reached the United States in 1906 in medical journals, it was only when he came to lecture at Clark University and published in English his *Interpretation of Dreams* in 1913 that his ideas about sex aroused general attention. The press and the public then made up for lost time, and not until the recent publications of Dr. Alfred Kinsey was sex, its urges, variations, and frustrations, so enthusiastically publicized. The *American Magazine* protested that "no other leading psychotherapist has accepted this sweeping and audacious theory," but by 1913 the public, at least for conversational purposes, had swallowed it whole. Pretended familiarity with libidos and egos became the mark of the up-to-date intellectual in some urban societies; analyzing one's friends' sex urges was a social pastime; in Greenwich Village and along Park Avenue, it was smart to be "psyched."

Freud's work was an important contribution to psychology, and it was not his fault that it encouraged what Agnes Repplier was calling "the repeal of reticence." Though most Americans either denounced his theories or smirked over them, the public was, more than it realized, indirectly absorbing them. Novelists and playrights immediately began to utilize his motivations, and magazines speculated *ad nauseam* on the neuroses behind every known case of murder and bed-wetting. A man seeking an excuse to do what he wanted to do found one in Freud, and society became cluttered with the rampant expression of egos. Conservatives might agree with the *Scientific American* that Freud's ideas were, on the whole, "disgusting and wild interpretations," but those interpretations had become part of the permanent canon of literature, the arts, and society.

There were, of course, reactions to the apparent breakdown of social standards. Men who had never read Gibbon's *Decline and Fall* cited it gloomily as a warning of what would happen to America if its society continued to hasten blithely down the primrose path. Ministers pleaded and condemned from their pulpits, but it was Dr. Alfred Wallace, "England's grand old man of science," speaking from the eminence of his ninety years, who outdid all the Cassandras when he announced that "there has been no advance either in intellect or in morals from the days of the early Egyptians."

Vestigial Puritans tried to curb new sin with new laws against dancing, slit skirts, Sunday baseball, and scanty bathing suits, but all four forms of self-expression continued to flourish. Prohibitionists blamed it all on Demon Rum. Nine states adopted Prohibition before 1914; various towns and counties went dry on local option, and there was alarm lest the new habits and drinks might rob American men of their virility. Yale's athletic coaches explained away a year of defeats by deploring undergraduates who spent their time dancing and drinking and riding about in automobiles instead of hardening their muscles by football and rowing. An American admiral protested that the new safety razor would remove, after the manner of Delilah, men's masculinity with their sideburns and mustaches. The Dallas *Times* commented on the fact that the effete easterner was beginning to wear a wrist watch: "In winter we think he looks better carrying a muff." Thomas Bailey Aldrich invoked nostalgia in verse of dubious quality:

The oldtime fire, the antique grace:
You will not find them anywhere.
Today we breathe a commonplace
Polemic, scientific air.

In spite of all the extravagances of action and reaction, however, family life was usually the same old blend of affection and irritation between generations, and grated along its familiar routines with only a little more than normal parental alarm and filial resentment. The young were more openly intolerant of the ways and conventions of the old, and the old were more openly disturbed at the conduct and callowness of youth, but the changes were gradual enough to leave the men and women of 1913 less conscious of their full significance than the chronicler with the hindsight of the fifties. This was partly because Americans were less interested in improving their children's minds and manners than in enlarging their children's opportunities. To that end parents would work and sacrifice with a devotion that was often magnificent. It was also often misdirected, since parents were confused between the new and old values. Like a later flower of popular culture, Marilyn Monroe, they tended to "believe in everything—a little." But beneath their uncertainties and dismays, most Americans clung to the solacing conviction that American progress and prosperity was due to the unique virtues of their democratic system, which had the special approval of the Almighty. In 1912 Meredith Nicholson ended his *Hoosier Chronicle* in that comfortably exalted strain:

It's certainly amazing how times change, and I want to live as long as I can and keep on changing with them. Why, these farmers that used to potter round all winter worrying over their debts to the insurance companies are now going to Lafayette every January to learn how to make corn pay, and they're putting bathrooms in their houses and combing the hay out of their whiskers. It's all pretty comfortable and cheerful and busy in Indiana, with lots of old-fashioned human kindness flowing about, and it's getting better all the time. And I guess it's always got to be that way, out here in God's country.

With human kindness, even in Indiana, described as "old-fashioned," and progress defined in terms of bathtubs and profits on corn, it was inevitable that new priests of the religion of commerce and consumption should appear to preach their virtues. The Age of the Huckster was dawning. The advertising profession bloomed almost overnight, and began its work of convincing Americans that possessions made happiness, and therefore more possessions would make more happiness. Even in 1913 these prophets of the ever-expanding economy saw the infinite possibilities of propaganda, and they set out to build a world in which every sale and purchase was a contribution to national virtue. High-pressure salesmanship became "service"; installment buying was elevated to a declaration of faith in the future of America. Possessions were civilization, standardization was democracy, mechanical gadgets were culture, and all three were Progress.

In the *Independent* magazine George French predicted with enthusiasm that "the proper and legitimate field for advertising is infinitely wider than the promotion of the sale of merchandise or service. It may be employed in religion, in ethics, in civics, in the promotion of great charities." He visualized "the wonderful phenomenon of advertising playing the part of the greatest purifying element in business."

No wonder the Italian historian Guglielmo Ferrero, writing on "The Riddle of America," asked whether American worship of materialism was not the greatest threat to Western culture since the Tartars and the Huns. Were Americans only "barbarians laden with gold," or would they ultimately elevate world society? On the surface their pursuit of mundane riches did not seem to menace the highest traditions of European culture. But beneath the surface, Ferrero hinted, American society was giving quantity its most stupendous triumph over moral and spiritual quality. If qualitative values vanished from America, how long would they survive in Europe?

Ferrero left his questions unanswered, but a Midwestern American would soon submit a very emphatic answer. Sinclair Lewis differed from the hucksters on the virtues of American commercial "progress": "It has become a force seeking to dominate the earth, to drain the hills and sea of color. . . . It is . . . the small busy men, crush-

ingly powerful in their common purpose, viewing themselves as men
of the world but keeping themselves men of the cash-register and
comic film, who make the town a sterile anarchy."

Whatever one might think of Americans in 1913, it was clear that
they were making progress in some direction, though not along the
precise road found by John Bunyan's Christian pilgrim.

XIX
Adjustment

The years that ended with 1914 have been called An Age of Complacency and an Age of Ferment, an Age of Progress and an Age of Decline, and each title has its half-truth. To its citizens, 1913 was first of all a year of adjustment to new forces and values. Americans adapted themselves with enthusiasm to the uses of mechanical progress. But their mental and spiritual adjustment was less easy and less successful.

From the seventeenth century to the Civil War men had conceived of the universe as a system created by God, the secrets of which men might gradually learn but the operation of which He would always direct. It was a static concept in which men played a passive role. But Darwin and the rationalists transferred the immediate direction of events from God to natural forces. The course of the stars did not appear to be preordained other than by physical laws, and the development of life seemed to be a fortuitous and wasteful flux of mathematical chance. If men could master those laws, they could order nature and perhaps direct their own fates.

The effect on established religious doctrines was obvious, but it did not occur to many people that in diminishing the part of God in the supervision of the universe the new concepts also diminished man. Man had been the special and favorite creation of an omnipotent Being, but now he was only an adventitious development from a primitive cell.

Most Americans seemed to take this new concept in their stride, or thought they did. They were too busy utilizing the fruits of science to be greatly troubled by its religious implications. Man's new power to conquer the elements seemed to augment their status in the world, and the loss of an Omnipotent Benevolence that watched every sparrow fall did not seem to matter very much if man himself was on the way to benevolent omnipotence. Already men were flying through the air, and angels could do no more. . . .

Nevertheless the substitution of faith in progress for the faith of their fathers left many Americans of 1913 with a feeling of emptiness within. Those who could no longer really believe all the doctrines of their churches felt without them a lack of guidance and an unfulfillment of spirit. Many tried to fill the vacuum by the applied Christianity of good works, and they and their churches turned from faith and humility to humanitarianism and welfare work. They saved the surface but lost the depths of spiritual security.

Others tried to fill the spiritual void with any kind of activity that would make them forget it, and they pursued the gregarious life for mutual support, like children afraid to be alone in the dark. It was such men who organized empires and country clubs, built cities and held barbecues, but, with no idols except their own creations, remained socially-minded pagans.

Given the conditions and the American character, those results were inevitable. Americans were more practiced at organizing their souls than searching them, and it came naturally to them to serve a diminished God by the practical methods of their weekday activities. Directing a boys' club, administering a church charity, or expanding a company to employ more unemployed offered more tangible service to whatever deity they envisaged than prayer and self-approbation. Soul searching in solitude, that uncomfortable refuge of prophets and saints, seemed unsocial if not downright egotistic. Social service was more generous than the pursuit of self-perfection, and men who felt no selfishness in pursuing personal prosperity felt almost embarrassed at the idea of individual salvation. Organized good works and spiritual togetherness acquired an aura of religious virtue.

Americans had not yet learned that beneficent activity does not alone give spiritual strength and that whenever science makes a discovery the devil grabs it while the angels are debating the best way to use it. By 1913 an increasing number of good citizens, without knowing what was wrong, were feeling spiritually undernourished and disoriented. Others, more conscious of the vacuum, tried to fill it with some quasi-religious patent medicine.

Even the names of the new panaceas were significant of the quest for newness. One of the most popular was called New Thought, a jumble of refurbished religious clichés, pseudopsychology, and semi-sublimated materialism. Another was Christian Science, which denied the existence of evil, and hence of sickness, except in men's minds. There were also the literary physicians of the sick soul, a few with depth and sincerity, but most motivated by finding popular medications profitable. Ralph Waldo Trine, in a few inspirational pages, told seekers for reassurance how to get In Tune with the Infinite. Orison Swett Marden's Law of Religious Success told them how to have all this and Heaven too. Men and women who had never read a word of Hindu poetry or philosophy were plunging into the tepid waters of Rabindranath Tagore's verse, and thousands would shortly be confidently intoning, after Dr. Emile Coué: "Every day in every way I am getting better and better."

Most of these narcotics dulled the spiritual discrimination of more men and women than they helped, until they could not tell sincerity from charlatanism. Meanwhile, the intellectuals put philosophic props under scientific materialism. William James formulated a philosophic system that he hoped would allow for human self-direction within scientific determinism. He pictured the universe as a game of un-finished creation in which men might join, and since the rules of the game had not been permanently established, men might share in their formulation. He threw out the old absolutes and replaced them by what developed into pragmatism or the rationalism of expediency. The logic of this philosophic tour de force was not understood by most Americans, but it cheered them to think that their mundane pursuits had the philosopher's blessing.

John Dewey twisted the James theory inside out to reach the heart-ening conclusion (except for some qualifications his public ignored) that philosophic truth was measured by human welfare. This was eminently satisfactory to those who measured human welfare by their own prosperity or by a rising standard of living. Dr. Dewey told them, as they understood it, that what they wanted to believe virtue became virtue, by the fact that they wanted to think it so. Those who had difficulty in untangling this thought nevertheless concluded happily that Dewey's up-to-date philosophy supported modern science, and consequently approved the booming American Way of Life. It is difficult to say whether Dr. Dewey rationalized his thinking more than his public rationalized his rationalizations, but whatever he really meant he fortified Americans in their convictions that change was progress, good works were religion, and prosperity was virtue, and that consequently they and their society were moving onward and upward.

Feuerbach pointed out the ultimate absurdity of trying to make a religion of science when he said that according to science "Man is what he eats," but to most Americans science was the road to the particular Utopia they were seeking. Because scientific "proof" seemed to laymen the one dependable basis of knowledge and action, they tried to apply science to areas of life and feeling where its "proofs" were merely adventures in myopia. Thorstein Veblen would soon comment:

"On any large question which is to be disposed of for good and all, the final appeal is by common consent to the scientist. The solution offered in the name of science is decisive, so long as it is not set aside by a still more searching inquiry."

Of course, the best of the scientists never claimed that science alone could solve problems of human relations or feeling, or take the place of religious faith. They admitted that scientific truths were sometimes only tentative, or relative, and therefore only half-truths. They denied the ability of physical science to unveil the infinite, but to most Americans the very name of science was a word to conjure with. Philosophy and religion began to borrow its terms. Institutions of all kinds refurbished themselves and enhanced their popular standing by adopting "scientific methods." History, politics, and economics seemed less dismal after they were renamed social sciences. There were vogues of scientific management, scientific organization, scientific salesmanship. There were human science, popular science, the science of living, the science of personality, of marriage and even of beauty, whose high priestesses would soon be known as beauticians and cosmetologists. A New York undertaker, exalted by scientific nomenclature to the title of mortician, advertised that he would provide, at moderate prices, not only a scientific embalming but a scientific casket. In every area of knowledge and half-knowledge the prestige of science was invoked.

By 1913 most educators had embraced, sometimes against their better judgment, the trend of the times. In their effort to be scientific, humane scholars became unimaginatively factual. "Social scientists" grubbed out statistics unsusceptible of significant interpretations. Literary researchers began to spade up from the lives of minor poets details previously regarded as unnecessary to an understanding of their verse. Philosophers plucked with their academic tweezers individual hairs from the eyebrows of Plato, and turned them into professional careers. The assumptions that all human truth is best seen through a microscope or an adding machine was beginning to turn culture into the pedantic accumulation of trivia, and universities into haystacks where scholars searched for smaller and smaller needles.

There is much to be said for facts. Science requires them and society needs them. "Facts are more powerful than arguments," as Tom Paine said, and Governor Al Smith would soon iterate with his "Let's look at the record." Everyone can understand most facts, and that makes facts democratic and *ipso facto* virtuous. Most facts are useful, and America is in love with utility. Facts can be acquired by memory, which uses only a small part of the brain. Facts are bread and butter to Americans, who are often bored or uncomfortable in the presence of ideas or abstractions. "General ideas," as De Tocqueville said, "alarm their minds, which are accustomed to positive calculations, and they hold practice more in honor than theory." Or, as Anatole France put it: "The sciences are beneficent; they keep men from thinking"—a stimulating half-truth.

The worship of science, the pursuit of the factual, and the socialization of religion were all parts of a new formula that made an alliance between prosperity and virtue the newest of the American affirmations. Since the nation's unprecedented progress proved that it must be In Tune with the Infinite, it was every good American's duty to keep in tune by personal success, and personal success was almost certain if a man pursued it hard enough—and honestly, of course. "Young man," the great Horace Greeley had pontificated, "I would have you know that success in life is within the reach of everyone who will truly and nobly seek it."

Andrew Carnegie, naturally an authority on ethics because he had made millions and then given some of them away, was one of those who told the public that if a man was rich it was prima facie evidence that he was good. As early as 1891 he threw the toga of virtue over the shoulders of plutocracy, and the editor of the *North American Review* pronounced his contribution "the finest article that I have ever published in the *Review*." The rich man was a public benefactor, since his activities created more wealth, more employment, and the stimulus to others to do likewise. All wealth getting was virtuous as long as the accumulator regarded his wealth as a "public trust" and ultimately gave it away—except perhaps what he needed to maintain a mansion on Fifth Avenue, a castle in Scotland, and a private yacht and railway car. This laissez-faire humanitarianism, this sanctified solution of the fact that you can't take it with you, reassured the rich and disarmed the poor. The camel was halfway through the eye of the needle.

The Carnegie creed was echoed from Mount Zion. One of the loudest voices in praise of plutocracy came from the Reverend Russell H. Conwell, Baptist minister of Philadelphia. It was an influential voice, for Dr. Conwell had a national audience. His inspirational lecture "Acres of Diamonds" was so pleasing to the rich, and encouraging to the ambitious poor, that he repeated it from some six thousand platforms across America, and it presumably brought him its own acres of diamonds from several printed editions as well. According to this oft-banqueted divine:

"To secure wealth is an honorable ambition, and is one great test of a person's usefulness to others. . . . Money is power. . . . Every man and woman ought to strive for power, and to do good with it when obtained. . . . I say, get rich, get rich! But get money honestly, or it will be a withering curse."

A still finer halo was added to the brow of the millionaire by a far more elevated divine. The distinguished Episcopalian Bishop William Lawrence of Massachusetts, whose birth and inheritance made him the most acceptable if not the most ascetic prelate in New England, associated with Carnegie in an encomium that, coming from a less ecclesiastical source, might have seemed blasphemy:

"In the long run it is only to the men of morality that wealth comes. Godliness is in league with riches. Material prosperity is helping to make the national character sweeter, more joyous, more unselfish, more Christlike."

Philadelphia and Boston preachers had come a long way from their Quaker and Puritan origins.

Those Americans who accepted the bishop's deification of mammon had some difficulty in reconciling the new Christianity of coupon clipping with the religious tenets of their inheritance. The easiest way to escape from a troubled conscience is to delegate ethical responsibility to someone else. Since Protestants have no Pope for that purpose, they make one out of the new concept of democracy by going along with the opinions of the popular majority. Forced by a complex society to be increasingly dependent on others; led by the latest thinking to think of himself as merely a unit in a social organism; made by propinquity, urbanism, and the press more conscious than ever before of the tastes and opinions of the people around him, the average American became more and more anxious to adapt his opinions to the mass. The new education preached adjustment of the individual to society, and looked askance at any man's vehement dissents from popular and hence democratic beliefs. All the social pressures of the new society were to substitute group direction for self-direction.

Adjustment to the group had additional attractions to men of 1913. By acquiescing to majority opinions a man could avoid not only personal responsibility but the necessity of having to think for himself and defend his own views. And the man uncertain of himself and his worth could find in his acceptance by the group a sense of security that religion and self-sufficiency formerly supplied. In yielding to the group a man's ego might lose in stature but it gained in comfort.

The move from inner- to other-direction brought changes in the characteristics of Americans. Success in the group depended upon adaptability, capacity for compromise, persuasive powers and, above all, personality. It is significant that about this time best sellers were written on How to Make Friends and Influence People. To make "friends" by the hundred, flexibility of mind is more successful than firm convictions. It is antisocial to be too dogged or dogmatic, and not to cooperate is to be antagonistic. In matters of right and wrong the only group morality is measured by group success; therefore whatever succeeds is moral. Ethics become pragmatic; the group ends justify the group means; moral indignation and ethical absolutes go out of fashion. In matters of principle the other-directed man pleads *nolo contendere*.

Other-direction consequently breeds men more sensitive to the reactions of others than to personal conscience, more cautious than downright, more elastic than stalwart. The perfect member of an other-directed society would, like the citizens of Aldous Huxley's *Brave New World*, not only defer to the majority but do so systematically, joyously, and with a conviction of virtue. "Its members," in the words of Erich Fromm, "must acquire the kind of character that makes them want to act the way they have to act."

Leadership in an other-directed society depends on a man's ability to sense what group opinion will be, and get the credit for stating and acting on it first. Other-directed education must condition each child to develop his personal radar set that will tell him what others think, and must condition him to think as they do—an "adjustment to society." Democratic government in an other-directed society consists in finding the lowest common multiple and then making it national policy. Public opinion in such a society tends to be volatile, since it has no criterion except the shifting sands of mass emotions. Unity in such a society is frail, for it is based, not on strong individual convictions, but on fragile acquiescence by those who have merely gone along with the crowd. The symbol of other-directed society is obviously the bandwagon.

Americans of 1913 had not reached that advanced stage of other-direction, but they were on their way. Even that rare individual who resisted mass values and mass opinions could not prevent his children from deferring to them as naturally as they breathed the air about them. He was merely postponing for a generation the new concepts of democracy, society, and morality that other-direction would bring.

The older affirmations could not hold their own against the new, not because they had ceased to be voiced but because they had ceased to be lived. The newer ones were more readily accepted because they seemed to fill vacuums of the spirit. The change was basic. Whether the change would elevate man and society remained to be seen, but it was already creating a different America.

XX

Portents

A familiar law of physics seemed to govern American attitudes in 1913 toward the likelihood of war in Europe: to every action there was an equal and contrary reaction. Each disturbing news item from overseas was promptly offset by a domestic reassurance. Each dire prediction by a European expert was countered by the optimism of an American authority. Potsdam might rattle the saber or France voice fresh alarm, but the next day someone would assure Americans that a major war was unlikely. This is not a history of European affairs, and will review the armaments race only to record American reactions to it.

At the beginning of 1913 the blackest clouds on the European horizon were the races in naval building between Germany and Britain, and in army expansion between Germany and France. Germany was forcing the pace in both, but the Germans insisted their policy was wholly defensive, forced by Britain's naval strength and the belligerence of France. Britain was determined to maintain whatever pace in naval construction Germany might set. In January, 1913, it was clear that a record year of warship building lay ahead. Germany was pressing its naval competition, and in Britain twelve more battleships were under construction. British shipyards were so busy building armed ships for themselves and their Allies that they were forced to refuse many orders for new commercial vessels.

Americans reacted to the naval race in several ways. Although they admired German efficiency, most of them did not approve Germany's effort to compete with Britain in sea power. They preferred to share the sovereignty of the seas with the British navy as their only equal partner, and feared the results of a European naval rivalry. Nearly all Americans hoped the President would find some way to persuade both Germany and Britain to stop building new battleships, though few agreed with Secretary Bryan that the United States should begin the disarmament parade by reducing its own navy unilaterally. Though most Americans opposed a large standing army, they thought the United States should have a navy equal in strength to that of Britain or any other nation. The American navy had two oceans and the Monroe Doctrine to defend; Americans had a new interest in their "manifest destiny" in the Pacific. The Navy League was urging on Congress "a consistent program of naval construction" and increases in the efficiency of naval personnel. But the House rejected by 174 to 156 a proposal to build two additional battleships, and the appropriation for navy development was not increased.

Nearly all Americans applauded when on March 26th the young First Lord of the Admiralty Winston Churchill proposed in a public speech that the leading Powers agree to a one-year holiday from the building of warships, and added: "I address this proposal to all nations, and to no nation with more sincerity than to our great neighbor over the North Sea." The American government expressed its sympathy with the proposal, but three days later Germany gave a cold answer by announcing plans to build a still more powerful fleet. Not all Germans were happy about that reply, and the New York *Times* correspondent in Berlin reported: "The German people is dazed by the magnitude of the sacrifices it is asked to make for the purpose of strengthening the army and navy, not only by land and sea, but also by air." The Kaiser tried to counter these doubts in the minds of his people by asserting, "The Empire is in peril." The naval race continued.

England repeated its proposal for a naval holiday later in the year, and Secretary Bryan, who was urging his own peace plan, officially supported the Churchill proposal. But Admiral von Tirpitz told a British reporter that Germany would continue its naval expansion as planned, and neither British nor Americans derived much comfort from the admiral's assurance: "The German navy has a purely defensive function and no aggressive purpose . . . a war of aggression is unthinkable to Germany." Even if one could believe the admiral, one did not need to be a military strategist to recognize that by taking a merely defensive role the German navy could act as a shield to aggressive moves by the German army on land. As for a war of aggression, aggression was a matter of definition; a nation seldom conceded that it had begun a war. The German public, influenced by Potsdam propaganda, might come to believe that the German empire was "in peril" and that to attack some small country like Belgium was a necessary defensive move.

It was only toward the end of the year that the United States government took modest steps to strengthen its navy. On December 1st Secretary of the Navy Josephus Daniels asked Congress for funds to build two new dreadnoughts, eight destroyers, and three submarines, and also urged that the federal government acquire and operate enough oil wells and refineries to assure the navy adequate supplies. He hastened to add that he did not ask expansion because the navy might be called upon to fight, but to enhance American prestige as a force toward world peace. So that these modest proposals would not be interpreted as entering the United States in the naval race, Secretary Daniels repeated his support of the Churchill proposal, and on December 9th the House approved, 317 to 11, its own naval-holiday resolution.

If the United States Navy, already strong, needed amplification, the situation of the army was far more drastic. Apart from small contingents outside the continental United States, the United States land forces of trained men ready for immediate active duty numbered some 35,000. This compared with Germany's trained force in being of some 700,000, with Russia's army still larger and France's only a little less. In his report as Chief of Staff, Major General Leonard Wood urged rapid rearmament because "a proper armament is the surest guarantee of peace." He said that a war would find America badly prepared; its military weakness was "shocking" although its tiny army was highly efficient. In May former President Taft, whom no one thought alarmist, told the readers of the *Times* that the country was "ludicrously unprepared," though his word "ludicrously" did not later seem the happiest adverb he could have used.

Nevertheless in late March Secretary of War Garrison told Congress that he would not ask for any increase in the size of the Army's regular forces, and added that General Wood had not "urged" such an increase. The Secretary did ask for an increase in effective army reserves but nearly every Secretary of War asked for that, so steps taken in that direction were made with bureaucratic deliberation, and the public did not take the proposal as indicating any real concern about a future war. The year consequently ended with no major administration requests or budget increases for army expansion. If Americans judged the European war danger only by the words and actions of their own government, they were justified in concluding that there was nothing to worry about.

Many Americans who posed as unofficial authorities were insisting that Germany was the most peaceful and civilized of nations. Price Collier, whose books on Europe were widely read, told his readers in 1913 after a visit to Germany that "The Germany army . . . is the greatest school of hygiene in the world . . . the best all-round university in the world . . . the German army takes the place of our West, of our games, of our sports. . . . My latest visit to Germany has converted me completely to the wisdom of compulsory [military] service." Andrew Carnegie appeared to regard the Kaiser as the greatest exponent of peace in Europe and was certain of the peaceful intentions of Germany. Writing on "The Baseless Fear of War" in the *Independent*, he asked and answered rhetorical questions in a sledgehammer style worthy of his success as a steelmaster:

"Has there ever been danger of war between Germany and ourselves, members of the same Teutonic race? Never has it been imagined. Not one of the additional warships demanded this year, if built, in all probability will ever fire a shot against the foe. . . . Forty-five million dollars needlessly squandered. . . . All nations are our friends and we are the friends of all."

The editors of the *Independent* supported Mr. Carnegie's opinion with the statement that "no living man is better qualified to write on this subject," and added their own conviction: "There is a deliberate movement now under way to plunge the country into the mad military scramble of the European nations. . . . Yet we do not have an enemy on the face of the earth, and we challenge anyone in seriousness to specify a single power that has the remotest intention of attacking us."

The attitude of the *Independent* was typical of American idealists and intellectuals, who simply would not believe that the peoples of Europe would let their governments go to war. If the German militarists, for example, tried to begin a war, the powerful German Socialist party would threaten a general strike. University people in particular believed that their opposite numbers of Europe would oppose war and that governments would not dare to fight without their support. Wishful thinking was never more potent in educated minds.

There were some Americans less certain that Germany's intentions were peaceful. Alfred H. Fried, in the New York *Times* of January 12th, said that Berlin was the most dangerous storm center in Europe. Theodore Roosevelt had written privately to his friend Cecil Spring-Rice, the British ambassador eight years earlier: "I should never dream of counting on [the Kaiser's] friendship for this country. He respects us because he thinks we have a pretty good navy with which to fight." Even the ovation T. R. received in Germany and the personal honors done him by the Kaiser did not disarm him altogether, for just after that last visit he wrote to the British historian G. M. Trevelyan: "Germany has the arrogance of a very strong power, as yet almost untouched by that feeble aspiration toward international equity which one or two other strong powers, notably England and America, do at least begin to feel." But in 1913 T. R. was only a private citizen, and most Americans did not know how strong were his reservations about the peaceful intentions of the Kaiser and the Potsdam crowd.

President David Starr Jordan, of Leland Stanford Junior University, revered especially by liberals and the religious-minded, struck manful blows against American preparedness. He wrote articles and speeches in which he estimated that the cost of a major European war would be some $55,000,000 a day, and said that the treasuries of Europe could not possibly afford it. What was more, "the common man . . . would have a word or two to say. . . . Therefore the great war will never come. Humanly speaking, it is impossible." Dr. Jordan's remarks were well timed, concurrent with the House debates on the Navy Construction bill and with the issuance of invitations to attend the fourth annual Peace Conference in St. Louis beginning on May 1st.

In spite of such reassurances from high places, disturbing facts, opinions, and rumors kept flooding in, and the American public could not dispose of all of them as merely alarmist. In the January *Atlantic Monthly* the Italian historian Ferrero, whom T. R.'s admiration had made a well-known name in America, wrote on "The Danger of War in Europe":

> The neglect of public duties by the class which once bore the entire responsibility is one of the most regrettable results of industrial development and universal wealth. . . . Standing between the alternatives of war on the one hand, and of lawlessness on the other, the European nations are all equally bewildered, while the approaching crisis is all the more serious because thinking men are giving up politics for business.

André Tardieu, editor of *La Revue des Deux Mondes*, wrote that war was possible, if for no other reason than "due to chance or a madman or a fool, and again because . . . there are feelings that are forces for war." And Sir Arthur Conan Doyle, distracted for the moment from Sherlock Holmes and the advocacy of a tunnel under the English Channel, reported that he had never seriously believed in the German menace but that war could come by "some insane act," and added that after reading Friedrich von Bernhardi's *Germany and the Next War* he feared such an insane act was more than possible.

This was talk, but in March German newspapers regarded as spokesmen for the government announced with striking uniformity that Germany must increase its rearming because it was threatened by France. "Never," said one of them, "were our relations with our western neighbor so strained as today. . . . The French made their Russian alliance and their English friendship for the sole purpose of recapturing Alsace-Lorraine." The following day the Berlin Bourse slumped badly, owing, everyone agreed, to "uneasiness," especially as to relations with France.

In Paris the report brought real alarm, particularly after *L'Intransigeant* announced that the French government had learned that on January 13th Germany had asked Italy whether it would be ready to join Germany and Austria-Hungary in a campaign, to begin in October, "to put an end by decisive action to the general uneasiness in Europe." The French government sharply rebuked the press for disseminating such a report without authorization, but it did not deny the story. Had it done so, the man on the boulevards would not have been reassured, for he would have concluded that even if the report were true his government would have found it expedient to deny it.

Such items of news from Europe were generally printed in only the largest metropolitan dailies in America, and then often on an inner page. On March 2nd, for example, foreign correspondents of the New York *Times* reported that the European nations were still increasing and hastening their preparations for war, but on the following day its editorial page concluded: "The nearer the Powers, armed to the teeth, come to war, the more they dread to enter upon it." The logic of that position, a little like that of a cold-war Secretary of State, implied that the best way to avoid falling over a precipice was for all concerned to lean as far as possible over the brink. Two days after the attack on France by German newspapers, the *Times* reported that the European war scare "is not being taken seriously by the New York bankers." Someone in Wall Street was taking it seriously, judging from suddenly declining stock prices, especially of European securities.

The German press attack on France was promptly followed by German government action. Potsdam announced on March 13th that it proposed to increase its standing army by another 150,000 men, making the total under arms of some 850,000, and said that the cost of this expansion would be met by a new tax on all personal property.

For once the dams restraining German public criticism of its government broke under the flood of protests. The Frankfurter *Zeitung*, for example, called the proposed tax "a proper product of the drunkenness over armaments." At this crucial point Karl Liebknecht, leader of the Socialist party in the Reichstag, charged that the growing militarism was being deliberately stimulated by secret agreements between members of the European steel and armaments cartels on the one hand and the militarists on the other. The industrialists were augmenting the war scare in order to secure larger orders and greater profits. Liebknecht said he could prove that officials of the Krupp Works and of the Imperial War Staff were together subsidizing certain newspapers to conduct a campaign of hate and fear against other nations. The Krupps, he said, were actually selling steel to France and other countries for 30 per cent less than they were charging the German government, and this was with the approval of certain German military leaders who paid the extra price in return for the Krupps' cooperation in stirring up war spirit.

The charge shocked or alarmed nearly everyone in Europe and even stirred American opinion. Were the Liebknecht charges true? It is interesting that on November 12th of the same year Sir William Tyrrell, Permanent Undersecretary for Foreign Affairs, told Colonel House privately, the colonel recorded, that "an armament trust was forcing all governments not only to pay excessive prices, but was creating war scares." The American reaction to the Liebknecht charges was that no German parliamentarian leader, not even a socialist, would make up such charges out of whole cloth and thus deliberately discredit his nation. If what Liebknecht said was not wholly true it was probably largely true, and something ought to be done about it. But in the long run Liebknecht's charges served more as a soporific than as a warning to Americans, who thought that now the corruption was revealed it would cease. The charges gave Americans the villain they had been looking for, and made the solution of European militarism seem simpler: arrest and publish the guilty parties, and the danger of war would end. The militarists and the cartels became the sole scapegoats, and the deeper factors pressing Europe into war were ignored by an American public relieved that now, at last, it understood the situation.

The effects of the latest German military plans were prompt and far-reaching. On June 15th the French Minister of War said: "Germany would not suddenly raise her effective forces from 700,000 to 880,000 unless she had designs. It is not for me to fathom those designs . . . but it is my duty as French Minister of War to take all due precautions. . . . We want peace."

In competing with Germany in manpower, the French were playing a losing game, but they could see no alternative. The French population was less than that of Germany, and its army numbered some 550,000 men. The French birth rate was lower, and still falling, and though its government had recently offered a subsidy to French fathers with more than three children, this production incentive would not provide more soldiers to defend France for another twenty years. Germany could increase its standing army by calling up still more young men; France could do so only by increasing the term of service. To most Frenchmen the prospect of a third year of compulsory service in the army was at least as unpalatable as the proposed 5 per cent tax on personal property was to most Germans.

French socialists and labor leaders threatened not to cooperate with the government if the three-year military service law was passed, and French businessmen were troubled at its effect on the labor market and at the increase of taxes necessary to finance an added military cost estimated at $115,000,000. There were mutinous incidents in three French army camps, and eight "syndicalists" were arrested on charges of inciting to desertion and rebellion. The only hope was that the Reichstag would not approve the proposed expansion. A group of distinguished French intellectuals, including thirty-five Sorbonne professors and Anatole France, issued a manifesto urging "calm consideration of the proposed military measures."

British alarm was not lessened by Sir Edward Grey's statement that Europe had been on the very edge of war a month or two earlier over the question of Albania. Englishmen began to talk seriously of what had always been anathema to them—universal peacetime con-

scription for military training and service. Russia promptly planned
to balance the German increase by enlarging its own army by three
new corps, and was reported to be planning to spend a billion dollars
over the next two years to expand its navy. Austria-Hungary, fearing
Russia, proposed to increase its army in proportion, and even Belgium
and Switzerland began to discuss enlarging their military forces.

The exchanges in Europe were so depressed that the fact was headline news on American financial pages. The bourses in Paris and Berlin were more nervous than ever, though in both cases the government
took undercover steps to bolster confidence. On June 8th the slump
on the London Exchange was so serious that it spoiled the holiday
spirits of the Derby Day weekend and left London theaters and restaurants half empty when they were usually crowded. Stocks in New
York on June 5th were the lowest in five years, owing to "foreign
liquidation to meet European capital and tax need and general political uncertainties"—financial jargon for "fear of war."

It became clear that German belligerency and distortion of truth
were not limited to the military set and the armaments interests. In
June, Americans got their first look at a preface the crown prince had
written to a new book entitled *Germany in Arms*. The prince announced: "The sword will remain the final and deciding factor until
the world's end. . . . Only with the support of our good sword we
maintain that place in the sun which is due us, but is not willingly
accorded to us." The German press, except for a few independent
liberal papers, was shouting defiance at other nations, and suddenly
made the United States the temporary target of virulent criticisms.
On June 29th the official periodical of the German National party
said: "In Woodrow Wilson one of the most dangerous agitators of
modern times has succeeded in attaining one of the highest political
offices in the world," and characterized his internal currency reforms
as "a new peril for the economic peace of the world . . . a frontal attack
against the concentration of capital [and] a demagogical appeal in
favor of impecunious money seekers." German government-controlled
newspapers denounced American policy toward Mexico as selfish,
weak, vacillating, bellicose, and absurd.

The German press of all parties pronounced Secretary Bryan incompetent, and so ignorant of foreign affairs that he had confused Germany with Russia and Bucharest with Budapest (which some Americans thought quite possible). Mr. Bryan's Chautauqua lecturing laid him open to blistering attacks by the German press, and they made the most of it. Perhaps the special irritation with Mr. Bryan was due to his announcement, more optimistic than meaningful, that his peace plan had received favorable responses from twenty nations, including Britain, France, Russia, and Germany.

The American belief that the intellectuals of Germany would resist the war spirit proved erroneous, for many of them rallied around the screaming German eagle. Professor Adolph Wagner announced: "We Germans are not sufficiently warlike. The military spirit came to us too late. Germany . . . is pacific, but [France] think[s] of nothing but Alsace and Lorraine. [Its] officers ceaselessly point out to their soldiers the eternal enemy—Germany." Hermann Sudermann, whose plays were being read and praised in American universities, offered a new version of history: "Prussia and Germany, since the Middle Ages, have never fought except to defend themselves." At a full-dress symposium, German scholars agreed that France was the bellicose villain that was forcing Germany to reluctant measures of defense. According to Maximilian Harden, editor of *Die Zukunft*, ". . . certain signs show that there is a France obsessed by warlike ardor . . . the hostility between Germany and France is being kept alive by France alone." Theodore Wolff of the *Berliner Tageblatt* said: "For fifteen years the German emperor, the government and the public have done everything possible toward reconciliation with [France]. They have received nothing but rebuffs."

The Reichstag's action on the new military proposals disappointed those who thought the liberal forces in Germany would rebel. On July 1st it passed the bill increasing the Germany army and the German taxes, with only the socialist, Alsatian, and Polish members opposing. A week later France passed its three-year conscription bill, and other European nations moved toward further armaments with an air of helpless inevitability. It is hard to see in 1960 why the handwriting on the wall was not then clear to all the world. But there were no devastating reactions in the world's money markets, probably because they had already discounted the Reichstag's action. For the balance of the year the financial centers appeared calm, probably with the fatalistic passivity of men prepared to hear the ship strike on the rocks at any moment. On July 11th the New York stock market had its dullest day in seventeen years, with stock sales totaling only 64,000 shares. The Paris Bourse remained throughout July "almost wholly inactive [owing] to indecision and lack of confidence." Financial experts believed that even if war did not come, the war budgets would wreck the economy of Europe and drive kings and governments to desperation.

Americans were still receiving reassurances from high places. Secretary Bryan orated mellifluously that "conditions promising world peace were never more favorable than now, and in saying that, I have special reference to those wars that might occur between great powers." David Starr Jordan continued to assure his countrymen that "great international wars are practically at an end"—a statement in which both speaker and audience ignored the qualifying adverb. Norman Angell of England, whose *The Great Illusion* was widely read in America, insisted: "Cessations of all military conflict between powers like France and Germany, or Germany and England, or Russia and Germany, has already come . . . nothing will induce them to take the immense risks of using their preposterous military instruments, if [again the ignored loophole] they can possibly avoid it." Roger Babson, the business expert, returned from Europe to announce his conviction that "Germany does not want war . . . she has not the funds nor the credit . . . she is too keen for making money," but he too qualified his dogmatism by the afterthought that none of the Powers would start war "this year . . . for none of them are ready." Mr. Babson's most original prediction was the one taken least seriously: "Russia will some day rule Europe."

Every statesman must occasionally lie a little for his country. Sir Edward Grey was a model of personal integrity, but some of his public statements expressed more optimism than he could have felt. In

August he told the House of Commons that the Concert of Europe was a reality, that the Powers were not ranged against each other in two separate groups, and that discord between them was unlikely. The effect of his words was, however, somewhat impaired by that irrepressible and, some thought, irresponsible future prime minister, David Lloyd George, who, on the very next day, gave the Commons a different estimate. He said the Powers were scaring each other into such great military expenditures that he feared it would end in disaster. As Chancellor of the Exchequer he probably meant financial disaster, and there were many businessmen in Europe and America who feared panic more than war.

The Philadelphia *Record* commented that "the world is not saving money fast enough to meet the requirements of governments and corporations," and one man from Wall Street suggested that the public could stop war by refusing to buy the bonds of the various European governments. Economists deplored the effects of taking from European productive activities several million young men for military service, and the *London Economist* pronounced: "The world is over-loaded and over-armed." Everyone agreed on one thing: "Now is a poor time to borrow money."

Elihu Root, former Secretary of State, brought a new note into the debate when he warned that the situation in Europe was no longer within the control of a few leaders. "It is not the governments but the people from whom the danger of war comes today, and will always come so long as they fail to exercise proper self-restraint and the courtesy that peace of the world demands."

If anyone hoped that the new American ambassador to Berlin would promptly ease the tensions of the Wilhelmstrasse, he underestimated the priorities of diplomacy. Mr. Gerard was busily engaged in finding what he regarded as "suitable quarters" for his embassy. The realization of his high standards proved so difficult that as late as October 12th he reported himself "spending most of his time" on that important matter. Such devotion to diplomatic duty eventually won its reward, for on November he was able to inform the State Department that he had rented Schwabach Palace, which he thought

would prove adequate to the prestige of his embassy. He felt compelled to add that the bill for rent and repairs might be higher than
the Department would be willing to pay, and he assured President
Wilson that if necessary he would contribute from his own pocket—
and that the proper redecoration of the palace would of course make
demands on his time as well as his purse. . . . It is fair to add that
Professor Charles Seymour, editor of the House letters, later wrote
that "Mr. Gerard was excelled by none in the dignity and capacity
with which he maintained the interests and furthered the policy of
his government."

The cold facts and hot emotions of Europe could have been mis-
interpreted only by wishful thinkers. It was clear that the psychology
of Europe was becoming almost as inflammable as its explosives. Late
in November there were antiwar and anti-German riots in German-
held Alsace, and "German bayonets dealt very harshly with the French
population"—so harshly that questions were asked in the Reichstag
by its socialist members. The futility of German opposition to Potsdam was made clear by the results. The Kaiser settled the matter by
making a personal statement approving the use of martial law and the
bloodstained bayonets of his troops in Alsace, and the social protest
ended.

In other cases the emotional reactions were more indicative than
the events that caused them. Certain German officers observing as
guests the peacetime maneuvers of the little British army reported
on their return that the British operations were "a fiasco . . . joy
rides by day and full-dress parties by night . . . no officer without a
valet, three changes of uniform and afternoon tea," while the enlisted
men went unfed because transport trains were lost in the confusion
and not found again until after the maneuvers had ended. Germans
did not conceal their delight in this somewhat erroneous report, which
however had enough truth in it to hurt, and destroyed what little
was left of British friendship for German military figures.

As December came, everyone in America seemed eager to forget
international alarms or convert them to the Christmas spirit. No one
tried harder than Secretary Bryan, who on December 11th told the

Canadian Society of New York that there would be no war between the United States and any other country during the Wilson administration. The American Association for International Conciliation carried conciliation toward farce by sending a year-end address to the Kaiser congratulating him for "the maintenance of twenty-five years of unbroken peace between Germany and the other nations of the world. . . . More than once during the past twenty-five years it has been the high privilege of Your Majesty not only to exercise peaceful forbearance but to inspire it in others." The document bore the signature of Nicholas Murray Butler and many other presidents of colleges dedicated to the discovery and dissemination of truth, as well as of Andrew Carnegie and the presidents of United States Steel, the National Academy of Design, the American Institute for Arbitration, the American Historical Association, the National Education Association, the American Bankers' Association, the American Bar Association, and the National Academy of Science. As a Christmas card, the message was a masterpiece of romantic fiction.

In its review of the year the New York *Times* stressed, as striking evidence of progress toward world peace, the new agreements reached during the year between the European Powers. Unfortunately most of them, such as those concerning Angola, Rhodesia, Mozambique, and the Portuguese colonies, were trivial compared to the issues the Great Powers had obviously not settled. The *Times* editors were forced to admit that world peace was still unfinished business.

This somewhat plumless pudding for a happy new year was generously sweetened by no less a person than the Prime Minister of Great Britain. Mr. Asquith assured the world that Anglo-German relations were never better. Those who read his statement did not know what Lord Asquith would write years later: that during 1912 European diplomats were conscious that they "were skating on the thinnest of ice and that the peace of Europe was at the mercy of a chapter of unforeseen and unforeseeable incidents." History, as recorded by the pen of a statesman, does not always repeat itself.

As for the American people, their attitude at the end of the year was probably as accurately pictured by Mark Sullivan as by any other man, when he wrote:

No one wanted war. We were sure we would never again be in a major war, even if, as a few thought possible, Europe went to war. We had an aggressive humanitarianism; we were trying arbitration treaties, international peace movements, naval holidays. But we could still joke about the "Wilson tango—one step forward, two steps backward; hesitate!"

XXI

Hindsight

"Epochs sometimes occur in the life of a nation when the old customs of a people are changed, public morality is destroyed, religious beliefs shaken, and the spell of tradition is broken."

De Tocqueville, writing of American democracy more than a century earlier, could hardly have been more prophetic. Americans of 1913 were among the victims and the creators of such an epoch. They did not think of themselves as either different or iconoclastic; the changes and demolitions came piecemeal, and seemed merely part of the day's work.

Neither the man in the street nor the man in the White House foresaw that 1913 would mark the end of the familiar world. Even the few who envisaged world war did not guess how different would be the society that survived it. The war itself was not the primary cause of change; it merely hastened and accentuated forces already germinating in society. In the long run the fall of Belgium was less significant than the collapse of religious faith; the victory sealed at Versailles less historic than the victories of factory over farm and determinism over free will. The war was merely the catalytic agent of spiritual dismay, and except for its physical destruction it wrought no changes that economic and social fermentation would not in their own good time have brought about.

The significance of 1913 lies in how Americans reacted to its events. Democracy offered them its greatest test of their foresight and self-control. The ways they met and failed to meet the issues of their time threw light on their democratic form of government as well as on the American character. Since that light reveals some weaknesses in both, let us record immediately that it also disclosed strengths. The greatest of these strengths was the nation's capacity to meet crisis. When faced with danger too great and imminent to be ignored—whether of war, economic crisis, political corruption, or plutocratic oligarchy—American society summoned up the courage and unity to overcome it. Under its surface flabbiness of mind and body, it proved there were good iron and muscle; that beneath its habitual self-indulgence lay some capacity for sacrifice; that from behind its façade of cynicism and expediency were strong foundations of subconscious idealism. And not the least of American strengths in such crises was a grumbling good nature and a wise-cracking humor that made all men partners and all trials endurable.

But even to those virtues one must attach qualifications. Such strengths appeared only when the challenge was clearly unavoidable, and did not outlast the immediate need. The national genius did not include the capacity to envisage the untoward logic of events or to prepare adequately for them, or to make the most, after victory, of the experience and opportunity. In its attitudes toward European war, industrial strife, and the problems of urbanization, the nation revealed in 1913 a tendency to be caught by events rather than to anticipate them—to face up to crises, but not to the lessons they should teach.

This is partly because Americans as a whole had not kept intellectually or spiritually fit; they had to be allowed time to think, to get into condition, to remember how to pray; and their best qualities did not emerge without delays, exhortations, and shocking wastes. Their process of getting ready, mentally and physically, was an expensive one. Geography and good luck have allowed them time; the future may not be so considerate.

Americans of 1913 were living simultaneously in two worlds, one dying and the other in creation. Products of one culture, they were developing another, and could not reconcile the two. They could not wholly shake off the emotional attachments of their past, or envisage and control a future they were eager to embrace. Like children eager to assert their independence, they were running away from the old home, but with many a backward glance, at once resisting and depending on parental faiths and securities.

Like children, too, they could not see the duality of their own natures or understand the emotions that pulled them back and forth. The man of 1913 illustrated how American culture has been determined more by popular emotion than by reason or leadership. He was not the first man in history to try to make the best of both worlds, but few of his predecessors straddled two worlds so different or attempted to reconcile the two with more naïveté and less success.

That was partly because Americans were still a young nation in history. And even younger in their group emotions. They used their short history as an excuse for their faults, and called them merely growing pains. They even considered their youth a virtue in itself, boasting their vigor, optimism, crudeness, breezy lack of subtlety, and juvenile pleasures and aims. They admired their young so much that they emulated them, and to be called boyish was a high compliment to a man of fifty. No society was ever more deferential to its children; it played up to them and down to them; it spoiled them, sacrificed for them, worried about them, and gave them everything except what their elders lacked—self-discipline and mature values. Americans delighted in perpetuating their children's adolescence, and their own.

An individual has reached maturity when he can reconcile his reason with his emotions and his outer life with his inner; when he can face events rationally and act his age. An immature person, unable to integrate his personality with his life, is thrown off balance when confronted with unforeseen problems and new situations. Reluctant to face unpleasant realities, he declines to recognize them, and retreats into the security of familiar patterns or escapes into his own world of illusions. Uncertain of his standards, he substitutes emotions for judgments; reluctant to admit his mistakes, he seeks a convenient scapegoat. Toward other people he alternates between aggressive overconfidence and alarmed retreat.

If a society can be measured by the same tests, then the devotion of Americans to the qualities of youth has significance. Their reactions to change were those of emotional adolescents. In their relations with the rest of the world they alternated between overconfidence and dismay, and withdrew from difficult problems into the false security of the traditional myth. When events displeased them, they sought for the mote in their neighbor's eye without considering their own, and demanded an investigation. They comforted their sense of virtue by preaching to other men and nations an ethic they no longer applied to themselves. When they felt their problems too difficult, they turned to some paternal power, like government or mass opinion. Their spiritual uncertainties betrayed themselves in their emotional volatility, so that in a single week events could lift them to excessive optimism or plunge them into excessive uncertainty. When all went well they exulted in their brave new world, but when that world troubled them they turned to the old affirmations as a nervous woman turns to narcotics. And like children bursting out of a schoolroom, they sought in noisy activity a remedy for the trying ordeal of abstract thinking. Are those characteristics still patent in American society of 1961?

As early as 1830 the perceptive De Tocqueville suggested that the freedoms of democracy might lead to a childlike passion of acquisitiveness. "When a child begins to move in the midst of objects that surround him, he is instinctively led to appropriate to himself everything he can lay his hands upon. . . . The lower orders, when they are first invested with political rights, stand in relation to those rights as a child does to the whole of nature." The men and women of 1913, surrounded by all the gifts of nature, were not unlike eager boys before the Christmas tree.

As De Tocqueville watched popular democracy of the Jacksonian era ride the crest of power, he observed its concentration on getting and spending. In 1848 he speculated: "Can it be believed that the democracy which has overthrown the feudal system and vanquished kings will retreat before tradesmen and capitalists?" and continue to neglect "the first of its duties . . . to educate democracy; to reawaken, if possible, its religious beliefs; to purify its morals; to mold its actions?" If he saw the America of 1848 as an exponent of rampant acquisitiveness, what would he have thought of the America of the Gilded Age and the new century?

It was not the outward symbols of the Acquisitive Age—its trusts, skyscrapers, automobiles, and great cities with their factories and slums—that threatened most seriously to undermine American character. A greater danger lay in the confusion of values such developments brought to men's minds and spirits. The orgy of materialism nearly submerged any higher aim and even affected the creative quality of those who wrote or painted or taught. Their realism was too often idealism turned cynical, their romanticism a flight from reality. "A people cannot recover the sentiments of their youth, any more than a man can return to the innocent tastes of childhood; such things may be regretted but cannot be renewed," according to our French prophet. That is why both the realists and the romanticists of the new century sometimes revealed a subtle estrangement from the worlds they painted and wrote about; why their romanticism seems thin and their realism a touch unreal. Like the reformers, the suffragettes, and the millionaires, the creative artists of 1913 found their liberations a little hollow and their triumphs a little brittle.

In trying to analyze national character and its causes, a difficulty arises. Are the strengths and weaknesses of Americans due to their innate character and heredity, or are they derived from the conditioning of a century and a half of their particular version of democracy? One cannot avoid the suspicion that some of the faults in America of 1913 were the creations of the democratic system—perhaps even the price of popular rule. If so, then democracy must be doubly on its guard against itself under the strains of 1961.

In 1913 Americans failed to see clearly and act firmly, not from mental myopia but from emotional rejection of unpleasant reality. American isolationism was deeper than history and geography; it was born of wishful thinking, national insecurity, and lack of emotional maturity. That psychic condition is still evident in current American reactions to every suggestion of economic or political involvement elsewhere in the world. Though public opinion has made great strides toward a more affirmative internationalism, those strides have not kept pace with the necessities of world events. Our present reluctance to make overseas commitments or maintain consistent policies of internationalism have the hallmarks of 1913's escapism.

Certainly one fiasco of 1913 can be laid at the door of democratic machinery. The California anti-Japanese legislation was tragic because it helped bring about Pearl Harbor, yet constitutionally the federal government was, or thought it was, powerless to prevent a state from actions that jeopardized international relations. That weakness in American democracy still exists when it is possible for a senator from Wisconsin and a governor from Arkansas to subvert American national policies and impair good will for America in every foreign country.

To a close observer the centrifugal forces of 1913 society seemed stronger than the unifying ones. The national unity so painfully gained in the nineteenth century suffered during the first years of the twentieth. Not only did the South remain sulkily unreconstructed but the forces of sectionalism asserted themselves in other parts of the nation. Class consciousness and resentments divided society vertically, while pressure groups divided it horizontally. Organized labor embarked on a course sometimes in conflict with the national welfare. It challenged both the economic system and the authority of the government to enforce law and order during industrial strife, while organized capital remained socially irresponsible. Millions of Negroes were refused constitutional rights, and other racial prejudices were growing. Samuel D. Burchard's notorious reference to "Rum, Romanism, and Rebellion," and the reactions to it, had long since revealed how conscious nearly every American was of the strains between Protestants and Catholics, and those strains had not diminished in 1913.

It can still be hoped that these were merely growing pains—though not one of them has yet been outgrown. Yet if they are not overcome, democracy is doomed. The unity of democracy must be based on mutually held principles that create common feelings and reactions among all its citizens. In 1913 the previously agreed-upon principles on which American unity had been originally based were carrying less authority, while no substitute affirmations had gained unanimous acceptance. The older affirmations, however inadequate for the new century, had provided individual Americans with a personal compass; when they lost real faith in those affirmations they lost the compass.

America's strength has been so great that it has thus far survived its weaknesses. The nation's progress has been a miraculous victory of its human and physical resources over its indecisions, ineptitudes, postponements, hypocrisies, disunities, and wastes. It is now challenged on all fronts: military, scientific, ideological, cultural, and, above all, moral. That challenge comes when Americans have largely abandoned their traditional affirmations and have found no new source of inner direction. Neglecting the advice of Caliban in crisis, every man is not shifting for all the rest.

Once again the nation meets its dangers spiritually unarmed and psychologically ill-prepared. Americans of 1961 are better aware of the gravity of their external crisis than were those of 1913, but awareness can bring hysteria rather than wisdom to people suffering from inner conflicts of mind and spirit. Americans of 1961, like their parents, do not see clearly the whole nature and gravity of the current world crisis—the challenge of our own spiritual and intellectual weaknesses.

Yet the future of the nation depends—at least as much as upon its military power—on the capacity of its individual citizens to reconcile mind and emotion, myth and reality, reason and faith. Only if Americans of today can shake off their habit of leaning on one another; only if they can find something more solid and elevating than other-direction to guide them; only if they think for themselves and make their thoughts kinetic; only if they can find, apply, and promulgate moral principles at once uplifting and dynamic, will they overcome, at home as well as abroad, the challenges of change and the threats of new barbarism.

Index